W9-BYJ-675

Bringing Home the Dharma

ALSO BY JACK KORNFIELD

After the Ecstasy, the Laundry
The Art of Forgiveness, Lovingkindness, and Peace
The Buddha Is Still Teaching
The Buddha's Little Instruction Book
A Lamp in the Darkness
Living Dharma
Meditation for Beginners
A Path with Heart
Seeking the Heart of Wisdom (with Joseph Goldstein)
Soul Food (with Christina Feldman)
A Still Forest Pool (with Paul Breiter)
Teachings of the Buddha
The Wise Heart

Bringing Home the Dharma

Awakening Right Where You Are

JACK KORNFIELD

Foreword by
Daniel J. Siegel, MD

SHAMBHALA
Boston & London
2011

Shambhala Publications, Inc.
Horticultural Hall
300 Massachusetts Avenue
Boston, Massachusetts 02115
www.shambhala.com

©2011 by Jack Kornfield

Pages 277–279 constitute an extension of this copyright page.

All rights reserved. No part of this book may be reproduced
in any form or by any means, electronic or mechanical, including
photocopying, recording, or by any information storage and retrieval
system, without permission in writing from the publisher.

9 8 7 6 5 4 3 2

Printed in the United States of America

⊗ This edition is printed on acid-free paper that meets the
American National Standards Institute z39.48 Standard.
♻ This book is printed on 30% postconsumer recycled paper.
For more information please visit www.shambhala.com.

Distributed in the United States by Random House, Inc.,
and in Canada by Random House of Canada Ltd

Designed by James D. Skatges

Library of Congress Cataloging-in-Publication Data
Kornfield, Jack, 1945–
Bringing home the dharma: awakening right where
you are / Jack Kornfield; foreword by Daniel J. Siegel.
p. cm.
ISBN 978-1-59030-913-1 (hardcover)
1. Spiritual life—Buddhism. I. Title.
BQ5405.K665 2011
294.3'444—dc22
2011014495

Dedicated to the thousands of sincere students
of dharma in the West

and

to the staff members of Spirit Rock and IMS
who have supported so many of these students

Contents

Foreword

Daniel J. Siegel, MD

Why would one of the world's most renowned teachers of mindfulness and Buddhist psychology ask a psychiatrist and mental-health educator to write the foreword to a book about everything from parenting to the nature of enlightenment? Perhaps because *Bringing Home the Dharma* is a compelling historical and personal exploration of the nature of the mind, and it contains teachings and perspectives that are important for our times.

The "dharma" is the nature of things, including the nature of our mental lives and the world in which we live. In these writings we learn about the Buddhist view of the mind and emotions and how personal transformation can be cultivated. We also see, through Jack Kornfield's wise and kind eyes, how his quest for nearly half a century has unfolded and informed his own experience. With great insight and humor, he shares the story of helping to bring Buddhist practice to the West, and he includes a captivating set of stories about the various teachers who have influenced this historic transfer of knowledge over the last century.

I first met Jack in preparation for a conference he had organized with a number of mindfulness teachers and Huston Smith, the celebrated authority on the world's religions. I am a scientist by training, and I had no background in the material Jack was presenting at the conference. I was also unfamiliar with Jack's writing and teaching. Yet at the meeting we found a tremendous common ground.

Listening to Jack and the other presenters, I could sense a deep devotion to understanding the nature of our mental lives—and how to bring those lives from suffering to clarity. In many ways, this was the exact oath I had taken as a physician, and so I was surprised to find that Buddhist views were actually more about a science of mind and a method of healing than about a "religion." Here I encountered Buddhism as a system of thought and understanding devoted to alleviating mental pain. How odd, I thought as a psychiatrist, that something in the realm of religious practice was actually more akin to clinical work in the field of mental health. And so began a relationship with Jack that has become both a deep friendship and a professional partnership in which we teach together throughout the United States on the connection between science and spirituality, linking the mindful brain with the wise heart.

Though our collaboration, I have come to see that "awakening" involves the capacity to train the mind to move our brains, and our relationships, toward the open plane of possibility. Rather than being swept up into engrained patterns of thought or feeling, constrained by prior expectation and filtered perception, we can intentionally move our mental lives toward openness and creativity. From this new emergence arises a sense of vitality and clarity, which lie at the heart of well-being.

A host of carefully conducted scientific research projects now clearly demonstrates how attention shapes the firing of neurons in the brain, which then creates structural changes in the brain's very architecture. In other words, the mind can change the brain. And yet if the brain has a propensity to become stuck in familiar patterns, our mental lives can go on autopilot and we may be at risk of becoming stuck in a chaotic or deadened life.

One example is the isolation that many people experience in modern culture, surrounded by so many and yet so alone. And this sense of a separate self makes us at risk for highly problematic impediments to health: As individuals, we may have the negative outcomes to our body that come from perceived loneliness and isolation. Within relationships, we may feel apart even in the company of others. And we also have a relationship with the planet at large. Our planet itself is at risk if we continue a pattern of material acquisition and energy consumption in which the one with the "most toys wins." If "I" am not a part of the larger "we" of our common humanity, we are at grave risk of destroying life on this shared home we call earth. The self does not have to be seen as a singular noun, but rather as a plural verb in which we are all both differentiated and linked to one another. This is the heart of integration, and the heart of awakening the mind.

We can promote a more integrated way of living through the power of mindful awareness. With integrative reflective practices, our relationships with one another can become filled with compassion and kindness. And for our planet, the hope of moving from "me" to "we" is filled with the potential of bringing health and healing to our precious and fragile home. This is the power and the promise of the paths to awakening the mind and integrating our lives.

Whatever your own background, this book is a treasure of discovery filled with jewels of wisdom that can elucidate both a secular and a spiritual understanding of this life we lead. We can be grateful to Jack Kornfield for sharing his illuminating journey and making the transformative practices of mindfulness and meditation accessible to all of us.

Introduction

Free your heart.
Travel like the moon among the stars.
　　—BUDDHA

What matters in life is simple. Are you free and loving? Are you bring-ing your gifts to the world that so badly needs them? The joyful news of the Buddha's way is that you can do so, you can live with freedom and compassion in every part of your life.

Mistakenly, people associate Buddhist teachings exclusively with sitting quietly in meditation. This error reflects our divided society where the body is relegated to the gym, work to the office, healing to the hospital, enjoyment to two weeks' vacation, and the sacred to weekly visits to church or temple. The wholeness of awakening is the message of this book.

All aspects of your life are your field of practice, the precise place to find freedom and compassion. From politics and parenting to med-itation and education, from sex and drugs to poetry and art, every part of your life is sacred. This very life, your work, your family, your commu-nity is the only place for awakening. In Zen this is called "no part left out."

This was the Buddha's message to all he met. For forty-five years the Buddha wandered the dusty byways and cool woods of India, meeting with farmers and mothers, merchants and politicians, priests and schol-ars, cobblers and gardeners, barbers and weavers, artisans and kings. His instructions could not have been more clear. All parts of your human experience must be included in an awakened life.

The Buddha's own words explain that awakening and freedom are found:

When sitting, standing, walking, and lying down;
through right speech, right action, right livelihood;
inwardly and outwardly,
with the whole body, feelings, mind, and relationships;
in solitude and community;
in prison, hut, farm, or palace;
in times of war or peace;
in sickness and in health.

These are empowering and ennobling words. Your life provides the perfect conditions for awakening freedom and compassion. Enlightenment and liberation are not found in the Himalayas, nor in some ancient monasteries. They are only found where you are. Thus they are possible for you! We can sense this truth. There is a way of moving wisely and graciously through the world, bestowing blessings and happiness upon yourself and others, in times of trouble and ease.

To find this freedom, you must learn how to quiet the mind and open the heart. This is the purpose of meditation. The teachings in this volume offer helpful directions in many dimensions of meditation. And then you must discover ways to embody this wisdom and compassion in the world. In these pages there are practical and visionary teachings on parenting, engaging in politics, creating community, and embodying a spiritual life. These chapters have been gathered and woven together from twenty-five years' of writings. Each of these chapters invites your wisdom to expand. They give permission, direction, and specific guidance so that your heart and body, mind and action can awaken together.

The perspectives and teachings in this book are dear to my heart. For over forty years I have been practicing in this way. I have become more tolerant, kinder, more understanding, joyful, and free. Not only in the meditation hall but in the grocery store, on the highways, at work, and at home. You can too. This is not idealistic. I can also still be foolish, awkward, and unconscious. But I have learned to bow with compassion to this too, to accept what Oscar Wilde calls the "tainted glory" of our humanity. And then to smile like the Buddha.

As the marvelous teachings of liberation spread to far lands, the Buddha counseled his disciples to "teach in the vernacular of the times."

In China and Japan, Ch'an and Zen arose. In Indonesia and Afghanistan, Tibet and Mongolia, Mahayana and Vajrayana Buddhist teachings flowered in new forms. Now Buddhism in the West has begun to appear. It is an honor to join together in this creation.

Read these words, consider, discover, practice, and embody their value and let your heart become wise and your life an expression of freedom.

May it be so.

JACK KORNFIELD
Spirit Rock Center
2011

PART ONE

Becoming Who We Are

1

The Liberating Practice
of Mindfulness

IN MYTHS FROM AROUND THE WORLD, men and women have
searched for an elixir that will bring protection from suffering. Buddhism's answer is mindfulness. How does mindfulness work? Let me
illustrate with a story that became the basis for the 1988 film *Gorillas in
the Mist*. This movie is about Dian Fossey, a courageous field biologist
who managed to befriend a tribe of gorillas. Fossey had gone to Africa
to follow in the footsteps of her mentor, George Schaller, a renowned
primate biologist who had returned from the wilds with more intimate
and compelling information about gorilla life than any scientist before.
When his colleagues asked how he was able to learn such remarkable
detail about the tribal structure, family life, and habits of gorillas, he
attributed it to one simple thing: he didn't carry a gun.

Previous generations of biologists had entered the territory of these
large animals with the assumption that they were dangerous. So the
scientists came with an aggressive spirit, large rifles in hand. The gorillas could sense the danger around these rifle-bearing men and kept a far
distance. By contrast, Schaller—and later his student Dian Fossey—entered their territory without weapons. They had to move slowly, gently,
and above all, respectfully toward these creatures. And, in time, sensing
the benevolence of these humans, the gorillas allowed them to come
right among them and learn their ways. Sitting still, hour after hour,
with careful, patient attention, Fossey finally understood what she saw.
As the African-American sage George Washington Carver explained,
"Anything will give up its secrets if you love it enough."

Mindfulness is this kind of attention. It is a nonjudging, receptive awareness, a respectful awareness. Unfortunately, much of the time we don't attend in this way. Instead, we react, judging whether we like, dislike, or can ignore what is happening. Or we measure our experience against our expectation. We evaluate ourselves and others with a stream of commentary and criticism. When people initially come to a meditation class to train in mindfulness, they hope to become calm and peaceful. Usually they are in for a big shock. The first hour of mindfulness meditation reveals its opposite, bringing an unseen stream of evaluation and judgment into stark relief. In the first hour many feel bored and dislike the boredom. We can hear a door slam and wish for quiet. Our knees hurt and we try to avoid the pain. We wish we had a better cushion. We can't feel our breath and we get frustrated. We notice our mind won't stop planning and we feel like a failure. Then we remember someone we're angry at and get upset, and if we notice how many judgments there are, we feel proud of ourselves for noticing.

But like George Schaller, we can put aside these weapons of judgment. We can become mindful. When we are mindful, it is as if we can bow to our experience without judgment or expectation. "Mindfulness," declared the Buddha, "is all-helpful."

Peter, a middle-aged computer designer, came to a meditation retreat looking for relief. He was coping with a recently failed business, a shaky marriage, and a sick mother. But meditation quickly became an agony. The anger and disappointment that pervaded his current situation rose up in the quiet room to fill his mind. His attempts to quiet himself by sensing his breath felt hopeless; his attention was repelled away from his body like water on a hot skillet. Then it got worse. A restless woman seated nearby began to cough loudly and frequently. She began to fidget and move and cough more as the first day wore on. Peter, who was struggling just to be with his own sorrow, became frustrated and angry and, as she continued coughing, enraged. He sought out my coteacher and good friend Debra Chamberlin-Taylor and insisted that meditation was the wrong approach and that he wanted to leave. Debra asked Peter to close his eyes and mindfully notice the state of his body. It was filled with tension and hurting. With Debra's help, Peter found he could hold the tension and hurt with more acceptance and kindness. He breathed, relaxed a little, and recognized that the medicine he needed was nothing other than attention to directly understand his own pain.

The next instruction he was given was simple: as you sit, keep a gentle mindfulness on your body and notice whatever happens. After only a few minutes, his fidgety neighbor began a long coughing spell. With each cough Peter felt his own muscles clench and his breath stop. Now he became more curious, interested in how his body was reacting. He began to notice that hearing each cough produced an internal clenching and a wave of anger, which subsided as he practiced relaxing between the spells. Finally, at the end of the sitting period, he got up to walk down to the lunchroom. As he arrived, he noticed this same difficult woman in line just ahead of him. Immediately he noticed how his stomach clenched and his breath stopped—just seeing her! Again, he relaxed. After lunch when he returned to the meditation hall he checked to see what time his name was listed for a private interview with his teacher. Farther down the same list he read the restless woman's name. Still paying attention, he was surprised. Just seeing her name made his stomach clench and his breath tighten! He relaxed again. He realized that his body had become a mirror, and that his mindfulness was showing him when he was caught and where he could let go.

As the retreat went on, his attention grew more precise. He noticed that his own anxious and angry thoughts about his family and business problems could trigger the same clenching and tightening as the woman's cough did. He had always tried to have things under control. Now that his life had proved out of control, the habits of anger, blame, and judgments toward himself were tying him in knots. With each reaction, he could feel the knots arise. After each one he would pause mindfully and bring in a touch of ease. He began to trust mindfulness. By the close of the retreat, he was grateful to the restless woman near him. He wanted to thank her for her teaching. With mindfulness Peter found relief. He also discovered the benefit of curiosity and openness, what Zen master Suzuki Roshi famously called beginner's mind. In Suzuki Roshi's words, "We pay attention with respect and interest, not in order to manipulate, but to understand what is true. And seeing what is true, the heart becomes free."

MINDFULNESS AS FEARLESS PRESENCE

The art of listening is neither careless drifting on the one hand nor fearful clinging on the other. It consists in being sensitive to each

moment, in regarding it as utterly new and unique, in having the
mind open and wholly receptive.
—ALAN WATTS

Sitting mindfully with our sorrows and fears, or with those of another, is an act of courage. It is not easy. Mary believed that to face her
rage might kill her. John's son's cystic fibrosis brought terrifying images
of wheelchairs and early death. Perry was afraid to face his infidelities
and sexual peculiarities. Ron could hardly bear to think of the carnage
he had seen during his work in Bosnia. For Angela, facing the recur-
rence of her cancer meant facing death. And Konda had longings and
joy and creativity that she had never dared to express.

With patience and courage, they gradually learned how to sit firmly
on the earth and sense the contraction and trembling of their bodies
without running away. They learned how to feel the floods of emotions—fear, grief, longing, and rage—and to allow them to slowly release with mindfulness. They learned to see the endless mental stories
of fear and judgment that repeat over and over, and with the help of
mindfulness to let them go and relax, to steady the mind and return to
the present.

In the Buddha's search for freedom he, too, turned his mindfulness
to overcoming his fears. In a text called "Overcoming Fear and Dread,"
he recounts his practice:

> How would it be if in the dark of the month, with no moon, I
> were to enter the most strange and frightening of places, near
> tombs and in the thick of the forest, that I might come to un-
> derstand fear and terror. And in so doing, a wild animal would
> approach or the wind rustle the leaves and I would think, "Per-
> haps the fear and terror now comes." And being resolved to
> dispel the hold of that fear and terror, I remained in whatever
> posture it arose, sitting or standing, walking or lying down. I
> did not change until I had faced that fear and terror in that very
> posture, until I was free of its hold upon me . . . And having this
> thought, I did so. By facing the fear and terror I became free.

In the traditional training at Ajahn Chah's forest monastery in
Thailand, we were sent to sit alone in the forest at night to practice the

meditations on death. Stories of monks who had encountered tigers and other wild animals were part of what kept us alert. There were many snakes, including cobras. At Ajahn Buddhadasa's forest monastery we were taught to tap our walking sticks on the paths at night so the snakes would "hear" us and move out of the way. There were moments when I was really frightened. At another monastery, I periodically sat all night at the charnel grounds. Every few weeks a body was brought for cremation. After the lighting of the funeral pyre and the chanting, most people would leave, with one or several monks left alone to tend the fire in the dark forest. Then, as a practice, one monk would be left, remaining there until dawn, contemplating death. Not everyone did these practices. But I was a young man, looking for initiation, eager to prove myself, so I gravitated toward these difficulties.

As it turned out, sitting in the dark forest with its tigers and snakes was easier than sitting with my inner demons—my insecurity, loneliness, shame, boredom; my frustrations and hurts. Sitting with these took more courage than practicing all night in the charnel ground. Little by little I learned to face them with mindfulness, to make a clearing within the dark woods of my own heart.

Mindfulness does not reject experience. It lets experience be the teacher. One Buddhist practitioner with severe asthma learned to bring a mindful attention to his breath and limit his attacks by being patient as the muscles in his throat and chest constricted, slowly relaxing the stress in his body. Another man undergoing a painful cancer treatment used mindfulness to quell his fear of the pain and added loving-kindness for his body as a complement to his chemotherapy. Through mindfulness a politician learned not to be discouraged by his attackers. A frazzled single mother of preschoolers used mindfulness to acknowledge feeling tense and overwhelmed, and to become more respectful and spacious with herself and her boys. Each of these practitioners learned to trust the space of mindful awareness. With mindfulness they entered the difficulties in their own lives, and like the Buddha in the thick of the forest, they found healing and freedom.

FOUR PRINCIPLES FOR MINDFUL TRANSFORMATION

Learning takes place only in a mind that is innocent and vulnerable.
—KRISHNAMURTI

RAIN is a useful acronym for the four key principles of mindful transformation of difficulties. RAIN stands for Recognition, Acceptance, Investigation, and Nonidentification. A line from Zen poetry reminds us, "the rain falls equally on all things." Like the nourishment of outer rain, the inner principles of RAIN can be applied to all our experiences, and can transform our difficulties.

Recognition

Recognition is the first step of mindfulness. When we feel stuck, we must begin with a willingness to see what is so. It is as if someone asks us gently, "What is happening now?" Do we reply brusquely, "Nothing"? Or do we pause and acknowledge the reality of our experience, here and now? With recognition we step out of denial. Denial undermines our freedom. The diabetic who denies his body is sick and ignores its needs is not free. Neither is the driven, stressed-out executive who denies the cost of her lifestyle, or the self-critical would-be painter who denies his love of making art. The society that denies its poverty and injustice has lost a part of its freedom as well. If we deny our dissatisfaction, our anger, our pain, our ambition, we will suffer. If we deny our values, our beliefs, our longings, or our goodness, we will suffer.

"The emergence and blossoming of understanding, love, and intelligence has nothing to do with any outer tradition," observes Zen teacher Toni Packer. "It happens completely on its own when a human being questions, wonders, listens, and looks without getting stuck in fear. When self-concern is quiet, in abeyance, heaven and earth are open."

With recognition our awareness becomes like the dignified host. We name and inwardly bow to our experience: "Ah, sorrow. Now excitement. Hmm, yes, conflict; and yes, tension. Oh, now pain, yes, and now, ah, the judging mind." Recognition moves us from delusion and ignorance toward freedom. "We can light a lamp in the darkness," says the Buddha. We can see what is so.

Acceptance

The next step of RAIN is acceptance. Acceptance allows us to relax and open to the facts before us. It is necessary because with recognition, there can come a subtle aversion, a resistance, a wish it weren't so. Acceptance does not mean that we cannot work to improve things. But just now, this is what is so. In Zen they say, "If you understand, things are just as they are. And if you don't understand, things are still just as they are."

Acceptance is not passivity. It is a courageous step in the process of transformation. "Trouble? Life is trouble. Only death is nice," Zorba the Greek declares. "To live is to roll up your sleeves and embrace trouble." Acceptance is a willing movement of the heart to include whatever is before it. In individual transformation we have to acknowledge the reality of our own suffering. For social transformation we have to start with the reality of collective suffering, of injustice, racism, greed, and hate. We can transform the world just as we learn to transform ourselves. As Carl Jung comments, "Perhaps I myself am the enemy who must be loved."

With acceptance and respect, problems that seem intractable often become workable. A man began to give large doses of cod liver oil to his Doberman because he had been told that the stuff was good for dogs. Each day he would hold the head of the protesting dog between his knees, force its jaws open, and pour the liquid down its throat. One day the dog broke loose and the fish oil spilled on the floor. Then, to the man's great surprise, the dog returned to lick the puddle. That is when the man discovered that what the dog had been fighting was not the oil but his lack of respect in administering it. With acceptance and respect, surprising transformations can occur.

Investigation

Recognition and acceptance lead to the third step of RAIN, investigation. Zen master Thich Nhat Hanh calls this "seeing deeply." In recognition and acceptance we recognize our dilemma and accept the truth of the whole situation. Now we must investigate more fully. Buddhism teaches that whenever we are stuck, it is because we have not looked deeply enough into the nature of the experience.

Buddhist practice systematically directs our investigation to four areas that are critical for understanding and freedom. These are called the four foundations of mindfulness—body, feelings, mind, and dharma—the underlying principles of experience.

Here is how we can apply them when working with a difficult experience. Starting with investigation in the body, we mindfully locate where our difficulties are held. Sometimes we find sensations of heat, contraction, hardness, or vibration. Sometimes we notice throbbing, numbness, a certain shape or color. We can investigate whether we are meeting this area with resistance or with mindfulness. We notice what happens as we hold these sensations with mindfulness and kindness. Do they open? Are there other layers? Is there a center? Do they intensify, move, expand, change, repeat, dissolve, or transform?

In the second foundation of mindfulness, we can investigate what feelings are part of this difficulty. Is the primary feeling tone pleasant, unpleasant, or neutral? Are we meeting this feeling with mindfulness? And what are the secondary feelings associated with it? Often we discover a constellation of feelings.

A man remembering his divorce may feel sadness, anger, jealousy, loss, fear, and loneliness. A woman who was unable to help her addicted nephew can feel longing, aversion, guilt, desire, emptiness, and unworthiness. With mindfulness, each feeling is recognized and accepted. We investigate how each emotion feels, whether it is pleasant or painful, contracted or relaxed, tense or sad. We notice where we feel the emotion in our body and what happens to it as it is held in mindfulness.

Next comes the mind. What thoughts and images are associated with this difficulty? What stories, judgments, and beliefs are we holding? When we look more closely, we often discover that many of them are one-sided, fixed points of view or outmoded, habitual perspectives. When we see that they are only stories, they loosen their hold on us. We cling less to them.

The fourth foundation to investigate is called mindfulness of the dharma. *Dharma* is an important and multifaceted word that can mean "the teachings and the path of Buddhism." It can also mean "the truth, the elements and patterns that make up experience." In mindfulness of the dharma we look into the principles and laws that are operating. We can notice if an experience is actually as solid as it appears. Is it unchanging or is it impermanent, moving, shifting, re-creating itself? We notice if the difficulty expands or contracts the space in our mind, if it is in our control or if it has its own life. We notice if it is self-constructed. We investigate whether we are clinging to it, struggling with it, or simply letting it be. We see whether our relationship to it is a source of suffering or happiness. And finally, we notice how much we identify with it. This leads us to the last step of RAIN, nonidentification.

Nonidentification

In nonidentification we stop taking the experience as "mine" or part of "me." We see how identification creates dependence, anxiety, and inauthenticity. In practicing nonidentification, we inquire of every state, experience, and story, is this who I really am? We see the tentativeness of this identity. Instead of identification with this difficulty, we let go and rest in awareness itself. This is the culmination of releasing difficulty through RAIN.

One Buddhist practitioner, David, identified himself as a failure. His life had many disappointments, and after a few years of Buddhist practice, he was disappointed by his meditation too. He became calmer but that was all. He was still plagued by unrelenting critical thoughts and self-judgments, leftovers from a harsh and painful past. He identified with these thoughts and his wounded history. Even the practice of compassion for himself brought little relief.

Then, during a ten-day mindfulness retreat, he was inspired by the teachings on nonidentification. He was touched by the stories of those who faced their demons and freed themselves. He remembered the account of the Buddha, who on the night of his enlightenment faced the armies and temptations of Mara, a powerful demon of Buddhist folklore who personifies our difficulties and obstacles on the path. David decided to stay up all night and directly face his own demons. For many hours, he tried to be mindful of his breath and body.

In between sittings, he took periods of walking meditation. At each sitting, he was washed over by familiar waves of sleepiness, body pains, and critical thoughts. Then he began to notice that each changing experience was met by one common element, awareness itself. In the middle of the night, he had an "aha" moment. He realized that awareness was not affected by any of these experiences, that it was open and untouched, like space itself. All his struggles, the painful feelings and thoughts, came and went without the slightest disturbance to awareness itself.

Awareness became his refuge. David decided to test his realization. The meditation hall was empty so he rolled on the floor. Awareness just noticed. He stood up, shouted, laughed, made funny animal noises.

Awareness just noticed. He ran around the room, he lay down quietly, he went outside to the edge of the forest, he picked up a stone and threw it, jumped up and down, laughed, came back and sat. Awareness just noticed it all. Finding this, he felt free. He watched the sun rise softly over the hills. Then he went back to sleep for a time. And when he re-awakened, his day was full of joy. Even when his doubts came back, awareness just noticed. Like the rain, his awareness allowed all things equally.

It would be too rosy to end this story here. Later in the retreat David again fell into periods of doubt, self-judgment, and depression. But now, even in the middle of it, he could recognize that it was just doubt, just judgment, just depression. He could not take it fully as his identity any-more. Awareness noticed this too. And was silent, free.

Buddhism calls nonidentification the abode of awakening, the end of clinging, true peace, nirvana. Without identification we can live with care, yet we are no longer bound by the fears and illusions of the small sense of self. We see the secret beauty behind all that we meet. Mindful-ness and fearless presence bring true protection. When we meet the world with recognition, acceptance, investigation, and nonidentifica-tion, we discover that wherever we are, freedom is possible, just as the rain falls on and nurtures all things equally.

.

2

The Art of Awakening

The Way of Meditation

A STORY IS TOLD OF THE BUDDHA when he was wandering in India shortly after his enlightenment. He was encountered by several men who recognized something quite extraordinary about this handsome prince now robed as a monk. Stopping to inquire, they asked, "Are you a god?" "No," he answered. "Well, are you a divine being or an angel?" "No," he replied. "Well, are you some kind of wizard or magician?" "No." "Are you a man?" "No." They were perplexed. Finally, they asked, "Then, what are you?" He replied simply, "I am awake." The word *buddha* means "one who is awake." How to awaken is all he taught.

Meditation can be thought of as the art of awakening. Through the mastering of this art we can learn new ways to approach our difficulties and bring wisdom and joy alive in our life. Through developing meditation's tools and practices, we can awaken the best of our spiritual and human capacities. The key to this art is the steadiness of our attention. When the fullness of our attention is cultivated together with a grateful and tender heart, our spiritual life will naturally grow.

For many people some healing of mind and body must take place as we start to sit quietly and meditate. To begin our healing, we must develop a basic level of calm and attention. We must find a way to develop our attention systematically and give ourselves to it quite fully. Otherwise, we will drift like a boat without a rudder. To learn to focus clearly, we must choose a prayer or a meditation practice and follow this path with commitment and steadiness, a willingness to work with our practice day after day, no matter what arises. This is not so easy for most people. They would like their spiritual life to show immediate and cosmic results. But what great art is ever learned quickly? Any deep training opens in direct proportion to how much we give ourselves to it.

Consider the other arts. Music, for example. How long would it take to learn to play the piano well? Suppose we take months' or years' of lessons once a week, practicing diligently every day. Initially, almost everyone struggles to learn which fingers go to which notes and how to read basic lines of music. After some weeks or months, we could play simple tunes, and perhaps after a year or two we could play a chosen type of music. However, to master the art so that we could play music well, alone or in a group, or join a band or an orchestra, we would have to give ourselves over to the discipline for a long time. It is the same in learning computer programming, oil painting, tennis, architecture, any of a thousand arts; we have to give ourselves to it fully and wholeheartedly over a period of time—there has to be a training, apprenticeship, cultivation. Nothing less is required in the spiritual arts. Perhaps even more is asked. Yet through this mastery we master ourselves and our lives. We learn the most human of arts, how to connect with our true self.

Suppose we begin with a period of meditation in the midst of our daily life. What happens when we actually try to meditate? The most frequent first experience—whether in prayer or chanting, meditation, or visualization—is that we encounter the disconnected and scattered mind. Buddhist psychology likens the untrained mind to a crazed monkey that dashes from thought to memory, from sight to sound, from plan to regret without ceasing.

To start, meditation is very much like training a puppy. You put the puppy down and say, "Stay." Does the puppy listen? It gets up and runs away. You sit the puppy back down again. "Stay." And the puppy runs away over and over again. Sometimes the puppy jumps up, runs over, and pees in the corner or makes some other mess. Our minds are much the same as the puppy, only they create even bigger messes. In training the mind, or the puppy, we have to start over and over again.

When you undertake a spiritual discipline, frustration comes with the territory. Nothing in our culture or our schooling has taught us to steady and calm our attention. Finding it difficult to concentrate, many people respond by forcing their attention on their breath or mantra or prayer with tense irritation and self-judgment, or worse. Is this the way you would train a puppy? Does it really help to beat it? Effective training of a dog or of our attention is never a matter of force or coercion. You simply pick up the puppy and place it where it needs to be; over and over, you gently return your attention to the here and now.

Developing a deep quality of interest in your spiritual practice is one of the keys to the whole art of attention. Steadiness is nourished by the degree of interest with which we focus our meditation. Yet, to the beginning student, many meditation subjects appear plain and uninteresting. There is a traditional story about a Zen student who complained to his master that following the breath was boring. The Zen master grabbed this student and held his head under water for quite a long time while the student struggled to come up. When he finally let the student up, the Zen master asked him whether he had found the breath boring in those moments under water. The focusing of attention on the breath is perhaps the most universal of the many hundreds of meditation objects used worldwide. Breathing meditation can quiet the mind, open the body, and develop a great power of concentration. The breath is available to us at any time of day and in any circumstance. When we have learned to use it, the breath becomes a support for awareness throughout our life.

Yet even with interest and a strong desire to steady our attention, distractions will arise. Distractions are the natural movement of mind, which is often like muddy or turbulent water. Each time an enticing image or an interesting memory floats by, it is our habit to react, to get entangled, or to get lost. When painful images or feelings arise, it is our habit to contract, to avoid them, or unknowingly distract ourselves. We can feel the power of these habits of desire and distraction, of fear and reaction. In many of us these forces are so great that after a few unfamiliar moments of calm, our mind rebels. We repeatedly encounter restlessness, busyness, plans, unfelt feelings, and these all interrupt our focus again and again. The heart of meditation practice is working with these distractions, steadying our canoe so to speak, letting the waves wobble us and pass by, coming back again and again to this moment in a quiet and collected way.

As you start to practice meditation, you will begin to recognize that certain external conditions are particularly helpful in developing concentration. Finding or creating a quiet and undistracting place for your practice is necessary. Select regular and suitable times that best fit your temperament and schedule; experiment to discover whether morning or evening meditations best support the silent aspects of your inner life. You may wish to begin with a short period of inspiring reading before sitting, or do some stretching or yoga first. Some people find it extremely helpful to sit regularly with a group or to go off to periodic retreats. Experiment with these external factors until you discover which are most helpful for your own inner peace. Then make them a regular part of your life. Creating suitable conditions means living wisely, providing the best soil for our spiritual hearts to be nourished and to grow.

As we give ourselves to the art of attention, over the weeks and months we discover that our concentration slowly begins to settle by itself. As we continue, the development of concentration brings us closer to life, like the focusing of a lens. If you take water from a pond and put it in a glass, it appears clear and still. But under the simplest microscope it shows itself to be alive with creatures and movement. In the same way, the more deeply we pay attention, we notice that every place we feel breath in our body can come alive with subtle vibrations, movement, tingles, flow. The steady power of our concentration shows each part of our life to be in change and flux, like a river, even as we feel it.

As we learn to let go into the present, the breath breathes itself, allowing the flow of sensations in the body to move and open. There can come an openness and ease. Like a skilled dancer, we allow the breath and the body to float and move unhindered, yet all the while being present to enjoy the opening.

As we become more skillful, we also discover that concentration has its own seasons. Sometimes we sit and settle easily. At other times, the conditions of mind and body are turbulent or tense. We can learn to navigate all these waters. When conditions show the mind is tight, we learn to soften and relax, to open our attention. When the mind is sleepy or flabby, we learn to sit up and focus with more energy. The Buddha compared this with the tuning of a lute, sensing when we are out of tune and gently strengthening or loosening our energy to come into balance.

In learning concentration, we feel as if we are always starting over, always losing our focus. But where have we actually gone? It is only that a mood or thought or doubt has swept through our mind. As soon as we recognize this, we can let go and settle back again in this next moment. We can always begin again. Gradually, as our interest grows and our awareness deepens, new layers of our meditation open. We find periods of deep peace and strength, like a great ship on a true course, although we can be distracted or lost sometime later. Little by little, we learn to trust our course and our steadiness grows.

Always remember that in training a puppy we want to end up with the puppy as our friend. In the same way, we must practice seeing our mind and body as "friend." Even its wanderings can be included in our meditation with a friendly interest and curiosity. Right away we can notice how it moves. The mind produces waves. Our breath is a wave, and the sensations of our body are a wave. We don't have to fight the waves. We can simply acknowledge, "Surf's up." "Here's a wave of memories from when I was three years old." "Here's a wave of planning the future." Then it's time to reconnect with the wave of the breath. It takes a gentleness and a kindhearted understanding to deepen the art of concentration. We can't be present for a long period without learning how to soften, drop into our bodies, come to rest. Any other kind of concentration, achieved by force and tension, will be short-lived. Our task is to train the puppy to become our lifelong friend.

The attitude or spirit with which we do our meditation helps us perhaps more than any other aspect. What is called for is a sense of perseverance and dedication combined with a basic friendliness. We need a willingness to directly relate again and again to what is actually here, with a lightness of heart and sense of humor. We do not want the training of our puppy to become too serious a matter.

The Christian desert fathers tell of a new student who was commanded by his master that for three years he must give money to everyone who insulted him. When this period of trial was over, the master said, "Now you can go to Alexandria and truly learn wisdom." When the student entered Alexandria, he met a certain wise man whose way of teaching was to sit at the city gate insulting everyone who came and went. He naturally insulted the student also, who immediately burst out laughing. "Why do you laugh when I insult you?" said the wise man. "Because," said the student, "for years I've been paying for this kind of thing, and now you give it to me for free!" "Enter the city," said the wise man. "It is all yours."

Meditation is a practice that can teach us to enter each moment with wisdom, lightness, and a sense of humor. It is an art of opening and letting go, rather than accumulation or struggle. Then, even within our frustrations and difficulties, a remarkable inner sense of support and perspective can grow. Breathing in, "Wow, this experience is interesting, isn't it? Let me take another breath. Ah, this one is difficult, even terrifying, isn't it?" Breathing out, "Ah." It is an amazing process we have entered when we can train our hearts and minds to be open, steady, and awake through it all.

3

A Mind Like Sky

Learning to Rest in Awareness

MEDITATION COMES ALIVE through a growing capacity to release our habitual entanglement in the stories and plans, conflicts and worries that make up the small sense of self, and to rest in awareness. In meditation we do this simply by acknowledging the moment-to-moment changing conditions—the pleasure and pain, the praise and blame, the litany of ideas and expectations that arise. Without identifying with them, we can rest in the awareness itself, beyond conditions, and experience what my teacher Ajahn Chah called *jai pongsai,* our natural lightness of heart. Developing this capacity to rest in awareness nourishes *samadhi* (concentration), which stabilizes and clarifies the mind, and *prajna* (wisdom), which sees things as they are.

We can employ this awareness, or wise attention, from the very start. When we first sit down to meditate, the best strategy is to simply notice whatever state of our body and mind is present. To establish the foundation of mindfulness, the Buddha instructs his followers "to observe whether the body and mind are distracted or steady, angry or peaceful, excited or worried, contracted or released, bound or free." Observing what is so, we can take a few deep breaths and relax, making space for whatever situation we find.

From this ground of acceptance we can learn to use the transformative power of attention in a flexible and malleable way. Wise attention—mindfulness—can function like a zoom lens. Often it is most helpful to steady our practice with close-up attention. In this, we bring a careful attention and a very close focus to our breath, to a sensation, or to the precise movement of feeling or thought. Over time we can eventually become so absorbed that subject and object disappear. We become the breath, we become the tingling in our foot, we become the sadness or joy. In this we sense ourselves being born and dying with each breath, each experience. Entanglement in our ordinary sense of self dissolves; our troubles and fears drop away. Our entire experience of the world shows itself to be impermanent, ungraspable, and selfless. Wisdom is born.

But sometimes in meditation such close focus of attention can create an unnecessary sense of tightness and struggle. So we must find a more open way to pay attention. Or perhaps when we are mindfully walking down the street, we realize it is not helpful to focus only on our breath or our feet. We will miss the traffic signals, the morning light, and the faces of the passersby. So we open the lens of awareness to a middle range. When we do this as we sit, instead of focusing on the breath alone, we can feel the energy of our whole body. As we walk, we can feel the rhythm of our whole movement and the circumstances through which we move. From this perspective it is almost as if awareness "sits on our shoulder" and respectfully acknowledges a breath, a pain in our legs, a thought about dinner, a feeling of sadness, a shop window we pass. Here wise attention has a gracious witnessing quality, acknowledging each event—whether boredom or jealousy, plans or excitement, gain or loss, pleasure or pain—with a slight bow. Moment by moment we release the illusion of getting "somewhere" and rest in the timeless present, witnessing with easy awareness all that passes by. As we let go, our innate freedom and wisdom manifest. Nothing to have, nothing to be. Ajahn Chah called this "resting in the One Who Knows."

Yet at times this middle level of attention does not serve our practice best. We may find ourselves caught in the grip of some repetitive thought pattern or painful situation, or lost in great physical or emotional suffering. Perhaps there is chaos and noise around us. We sit and our heart is tight, our body and mind are neither relaxed nor gracious, and even the witnessing can seem tedious, forced, effortful.

In this circumstance we can open the lens of attention to its widest angle and let our awareness become like space or the sky. As the Buddha instructs in the Majjhima Nikaya, "Develop a mind that is vast like space, where experiences both pleasant and unpleasant can appear and disappear without conflict, struggle, or harm. Rest in a mind like vast sky."

From this broad perspective, when we sit or walk in meditation, we open our attention like space, letting experiences arise without any boundaries, without inside or outside. Instead of the ordinary orientation where our mind is felt to be inside our head, we can let go and experience the mind's awareness as open, boundless, and vast. We allow awareness to experience consciousness that is not entangled in the particular conditions of sight, sound, and feelings, but consciousness that is independent of changing conditions—the unconditioned. Ajahn Jumnien, a Thai forest elder, speaks of this form of practice as *maha vipassana*, resting in pure awareness itself, timeless and unborn. For the meditator, this is not an ideal or a distant experience. It is always immediate, ever present, liberating; it becomes the resting place of the wise heart.

Fully absorbed, graciously witnessing, or open and spacious—which of these lenses is the best way to practice awareness? Is there an optimal way to pay attention? The answer is "all of the above." Awareness is infinitely malleable, and it is important not to fixate on any one form as best. Mistakenly, some traditions teach that losing the self and dissolving into a breath or absorbing into an experience is the optimal form of attention. Other traditions erroneously believe that resting in the widest angle, the open consciousness of space, is the highest teaching. Still others say that the middle ground—an ordinary, free, and relaxed awareness of whatever arises here and now, a quality of "nothing special"—is the highest attainment. Yet in its true nature, awareness cannot be limited. Consciousness itself is both large and small, particular and universal. At different times our practice will require that we embrace all these perspectives.

Every form of genuine awareness is liberating. Each moment we release entanglement and identification is selfless and free. But remember too that every practice of awareness can create a shadow when we mistakenly cling to it. A misuse of space can easily lead us to become spaced-out and unfocused. A misuse of absorption can lead to denial, the ignoring of other experiences; and a misuse of ordinary awareness can create a false sense of "self" as a witness. These shadows are subtle veils of meditative clinging. See them for what they are and let them go. And learn to work with all the lenses of awareness to serve your wise attention.

The more you experience the power of wise attention, the more your trust in the ground of awareness itself will grow. You will learn to relax and let go. In any moment of being caught, awareness will appear, a presence without judging or resisting. Close-in or vast, near or far, awareness illuminates the ungraspable nature of the universe. It returns the heart and mind to its birthright, naturally luminous and free.

While focused and absorbed attention might be familiar, and ordinary awareness more natural, the wide-angle practice of mind like sky may be less familiar. To amplify and deepen an understanding of how to practice with awareness as space, the following instructions can be helpful. One of the most accessible ways to open to spacious awareness is through the ear door, listening to the sounds of the universe around us. Because the river of sound comes and goes so naturally, and is so obviously out of our control, listening brings the mind to a naturally balanced state of openness and attention. I learned this particular practice of sound as a gateway to space from my colleague Joseph Goldstein more than twenty-five years ago and have used it ever since. Awareness of sound in space can be an excellent way to begin practice because it initiates the sitting period with the flavor of wakeful ease and spacious letting go. Or it can be used after a period of focused attention.

Whenever you begin, sit comfortably and at ease. Let your body be at rest and your breathing be natural. Close your eyes. Take several full breaths and let each release gently. Allow yourself to be still.

Now shift awareness away from the breath. Begin to listen to the play of sounds around you. Notice those that are loud and soft, far and near. Just listen. Notice how all sounds arise and vanish on their own, leaving no trace. Listen for a time in a relaxed, open way.

As you listen, let yourself sense or feel or imagine that your mind is not limited to your head. Sense that your mind is expanding to be like the sky—open, clear, vast, like space. There is no inside or outside. Let the awareness of your mind extend in every direction like the sky.

Now all the sounds you hear will arise and pass away in the open space of your own mind. Relax in this openness and just listen. Let the sounds that come and go, whether far or near, be like clouds in the vast sky of your own awareness. The play of sounds moves through the sky, appearing and disappearing without resistance.

After you rest in this open awareness for a time, notice how thoughts and images also arise and vanish like sounds. Let the thoughts and images come and go without struggle or resistance. Pleasant and unpleasant thoughts, pictures, words, and feelings move unrestricted in the space of mind. Problems, possibilities, joys, and sorrows come and go like clouds in the clear sky of mind.

After a time, let this spacious awareness notice the body. Become aware of how the sensations of breath and body float and change in the same open sky of awareness. The breath breathes itself, it moves like a breeze. If you feel carefully you will sense that the body is not solid. It is experienced as areas of hardness and softness, pressure and tingling, warm and cool sensation, all floating in the space of the mind's awareness.

Let the breath move like a breeze. Rest in this openness. Let sensations float and change. Allow all thoughts and images, feelings and sounds to come and go like clouds in the clear open space of awareness.

Finally, pay attention to awareness itself. Notice how the open space of awareness is naturally clear, transparent, timeless, and without conflict—allowing all things, but not limited by them.

The Buddha said, "O Nobly Born, remember the pure open sky of your own true nature. Return to it. Trust it. It is home."

4

Realizing Our Full Potential

Cultivating Love and Joy

With wisdom let your mind full of love pervade one-quarter of the world, and so too the second, third and fourth quarter. Fill the whole wide world, above, below, around, pervade the world with love-filled thought, free from any ill will, love abounding, sublime, beyond measure.
—BUDDHA

If we cannot be happy in spite of our difficulties, what good is our spiritual practice?
—MAHA GHOSANANDA

Who, being loved, is poor?
—OSCAR WILDE

WE HAVE WITHIN US an extraordinary capacity for love, joy, and unshakable freedom. One of my Buddhist teachers, Dipa Ma Barua, demonstrated this to me. When I studied with her, Dipa Ma was a grandmother and householder in Calcutta, India, and also one of the most accomplished meditators of the Theravada lineage. Until her mid-thirties, Dipa Ma had been an ordinary, devout Buddhist. Then in the space of a few years she lost two of her three young children to illness. Her engineer husband, devastated, died of a heart attack soon thereafter. After a year of lying in bed with paralyzing grief, Dipa Ma dragged herself to a temple to practice meditation. Desperate, she threw herself into her practice, and through her ardent nature and innate ability, she emerged with a deep realization. Dipa Ma was then trained and became a master of dozens of kinds of meditation. Through her intense dedication and shining spirit, she became a revered teacher for many.

In the late 1970s, I traveled to Calcutta to see Dipa Ma again. I had been meditating for a month in Bodh Gaya, India. Because of difficulty with my airplane ticket, I had only one day to spend with her. It was a hot day, over a hundred degrees. The air in Calcutta was smoggy and dirty. After I paid my respects to her, we spent some hours in deep conversation. Although I had been teaching successfully for five years, I was having a hard time. I had been suffering severe back pain, I was upset about a failed relationship, and before coming to India I had been working sixty hours a week for months. Given all this suffering and stress, I told her that I had begun to doubt my own capacities and ability to embody the teachings. Though she could see how shaky I was, she encouraged me to be steady in spite of it all. When it was time for me to go, Dipa Ma gave me her usual Bengali bear hug. Then she said she had a special blessing for me. Because she was so tiny, when I got down on my knees for the blessing, I was equal to her in height.

With great care and attention, Dipa Ma stroked her hands across my head and my whole body. She blew her breath on me and recited loving-kindness chants at the same time. At first it seemed like a very long prayer, but as she continued blessing me, I started to feel better and better. After ten long minutes my whole body was tingling and open. I was smiling from ear to ear. "Go and teach a good retreat for all those people," she said at last. "Go with mother's blessings." I felt as though a loving grandmother had sent me off with her good wishes, amplified with special yogic powers. I was in bliss.

I walked out into the sweltering Calcutta street and caught a taxi to Dum Dum Airport (its real name). It took two hours to get there, with the driver leaning on his horn the whole way, dodging between rickshaws and traffic, cows and fumes and trash. At the airport I went through the tedious Indian Customs, hours of standing around while officials looked through my stuff, grilled me, and stamped my documents. Eventually I got on the airplane for the three-hour flight to Bangkok. Bangkok was also hot and busy. The airport had long lines and more Customs. Then I spent an hour and a half riding to my hotel through the slow, crowded Bangkok traffic.

All the while I could not stop grinning. Through the Customs lines, plane rides, taxi rides, and traffic jams, I sat there with this huge smile on my face. It did not wear off. I went to sleep smiling and woke up smiling. I smiled continuously for days and felt uplifted for months following Dipa Ma's blessing.

Dipa Ma and other Buddhist teachers demonstrate the remarkable possibilities of the awakened heart. In *Transformations of Consciousness,* Harvard psychologist Jack Engler reports on his study of Dipa Ma and other advanced meditators. He found a degree of mental health and well-being among this group of subjects that was remarkable and hadn't been previously described in psychological research.

Engler gave these meditation masters an extensive battery of tests, including the Rorschach and Thematic Apperception tests, which measure personality and perception. Dipa Ma's tests confirmed that she had cultivated an unusually peaceful mind, completely untroubled by anger, fear, greed, or conflict of any kind. Engler reports, "The tests show a cognitive-emotional transformation and integration that reflected the deepest levels of inner liberation. Dipa Ma spontaneously wove her test responses into an ongoing spiritual story, a narrative that revealed the whole teaching of the dharma and at the same time showed clear comprehension of the tests—a remarkable achievement none of the researchers had ever witnessed."

Dipa Ma shows what is possible when we return to our Buddha nature. But let us remember that this kind of shining of the heart is not unique to meditation masters or advanced practitioners. It is already present and available in all of us. My colleague Sharon Salzberg tells a story demonstrating this, from a daylong loving-kindness retreat in Oakland, California.

"Whenever I teach loving-kindness retreats in an urban setting," Sharon explains, "I ask students to do their walking meditation out on the streets. I suggest they choose individuals they see and, with care and awareness, wish them well by silently repeating the traditional phrases of the loving-kindness practice, 'May you be happy, may you be peaceful.' I tell them that even if they don't feel loving, the power of their intention to offer love is not diminished. On this day our retreat took place a few blocks from downtown Oakland. Since we were directly across the street from the Amtrak station, several people chose to do their practice on the train platform.

"When a train pulled in, one woman from the class noticed a man disembark and decided to make him the recipient of her loving-kindness meditation. Silently she began reciting the phrases for him. Almost immediately she began judging herself: I must not be doing it right because I feel so distant. I don't feel a great wash of warm feeling coming over me. Nonetheless, reaffirming her intention to look on all beings with kindness instead of estrangement, she continued thinking, 'May you be happy, may you be peaceful.' Taking another look at the man, who was dressed in a suit and tie and seemed nervous, she began judging him: He looks so rigid and uptight. Judging herself, she thought, Here I am trying to send loving-kindness to someone and instead I'm disparaging him. Still, she continued repeating the phrases, aligning her energy with her deep intention: to be a force of love in the world. At that moment the man walked over to her and said, 'I've never done anything like this before in my life, but I'd like to ask you to pray for me. I am about to face a very difficult situation in my life. Somehow, you seem to have a really loving heart, and I'd just like to know that you're praying for me.'"

THE FOUR RADIANT ABODES

The old Buddhist list makers had a joyous time mapping the highest possibilities of human development. They enumerate the four degrees of noble hearts, five spiritual powers, five ranks, eight satoris, ten ox-herding pictures, ten stages of a bodhisattva, and thirty-seven factors of enlightenment. But the most treasured description of human awakening, what we in the West might call optimal mental health, is the four radiant abodes.

These four radiant abodes are loving-kindness, compassion, joy, and equanimity (or peace). These abodes are the expression of natural human happiness. They are immediate and simple, the universal description of an open heart. Even when we hear their names—love, compassion, joy, peace—they touch us directly. When we meet another who is filled with these qualities, our heart lights up. When we touch peace, love, joy, and compassion in ourselves, we are transformed.

Love is our true nature, but it is often covered over by a protective layer of fear. Buddhist practices can help us to unearth the gold beneath the clay and return us to our natural goodness. Even though this love is innate, the Buddhist path also uses systematic trainings to cultivate this love. They strengthen our capacity for love, compassion, joy, and peace. The practices that develop these qualities involve invoking and repeating certain intentions, phrases, visualizations, and feelings. These trainings have been employed by millions of practitioners to transform their hearts.

When the radiant abodes are developed, their complementary qualities help to balance one another. This balance is considered essential in Buddhist psychology. Because love, compassion, and joy can lead to excessive attachment, their warmth needs to be balanced with equanimity. Because equanimity can lead to excessive detachment, its coolness needs to be balanced with love, compassion, and joy. Established together, these radiant qualities express mental harmony.

The flow of these awakened qualities begins with natural inner peace. When consciousness is peaceful and open, we rest in equanimity. As our peaceful heart meets other beings, it fills with love. When this love meets pain, it transforms itself naturally into compassion. And when this same openhearted love meets happiness, it becomes joy. In this way, the radiant abodes spontaneously reflect and connect the whole of the world.

Awakening Love

Loving-kindness is the first of the radiant abodes, and there are practices for its cultivation. In the initial stages of loving-kindness practice, students are asked to direct love first toward themselves, repeating four or five tradition phrases of well-wishing, such as "May I be safe and healthy. May I be happy." Along with the recitation, students are encouraged to invite the quality of loving-kindness to be present in their body and mind.

The quality of loving-kindness develops as we repeat these phrases thousands of times, over days and months. Initially it can feel difficult to offer love to yourself: for many it can trigger feelings of shame and unworthiness. Yet it is a particularly powerful practice, because whatever we do not love in our own self, we will not accept in another. Buddhist teachings explain, "You can search the whole universe and not find any being more worthy of love than yourself."

After many repetitions, love and care for yourself can grow. Then the same loving-kindness is systematically extended to others, by categories. First we visualize and offer love to our benefactors, then our loved ones, our friends, neutral people, and eventually difficult people, and then finally even to our enemies. Then we extend the well-wishing of loving-kindness further—to all humans, animals, and insects, to beings of the earth, water, and air, to beings large and small, young and old, visible and not visible—until beings in every direction are included. At each step of the process, we deliberately extend our field of loving consciousness. If we find difficulty opening to the next area of loving-kindness, we try to gradually let go and forgive, repeatedly offering loving intentions until the obstacles dissolve.

Ruby has been a Buddhist practitioner for fifteen years. Today Ruby exudes happiness and joy, but this is not because her life has been easy. Several years ago, Ruby asked me what might be helpful next steps in her training and development. In addition to her work as a university administrator, she was caring for her mother and helping with two grandchildren, so she could not go on long retreats.

To balance Ruby's caring for others, I suggested that she undertake a year of loving-kindness practice just for herself. At first she resisted. "You mean a year of wishing that I be happy? It feels so self-centered. I don't know if I could do it." But she decided to try it. In her morning meditation, and throughout the day, Ruby wished herself well, with loving intention, at work, driving, shopping. At times the meditation felt tedious and difficult, but she stuck to it. Over the year Ruby became happier and more radiant. Then, I suggested she attend a weeklong retreat of loving-kindness meditation.

After two days of resistance, Ruby dropped into a silent and concentrated stillness. Through her practice, Ruby had learned not to resist her resistance, to allow all her experience to be held in love. As she did, the loving-kindness grew. Over the next days Ruby experienced a stream of luminous energy filling up the core of her body, expanding to a boundless ocean of love. She was incredibly happy. "I have opened," she exclaimed one morning. "I am nothing and I am the whole world. I am the crab apple tree and the frog by the stream and the tired cooks in the evening kitchen and the mud on my shoes and the stars. When my mind thinks about past and future, it is only telling stories. In loving-kindness, there is no past or future, only silence and love."

Ruby had graduated. Love was no longer a training or a practice, it was her life. It was love that Ruby brought to her mother's bedside through her long illness. Now Ruby tells me she doesn't practice loving-kindness meditation formally for herself or others much anymore, because "it just comes." She says, "We're not separate, and love is just what we are."

The experience of practicing loving-kindness in this systematic way illuminates new possibilities. For example, when we shift our attention from benefactors and friends to neutral people, a whole new category of love opens up. In this practice, neutral people are defined as people we see regularly but don't pay much attention to. We might choose our regular bank teller or a waitress at a local restaurant as our first neutral person. On one long retreat, I chose an old local gardener. I spent several days and nights picturing him and wishing him well in my meditation. Later I unexpectedly ran into him. Even though I didn't know his name, I was so happy to see him, I swooned: Oh, my beloved neutral person! Then I realized how many other neutral people I had ignored. As I included them in the practice of loving-kindness, my love grew deeper around me.

From neutral people, the practice of loving-kindness extends to difficult people and enemies. But this is not where we start. Only when our heart is open and our loving-kindness is strong do we bring in someone for whom we have strong aversion, someone by whom we've felt wronged, someone we've come to think of as an enemy. As we do, at first the heart shrivels and closes: After what you did to me, I'm never going to love or forgive you, ever. But as this hatred arises, we lose the joy of our own open heart. Seeing this, we understand the cost of hatred. We realize, for our own sake, that the cost is too high. Finally we think, OK, I'll forgive. I'll let even you into my loving-kindness—a little at first—so that I can keep my heart open. Through this repeated practice we learn to keep our heart open even in difficulty. As we cultivate this training in kindness, eventually we can end up like Dipa Ma, radiating love to all we meet.

My colleague Sylvia Boorstein tells of Phil, a Buddhist practitioner in New York who had worked with loving-kindness practice for years. One evening on a small side street in SoHo, a disheveled man with a scraggly beard and dirty blond hair accosted Phil, pointed a gun at him, and demanded his money. Phil was carrying more than six hundred dollars in his wallet and he handed it all over. The mugger shook his gun and demanded more. Stalling for time, Phil gave him his credit cards and then the whole wallet. Looking dazed and high on some drug, the mugger said, "I'm gonna shoot you." Phil responded, "No, wait, here's my watch—it's an expensive one." Disoriented, the mugger took the watch, waved the gun, and said again, "I'm gonna shoot you." Somehow Phil managed to look at him with loving-kindness and said, "You don't have to shoot me. You did good. Look, you got nearly seven hundred dollars; you got credit cards and an expensive watch. You don't have to shoot me. You did really good." The mugger, confused, lowered the gun slowly. "I did good?" he asked. "You did really good. Go and tell your friends, you did good." Dazed, the mugger wandered off, saying softly to himself, "I did good."

Whenever our goodness is seen, it is a blessing. Every culture and tradition understands the importance of seeing one another with love. An old Hasidic rabbi once asked his pupils how they could tell exactly when the night had ended and the day begun (daybreak is the time for certain holy prayers). "Is it when you can see an animal in the distance and tell whether it is a sheep or a dog?" one student proposed. "No," answered the rabbi. "Is it when you can clearly see the lines on your own palm?" another asked. "Is it when you can look at a tree in the distance and tell if it is a fig or a pear tree?" "No," answered the rabbi each time. "Then, what is it?" the pupils demanded. "It is when you can look on the face of any man or woman and see that they are your sister or brother. Until then it is still night."

Natural Joy

When Harvard psychologist Jack Engler was doing his research with Dipa Ma, he asked her about one of the common misunderstandings of Buddhist teachings. "If we get rid of greed, hate, and ignorance, it sounds like life might become sort of gray and dull," he said. "Where's the juice?" Dipa Ma burst out laughing. "Oh, you don't understand! There is so much sameness in ordinary life. We are always experiencing everything through the same set of lenses. Once greed, hatred, and delusion are gone, you see everything fresh and new all the time. Every moment is new. Life was dull before. Now, every day, every moment, is full of taste and zest."

When love meets pain, it becomes compassion and there will be many pages devoted to the path of compassion later in this book. When love meets happiness, it becomes joy. Joy is an expression of the liberated and awakened heart. A few years ago the Dalai Lama was cohost of a large scientific meeting in Washington, D.C. He met with physicians, neuroscientists, and several Buddhist teachers (including myself) to explore the latest clinical research on meditation and neurobiology. One morning a network television reporter interviewed him and asked about meditation and happiness. "You're the author of *The New York Times* best-selling book *The Art of Happiness,* and you frequently teach about happiness. Could you tell our viewers about the happiest moment in your life?" The Dalai Lama considered for a moment, smiled, and said, "I think, now."

When we live in the present, joy arises for no reason. This is the happiness of consciousness that is not dependent on particular conditions. Children know this joy. Maurice Sendak, author of *Where the Wild Things Are,* tells the story of a boy who wrote to him. "He sent me a charming card with a drawing. I loved it. I answer all my children's letters—sometimes very hastily—but this one I lingered over. I sent him a postcard and I drew a picture of a Wild Thing on it. I wrote, 'Dear Jim, I loved your card.' Then I got a letter back from his mother and she said, 'Jim loved your card so much he ate it.' That to me was one of the highest compliments I've ever received. He didn't care that it was an original drawing or anything. He saw it, he loved it, he ate it."

Joy can come spontaneously in deep meditation. Students describe trembling, tears of laughter, cool waves, ripples of ecstasy, floating joy, joy like turquoise water, bodily thrilling, grateful joy, playful and delighting joy, and ecstasy of stillness. They describe joy in the body, heart, and mind, joy in the beauty of the world, and joy in the happiness of others.

Nonetheless, sometimes people mistake Buddhism for a pessimistic view of life. Certainly the Noble Truths teach about suffering and its causes, and in Buddhist countries there are a few very serious, grim, duty-type meditation masters. I myself, like many other Westerners, sought them out. I was so determined to transform myself and maybe to discover some special experiences that I went to the strictest monasteries and retreats, where we practiced eighteen hours a day and sat unmoving in the face of enormous pain. And at these monasteries I learned many important things.

But somehow in the seriousness of my quest, I failed to notice the extraordinary buoyancy of the Buddhist cultures around me. Thai, Lao, Tibetan, Burmese, and Nepali cultures are lighthearted; the people are filled with laughter. The children enchant you with their happy smiles. The grown-ups work, play, and pray with a light spirit. Seeking austerity, we serious Westerners failed to notice that most Buddhist temples are a riot of colors, filled with elaborate paintings and statues and images of fantastic stories of angels, *devas*, bodhisattvas, and buddhas. We ignored the playful community life that centered around the temples, the cycles of rituals, dances, celebrations, feasts, and festivals. In our ardor, we did not appreciate how many of our greatest teachers—Ajahn Chah, Maha Ghosananda, Ananda Maitreya, the Sixteenth Karmapa Lama, Anagarika Munindra—had marvelous, easy laughs and an infectious sense of joy.

When I returned to the United States and began to teach, my colleagues and I tended to emphasize the Buddha's teaching on suffering and the need to awaken. We were young and the focus on human suffering gave our retreats gravitas. But suffering is not the goal, it is the beginning of the path. Now in the retreats I teach, I also encourage participants to awaken to their innate joy. From the very beginning I encourage them to allow the moments of joy and well-being to deepen, to spread throughout their body and mind. Many of us are conditioned to fear joy and happiness, yet joy is necessary for awakening. As the Persian mystic Rumi instructs us, "When you go to a garden, do you look at thorns or flowers? Spend more time with roses and jasmine." André Gide, the French novelist and philosopher, enjoins us, "Know that joy is rarer, more difficult, and more beautiful than sadness. Once you make this all-important discovery, you must embrace joy as a moral obligation."

Psychologists working with the Tibetan community in exile have noted the remarkable resiliency and joyfulness among the people, even though many are survivors of great trauma and loss. Most surprising are the responses of nuns and monks who have been imprisoned and tortured. According to a study by Harvard psychologists, many show few or none of the ordinary signs of trauma, but instead have deepened in compassion and joyful appreciation of life. Their trainings in loving-kindness, compassion, and wisdom led them to pray for their enemies. One old lama recounted that over the twenty years of prison and torture, his only true fear was that he would lose his compassion and close his heart. If we want to understand optimal mental health, these monks and nuns are a striking example.

Debra Chamberlin-Taylor, a Buddhist teacher and colleague, tells the story of a community activist who participated in her yearlong training group for people of color. This woman had experienced a child-hood of poverty, trauma, and abuse. She had faced the death of a parent, illness, divorce from a painful marriage, racism, and the single parent-ing of two children. She talked about her years of struggle to educate herself, to stand up for what she believed. She described how she had become a radical to fight for justice in local and national politics. Fi-nally, at the last meeting, this woman announced, "After all the strug-gles and troubles I've lived through, I've decided to do something really radical! I am going to be happy."

Just as we can awaken to loving-kindness and compassion, we can awaken to joy. It is innate to consciousness. As we find it in ourselves, we can see it in others. On one long spring retreat, Lorna, a young woman, came to me to talk about her reaction to one of the retreatants. She was having trouble with a big man seated nearby. He moved too often. Bud was an old ex-marine whose T-shirts revealed lots of tattoos. He smelled of tobacco smoke. His energy frightened her. Lorna tried to understand. She used loving-kindness practice and discovered how Bud triggered her painful history with men. Gradually, Lorna realized that most of what bothered her was her own imagination. Still, it seemed like a scary thing to talk to someone like Bud. Then, in the last week of the retreat, Lorna came in to see me, grinning. "I'm not afraid of him anymore." She explained that after breakfast she had walked down to the stream below the dining hall. She came upon the marine there among the banks of flowers, cupping each one deliberately in his hands to smell its fragrance. On the last day of the retreat, I saw Lorna in a joyful and animated conversation with Bud, standing near the flowers.

Like loving-kindness, there is a practice for joy. We begin by pictur-ing someone we love as they experience a happy moment. We feel their well-being. Then we recite the intention "May your happiness and joy increase. May the causes for your happiness increase," repeating these intentions again and again, through any resistance, through tiredness, comparing, or jealousy, over and over until our sense of joy becomes strong. Next, we systemically extend this practice to others we love, one after another, until the quality of joy in their happiness grows even more available. Then we turn the practice of joy to ourselves, including our own joy and happiness in the well-wishing. From this we systemically and gradually open our practice of joy to all categories of beings. As we train ourselves to celebrate the joy and success of others, we awaken the radiant abode of joy. With joy, whatever we do becomes holy. Martin Luther King, Jr., understood this when he said, "If a person sweeps streets for a living, he should sweep them as Michelangelo painted, as Beethoven composed music, as Shakespeare wrote his plays."

As a support for the cultivation of joy, we can also include the practice of gratitude. Buddhist monks begin each day with a chant of gratitude for the blessings of their life. In the same way, Native American elders begin each ceremony with grateful prayers to Mother Earth and Father Sky, to the four directions, and to the animal, plant, and mineral brothers and sisters who share our earth and support our life.

Gratitude is a gracious acknowledgment of all that sustains us, a bow to our blessings, great and small. Gratitude is confidence in life itself. In it we feel how the same force that pushes grass through cracks in the sidewalk invigorates our own life. In Tibet, the monks and nuns offer prayers of gratitude even for the suffering they have experienced: "Grant that I might have enough suffering to awaken in me the deepest possible compassion and wisdom." Gratitude does not envy or compare. Gratitude receives in wonder the myriad offerings of rain and sunlight, the care that supports every single life.

As gratitude grows, it gives rise to joy. We experience the courage to rejoice in our own good fortune and in the good fortune of others. In joy, we are not afraid of pleasure. We do not mistakenly believe it is disloyal to the suffering of the world to honor the happiness we have been given. Joy gladdens the heart. We can be joyful for people we love, for moments of goodness, for sunlight and trees, and for the very breath within our lungs. Like an innocent child, we can rejoice in life itself, in being alive.

The world we live in is a temple, and the miraculous light of the first stars is shining through it all the time. In place of original sin, we celebrate original goodness. Saint Teresa of Ávila explains, "God does not desire the soul to undertake any labor, but only to take delight in the first fragrance of the flowers . . . the soul can obtain sufficient nourishment from its own garden." In every meeting of the eyes and every leafing tree, in every taste of tangerine and avocado, a blessing occurs. This is true mental health.

FREEDOM HERE AND NOW

The radiant abodes express the fruit of mental development. When they are in balance, loving-kindness, compassion, and joy rest in an unshakable equanimity. This peace is not indifference or emotional resignation; it is the still point, the living reality of the present. This dynamic stillness is what Dipa Ma calls the crowning stage of Buddhist training, "where consciousness becomes a symphony of loving-kindness, playing in a silent ocean of equanimity."

We have now come full circle, arriving here where we started, and, as T. S. Eliot writes, "knowing the place for the first time." Coming to rest in the present, wherever we are, becomes the seat of awakening. We are now truly alive, able to care, to work, to love, to enter life fully, with an open heart. We see the lawfulness of life unfolding, the causes of sorrow, and the choice for freedom. We do whatever we can to reduce suffering, and all along we are free. This is the final message Buddhist teaching communicates to its followers: you are free. This freedom is the very nature of our own heart and mind.

Each of us will reflect our inner freedom in a unique way, through our temperament, body, and culture. There are those who express their freedom primarily through silence, others through joy. There are those who express freedom through peacefulness and others through service and love. A free and awakened consciousness is experienced as a many-faceted crystal. One facet is peace, another is love; one is strength, another is clarity; one is gratitude, others include integrity, compassion, courage, creativity, joyfulness, and abundance. Each of these qualities can fill consciousness and shine through our body, heart, and mind. This is not simply a metaphor. It becomes our actual experience. We are illuminated by these qualities, one or several at a time.

When we find freedom, even pain and illness become part of the grace of life, and they are our teachers. The Dalai Lama said, "When, at some point in our lives, we meet a real tragedy —which could happen to any one of us—we can react in two ways. Obviously, we can lose hope, let ourselves slip into discouragement, into alcohol, drugs, and unending sadness. Or else we can wake ourselves up, discover in ourselves an energy that was hidden there, and act with genuine clarity and compassion." Imperfections are part of the display of life. Joy and sorrow, birth and death are the dance of existence throughout which our awakened consciousness can shine.

This perspective is called finding the goodness in everything. As proof of the human capacity to do so, here is a prayer written by an unknown prisoner in the Ravensbrück concentration camp and left beside the body of a dead child: "O Lord, remember not only the men and women of goodwill, but also those of ill will. But do not remember only the suffering they have inflicted on us; remember too the fruits we brought forth thanks to this suffering—our comradeship, our loyalty, our humility, our courage, our generosity, the greatness of heart which has grown out of all this. And when they come to judgment, let all the fruits which we have borne be their forgiveness."

The Thai Buddhist teacher Ajahn Buddhadasa says that finding goodness everywhere allows us to be servants of peace. Buddhadasa means "servant of awakening" or "servant of peace." He called his monastery "the garden of peace." Amid the ancient forests, beautiful pools, bamboo, and stone sculptures, Ajahn Buddhadasa offered the teachings of loving-kindness, compassion, and peace. For fifty years, through cycles of war and truce, insurgency, simplicity, and modernization, tens of thousands came to hear his teachings of peace. As we awaken, we too become servants of peace, taking our place in the garden.

This is the culmination of the psychology of the wise heart. We are the beauty we have been seeking all our lives. We are consciousness knowing itself. Empty and spacious, compassionate and joyful, our very peace and equanimity begin to transform the world around us. Buddhist psychology helps us rediscover that freedom and joy are our original nature. "O Nobly Born, do not forget the luminous nature of your own mind. Trust it. It is home."

5

Make Your Heart
a Zone of Peace

Dharma and Politics

MANY BUDDHIST PRACTITIONERS have questioned how to apply
such teachings as mindfulness and loving-kindness in these turbulent
times. The modern world is in need of a spiritual perspective. The
dharma is a universal medicine. The teachings of generosity, virtue,
loving-kindness, and wisdom are nonpartisan. The benefits of dharma
teachings can be used by Republicans and by Democrats, by members
of the Green Party and by Libertarians, by Iraqis and by Israelis. The
dharma welcomes everyone and encourages all to awaken together.

But where, as dharma practitioners, do we start? In a complex political world how do we find a way toward peace? Our first task is to
make our own heart a zone of peace. Instead of becoming entangled in
the bitterness and cynicism that exist externally, we need to begin to
heal those qualities within ourselves. We have to face our own suffering,
our own fear, and transform them into compassion. Only then can we
become ready to offer genuine help to the outside world. Albert Camus
writes, "We all carry within us our places of exile, our crimes, our rav-
ages. Our task is not to unleash them on the world; it is to transform
them in ourselves."

Dharma practitioners who want to act in the sphere of politics must
quiet their minds and open their hearts. Meditate, turn off the news,
turn on Mozart, walk through the forest or the mountains, and begin to
make yourselves peaceful. Make yourselves an example of peace, and
allow the sensitivity and compassion that grows from our interconnec-

tion to extend to all beings. If we're not peaceful, how can we create harmony in the world? If our own minds are not peaceful, how can we expect peace to come through the actions that we take?

We can either react to terrorism and insecurity with fear—and create a frightened, barricaded society, a fortress America—or we can use the teachings of dharma to respond calmly, with both prudent action and a fearless, steady heart. Zen monk Thich Nhat Hanh tells us of the boat people who fled Vietnam in the 1970s, writing, "When the crowded refugee boats met with storms or pirates, if everyone panicked, all would be lost. But if even one person stayed calm, it was enough. It showed the way for everyone to survive."

Through practice, we can learn to make our own hearts a place of peace and integrity. With a quiet mind and an open heart we can sense the reality of interdependence. Inner and outer are not separate. We are all in the same boat. Once we see this clearly, we can extend the same principles of love and mindfulness to every area. Buddhist teachings explain that life cannot be divided into compartments. Our relationships with others, right speech, right action, right livelihood, are all part of the eightfold path. They are factors of enlightenment. Our relations and our society as a whole are expressions of the enlightened heart. Thus we can understand Gandhi's challenge: "Those who say spirituality has nothing to do with politics, they do not know what spirituality really means."

As we understand this, our task is to see for ourselves what is needed to bring to benefit to the world. How does peace come about? What are the conditions for peace? The Buddha taught that peace is possible both individually and collectively but that it depends on skillful causes and conditions. Inner peace requires mindfulness, compassion, and respect. Outwardly, it grows from the same conditions. When asked about the creation of a wise society, the Buddha counseled visiting ministers that when a society comes together to make decisions in harmony, when it honors its elders and the wise ways they have established, when it cares for its most vulnerable members—women and children—when it respects the environment and listens to its citizens and its neighbors, it can be expected to prosper and not decline. For the Buddha, a wise society is not based on greed, on hatred or delusion, but on generosity, respect, mindfulness, and compassion.

In the modern political climate we are bombarded with propaganda from every political point of view. This dulls the senses and overpowers our inner value system. Whatever our political perspective, we will encounter troubling images and feel anger, frustration, even outrage and impatience. If we stop and breathe and meditate, we will feel underneath these reactions our fear, and under this our caring and connection. If our actions come from this deep sense of caring, they will bring greater benefit and greater peace. From a quiet heart, we have the ability to look and see how our society treats its most vulnerable members. How does it treat the poor, the elderly, and the young? Is it acting in ways that foster greed, hate, fear, and ignorance? What can we do nationally and internationally to support generosity and respect, to end racism and exploitation, and to minimize violence? What rings true for each of us as followers of the dharma? We need to take an honest look and see what we are supporting as a society. And then we speak out truthfully, and stand up for what is wise.

America has sometimes confused power with greatness. But genuine greatness is not a matter of mere power; it is a matter of integrity. When we envision a society of compassion and justice—and as a nation we are called upon to do this—our actions can stem from respect for all beings, and peace is the result.

Once we have looked clearly, we can set a long-term intention and dedicate ourselves to a vision of a wise and compassionate society. This is a bodhisattva's act. Like setting the compass of the heart, this intention expresses our deepest values. If we set a long-term intention, it remains empowering no matter who wins a particular election, or what governments rise and fall. It becomes our way of practice. Thomas Merton taught, "Do not worry about immediate results. More and more you must concentrate on the value, the rightness, the truth of the work itself." With a dedicated intention we are willing to face the sufferings of the world and not shy away, to follow what we know is true, however long it takes. This is a powerful act of the heart, to stay true to our values and live by them.

A beautiful example of a long-term intention was presented by A. T. Ariyaratane, a Buddhist elder, who is considered to be the Gandhi of Sri Lanka. For seventeen years there had been a terrible civil war in Sri Lanka. At one point, the Norwegians were able to broker peace, and once the peace treaty was in effect, Ariyaratane called the followers of his Sarvodaya movement together. Sarvodaya combines Buddhist principles of right livelihood, right action, right understanding, and compassion and has organized citizens in one-third of that nation's villages to dig wells, build schools, meditate, and collaborate as a form of spiritual practice. Over 650,000 people came to the gathering to hear how he envisioned the future of Sri Lanka. At this gathering he proposed a five-hundred-year peace plan, saying, "The Buddha teaches we must understand causes and conditions. It's taken us five hundred years to create the suffering that we are in now." Ari described the effects of four hundred years of colonialism, of five hundred years of struggle between Hindus, Muslims, and Buddhists, and of several centuries of economic disparity. He went on, "It will take us five hundred years to change these conditions." Ariyaratane then offered solutions, proposing a plan to heal the country.

The plan begins with five years of cease-fire and ten years of rebuilding roads and schools. Then it goes on for twenty-five years of programs to learn one another's languages and cultures, and fifty years of work to right economic injustice, and to bring the islanders back together as a whole. And every hundred years there will be a grand council of elders to take stock on how the plan is going. This is a sacred intention, the long-term vision of an elder.

In the same way, if we envision the fulfillment of wisdom and compassion in the United States, it becomes clear that the richest nation on earth must provide health care for its children; that the most productive nation on earth must find ways to combine trade with justice; that a creative society must find ways to grow and to protect the environment and plan sustainable development for generations ahead. A nation founded on democracy must bring enfranchisement to all citizens at home and then offer the same spirit of international cooperation and respect globally. We are all in this together.

Seeing clearly, we need to act. To empower our vision, we need to start now, and be willing to plant seeds, for however long it takes, to benefit our society and ourselves. At Spirit Rock Meditation Center, Sylvia Boorstein has taught a class called Informed Citizenship as Spiritual Practice, which encourages people to ask themselves, What can I do as a wisdom holder, as a bodhisattva, and as a member of this society to best contribute to the world in these times? It might be registering people to vote, or working politically, or making our vision heard in organizations of power or in the government, speaking up or writing. It might include working with children, or helping to create a business climate of responsibility and integrity, or working internationally, or tending to poverty, racism, and injustice locally. Each person has to find specific steps to offer their vision and energy to society, and to empower those around them. If we don't do this, change won't happen. The vision will not be fulfilled.

The Buddha's teachings of compassion and wisdom are empowering; they encourage us to act. Do not doubt that your good actions will bear fruit, and that change for the better can be born from your life. Gandhi reminds us, "I claim to be no more than an average person with less than average ability. I have not the shadow of a doubt that any man or woman can achieve what I have if he or she would simply make the same effort and cultivate the same hope and faith."

6

Our Children Will Learn What They Live

Becoming More Conscious Parents

JUST AS THERE IS an environmental crisis, and just as there are social and political crises, there is also a crisis in parenting. The same loss of connection with nature, the same loss of community and village, the same loss of the values of the heart that creates these other crises creates the crisis in child rearing.

Some days, I find it a terrible thing to go to the supermarket. I'll see a two-year-old boy walking alongside his mother or father, and the boy accidentally knocks something over. Immediately the parent turns back, smacks the kid, and yells, "Don't you dare do that!" And the poor toddler is shaken up and doesn't understand. What do they want from me? he wonders. I'm just learning to walk. It was an accident. Right then, this child learns that he's bad, and he also learns that if you don't like what happens, you hit somebody.

It's not that these parents don't love their kids, but that they don't know what to do. Often mama and papa are tired. They've got three kids and financial troubles or a bad marriage, and they haven't been sleeping well. All those difficulties enter into the way they relate to their children.

Even when you don't actually see the parenting, you can see its effect on the children. From time to time, I used to volunteer in an elementary school class. Nearly half the children live in single-parent homes. When I worked in the classroom, I saw kids who lived in the midst of family crises or were being raised primarily by TV and fast food. You can feel their pain, their fears, their confusion, and self-doubt.

At the other extreme are the many children suffering from the "hurried-child syndrome" or from the hovering of "helicopter parents," who seem always to be there, pushing their children to become successful even before they reach kindergarten. Frequently, the effect of all this is that by age eight these kids are being treated by doctors because they're suffering from stress, fatigue, and the fear that they will not get into an elite university.

But no one is allowed to say anything to parents in supermarkets and playgrounds or even to the parents of your child's classmates. It's a taboo, as if children are their parents' possessions. Yet parents are also beset by guilt, worry, pain, and fear of doing it right or wrong.

THE LOSS OF COMMUNITY

Our country's postindustrial culture has left us to raise our children apart from a community of neighbors and wise elders. There aren't many grandparents around—they all live somewhere else or they're at work, like most of the parents.

Instead of village elders, American parents have turned to various "experts" and whatever fad or theory those experts have come up with. In the 1920s, an influential school of child psychology actually taught parents that it was bad to touch their children. Several decades later, parents all across America read books that insisted that we bottle-feed (not breast-feed) an infant every four hours and that we should not pick up a crying baby but just let him "cry himself out."

Other cultures know that when babies cry, they cry for a reason, and that that is when to pick them up and feed them or hold them and comfort them. Countless educators and psychologists have been working in recent years to restore our respect for children from the first year of life.

When children are valued in this way, the whole of society benefits. In this spirit, there's a tribe in West Africa whose members count the birthday of a child from the day the child is first a thought in its mother's mind. On that day, a woman goes out and sits under a tree and quietly listens and waits until she can hear the song of her child. When she has heard the song, she returns to her village and teaches it to the man whom she has envisioned as the child's father so that they can sing the song when they make love, inviting their child to join them. The expectant mother then sings this song to the child in her womb and teaches it to the midwives, who sing it when the child is born. And the villagers all learn the child's song, so that whenever the child cries or hurts itself, they pick it up, hold it in their arms, and sing the song. The song is also sung when the young man or woman goes through a rite of passage, when he or she marries, and then, for a last time, when he or she is about to die.

What a beautiful way for human beings to listen to and to comfort other human beings! To know each other's song. This is the spirit of conscious parenting, to listen to the song of the child in front of you and to sing that child's song to him or her. When a child is crying, we need to ask why this child is singing the crying song, what frustration this child is feeling.

CHILDREN WITH A HOLE INSIDE

Yet when our culture tells us to ignore our instincts, to distrust our intuition, children grow up raised more by electronic screens than by an adult. The average American child sees, via the modern media, tens of thousands of murders and violent acts, and an ocean of advertisements. We're raising our children on violence and materialism. We are feeding the next generation the recipe for the very greed and hate we later attempt to undo in our spiritual practice. With the highest rate of infant mortality of any industrialized nation and millions of "latchkey kids," we have given up caring for our children. An increasing number are raised by day care and TV. We will end up with a new generation of Americans more wired by texts and tweets and more connected to TV and video games (often violent ones) than to other people. We will have more wars and violent crimes than successful marriages. It is a questionable experiment to raise our children more with screens and electronics than with people. Yet when children are not held enough when they are young, not valued enough and respected enough, not listened to or sung to, they can grow up with a hole inside, with no real sense of what it means to love, with no real capacity for intimacy.

The Dalai Lama, speaking with a group of Western psychologists, said that he couldn't understand why he heard so much talk about self-hatred and unworthiness. He was so astonished that he went around the room and asked everyone, "Do you feel unworthiness and self-hatred sometimes?" "Yes." "Do you feel it?" "Yes." Everyone in the room nodded yes. He couldn't believe it. He was also astonished that in our culture people more commonly talk about their difficulty with their parents instead of honoring their parents.

Contrast this with stories of the healthy childhoods of the people of the Buddha's time. The Buddha himself was raised by his mother's sister after his mother died, and he was given all the nurturance, natural respect, care, and attention that every child needs. Later, when he left home to practice as a yogi, he had the inner strength and integrity to undertake six years of intensely ascetic practice—he followed every available ascetic discipline, hoping through them to rid himself of his desires and fears, to overcome his anger, and to master his body and mind. The rigors almost killed him, but he did not succeed in the fight against himself.

Exhausted by this struggle, he sat down, and a vision came to him from his childhood that led directly to the path of his enlightenment. He remembered being a young boy sitting in his father's garden under a rose apple tree. It was at the time of the spring plowing festival. He remembered sitting there and experiencing a sense of stillness and wholeness, a state of great concentration and wonderful well-being. He realized that ascetic self-denial had taken him in the wrong direction and that the basis for spiritual life was well-being—not fighting against one's body, heart, and mind. From this great insight he discovered the Middle Way between denial and indulgence. He then took nourishment and began to care for himself. His strength returned, his loving-kindness returned, and eventually he became enlightened.

The Buddha had this vision of well-being from his childhood to draw upon in his practice. Many of us, though, have not had such an experience as children. And so the first years of our spiritual practice are spent dealing with grief, unworthiness, judgment, self-hatred, abuse, addiction, rage. This is common in our culture. Of course, spiritual practice brings us to face the deep grief and sorrow and pain of the world, but for Americans, much of our pain is a hole in our souls, and empty space in ourselves that longs to be connected, that longs for intimacy and love. We all face this to the extent that we didn't experience a sense of well-being in childhood. For the next generation, this suffering will be even more pervasive unless we bring a healing wisdom to parenting.

PARENTING AS PRACTICE

Parenting is a labor of love. It's a path of service and surrender and, like the practice of a Buddha or a bodhisattva, it demands patience and understanding and tremendous sacrifice. It is also a way to reconnect with the mystery of life and to reconnect with ourselves. Young children have that sense of mystery. When my daughter Caroline was seven, I could see her sense of mystery getting fainter. That Christmas she announced, "I don't believe in Santa Claus anymore. My friends told me. Besides which, I don't see how he could fit down our chimney. He's too big."

At seven, she began to trade in the mystery of things for concrete explanations. Up until then she had mostly been living in a mythological, timeless world, where reindeer fly and Santa Claus appears. Then she grew bigger and decided to take out the tape and measure the width of the chimney. But long after she proclaims herself "too old" to believe in Santa Claus, there will be new mysteries. Anyone who has teenage kids is reminded that no one understands the mystery of sex. Teenagers don't ask you directly about it, but you can feel it in the air. As teenagers grapple with love and sex and hormones and embarrassment, we do too. "What did you do in school today?" a father asks his teenage son. "Oh, we had sex ed," he replies. "What did they tell you?" "Well, first a priest told us why we shouldn't. Then a doctor told us how we shouldn't. Finally the principal gave us a talk on where we shouldn't."

Children give us the opportunity to awaken, to look at ourselves, our lives, and the mystery around us with beginner's mind. Suppose we look at child rearing in the spirit of the Buddha's discourses on mindfulness. In the text, we are instructed to pay attention to breathing in and out; to be aware when standing up, bending, stretching, or moving forward or backward; to be aware when eating or sitting or going to the bathroom; to be aware when the mind is contracted, fearful, or agitated; and to be aware as we learn to let go, when the mind is balanced and filled with equanimity and understanding and peace. To further develop our awareness, the Buddha recommends sitting in meditation, practicing by staying up all night and contemplating the sickness of the body or aging, developing a loving empathy for the suffering of all beings, and bringing wisdom and compassion to them.

Suppose the Buddha gave similarly detailed instructions for using parenting as practice. It would be a nearly identical teaching. We would be instructed to be as mindful of our children's bodies as we are of our own. To be aware as they walk and eat and go to the bathroom. Then, instead of sitting up all night in meditation, we can sit up mindfully all night when our children are sick. We can be mindful when they're afraid and when it's time to hold them or comfort them with loving-kindness and compassion. We can practice patience and surrender. We can become aware of our own reactions and grasping. We can learn to let go over and over and over again as our children age. This is giving generously to the garden of the next generation, for giving and awareness is the path of awakening.

CONSCIOUS PARENTING

Along with undertaking the practice of mindfulness, I suggest four other principles of conscious parenting: attentive listening, respect, integrity, and loving-kindness. The principle of attentive listening means listening to the Tao of our children's seasons, bringing awareness to our human intuition and our instincts, to our children. Here's a story about listening: A five-year-old boy was watching the news with his father during the Persian Gulf War. The boy kept asking his father questions: "How big is the war? How did it start? What is war?" The father tried to explain why countries went to war, why some people thought wars were necessary and other people thought wars were wrong. But the boy kept asking the same questions night after night. Finally, the father heard what his son was really asking, and he sat the little boy down and said, "You don't have to worry. We are safe here. Our house is not going to be bombed. We will be safe, and we will do whatever we can to help keep other families safe." Then the little boy became peaceful because that was the reassurance his heart had been asking for.

This is the principle of attentive listening. Do we hear what our children are trying to tell us? It's like listening to the Tao. How long should we nurse our babies, or how late should we allow our teenagers to stay out on dates? To answer those questions, we have to listen and pay attention to the rhythms of life. Just as we learn to be aware of breathing in and breathing out, we can learn to sense how deeply children want to grow. Just as we learn in meditation to let go and trust, we can learn to develop a trust in our children so that they can trust themselves.

Some of us are confused by children's needs for both dependency and independence, and instead of listening to them, we impatiently hurry them along. In an article on dependency in *Mothering,* a parenting magazine I respect, Peggy O'Mara, the editor, wrote,

We have a cultural bias against dependency, against any emotion or behavior that indicates weakness. This is nowhere more tragically evident than in the way we push our children beyond their limitations and timetables. We establish outside standards as more important than inner experience when we wean our children rather than trusting that they will wean themselves, when we insist that our children sit at the table and finish their meals rather than trusting that they will eat well if healthful food is provided on a regular basis, and when we toilet train them at an early age rather than trusting that they will learn to use the toilet when they are ready to do so.

It is the nature of the child to be dependent and it is the nature of dependence to be outgrown. Dependency, insecurity, and weakness are natural states for a child. They're the natural states of all of us at times, but for children, especially young ones, they are predominant conditions and they are outgrown. Just as we grow from crawling to walking, from babbling to talking, from puberty into sexuality, as humans we move from weakness to strength, from uncertainty to mastery. When we refuse to acknowledge the stages prior to mastery, we teach our children to hate and distrust their weaknesses, and we start them on a journey of a lifetime of conflict, conflict with themselves, using external standards to set up an inner duality, a conflict between what is immediately their experience and how they're supposed to be. Begrudging dependency because it is not independence is like begrudging winter because it is not yet spring. Dependency blossoms into independence in its own sweet time.

We need to relearn how to value dependence and interdependence with patience and mindfulness; this is at the heart of both parenting and our spiritual practice. A more mature way to understand this dynamic is the emphasis Buddhist teaching places not on independence but on interdependence. When our children are taught to value their place in the web of life, they grow to honor their place and contribution at every stage of development. They learn to trust their bodies, their instincts, their feelings, and their own minds. With interdependence they also learn to value the feelings, connections, and collaboration with others. Unfortunately for all children, most especially for teenage girls, our ambitious society devalues these very qualities, and the wisdom of the feminine they carry is undermined along with their own vision and self-confidence.

This leads to the second principle for parenting, which is respect. All beings on earth—pets, plants, coworkers, lovers, children—thrive on respect, bloom when treated with respect. A story: A family settled down for dinner at a restaurant. The waitress took the orders of the adults, then turned to the seven-year-old. "What will you have?" she asked. The boy looked around the table timidly and said, "I would like to have a hot dog." "No," the mother interrupted, "not a hot dog. Get him meat loaf with mashed potatoes and carrots." As she turned to go, the waitress asked the boy, "Do you want ketchup or mustard on your hot dog?" "Ketchup," he said. "Coming up," she said, and she started for the kitchen. There was a stunned silence at the table. Finally, the boy looked at his family and said, "You know what? She thinks I'm real."

I saw the power this respect holds in traditional cultures on our family sabbatical to Thailand and Bali. My daughter Caroline studied Balinese dance for two months with a wonderful teacher, and he proposed to stage a farewell recital for her at his school, which is also his home. When we arrived, they set up the stage, got the music ready, and then started to dress Caroline. They took a very long time dressing a six-year-old whose average attention span is about five minutes. First they draped her in a silk sarong, with a beautiful chain around her waist. Then they wrapped embroidered silk fifteen times around her chest. They put on gold armbands and bracelets. They arranged her hair and put golden flowers in it. They put on more makeup than a six-year-old could dream of. Meanwhile, I sat there getting impatient, the proud father eager to take pictures. It was getting dark. "When are they going to finish dressing her and get on with the recital?" Thirty minutes, forty-five minutes. Finally the teacher's wife came out and took off her own golden necklace and put it around my daughter's neck. Caroline was thrilled.

When I let go of my impatience, I realized what a wonderful thing was happening. In Bali, whether a dancer is six or twenty-six, she is equally honored and respected. She is an artist who performs not for the audience but for the gods. The level of respect that Caroline was given as an artist allowed her to dance beautifully. Imagine how you would feel if you were given that respect as a child. We need to learn respect for ourselves, for one another, to value our children through valuing their bodies, their feelings, their minds. Children may be limited in what they can do, but their spirit isn't limited.

Another measure of respect comes in the setting of boundaries and limits appropriate to our child. As parents, we can set limits in a respectful way, with a compassionate no and an explanation of why something is out of bounds.

Sometimes, if we didn't get respect ourselves when we were children, we may have such a hole in our spirit that we need therapy and spiritual practice to make ourselves whole again. We may need to relearn self-respect before we can treat our children with respect or teach them self-respect. Children are aware of how we treat them, but they are also aware of how we treat ourselves, how we treat our bodies, how we respect our own feelings. Is it OK for us to cry or to touch one another or to be sad or angry?

That leads me to a third principle, integrity. Children learn by example, by who we are and what we do. They watch us, and we communicate to them by the way we live, the way we talk about others, and how we treat people on the street. Another story: An old sailor gave up smoking when his pet parrot developed a persistent cough. He was worried that the pipe smoke was damaging his parrot's health. He had a vet examine the bird. After a thorough checkup, the vet concluded that the parrot didn't have a respiratory disease. It had merely been imitating the cough of its pipe-smoking owner.

This is how children learn. We teach them by our being. Are we at ease or are we agitated, are we impatient or are we forgiving? Students used to ask the Tibetan master Kalu Rinpoche, "At what stage should we start to teach our children meditation and spiritual practice?" He said, "How do you know that you should teach it to them at all? Don't bother doing that. What your children need to learn is what you communicate from how you are. What matters is not that you give them any spiritual practice but that you do your own."

In a similar vein, Dorothy Law Nolte has written a poem:

Children Learn What They Live

If children live with criticism, they learn to condemn.
If children live with hostility, they learn to fight.
If children live with ridicule, they learn to feel shy.
If children live with shame, they learn to feel guilty.
If children live with encouragement, they learn confidence.
If children live with tolerance, they learn patience.
If children live with praise, they learn appreciation.
If children live with acceptance, they learn to love.
If children live with approval, they learn to like themselves.
If children live with honesty, they learn truthfulness.
If children live with security, they learn to have faith in themselves
     and in those about them.
If children live with friendliness, they learn the world is a nice place
     in which to live.

If we are to offer this kind of respect and integrity to our children, we have to slow down, to make time for our children, to participate in their schools. If you don't have a child of your own, befriend a neighbor's child, or help the children of a refugee family in your community. Often we think that we're too busy, that we should be working longer hours to earn more money; there's great social pressure to work and to produce. Let's not fall for that. Let's take the time to raise our kids, to play with them, to read to them. Let's allow our children to help each of us reclaim the spirit of our child.

The last principle of conscious child rearing is loving-kindness. The central image in the Buddha's teaching of loving-kindness is a mother "holding and protecting her beloved child." Develop loving-kindness for yourself, for your own children, and for all beings in the world.

Many of us try to control kids with discipline, by shaming them, by hitting them, by blaming them. But when we come to sit in meditation, we see how much pain we carry from blaming ourselves. We find judgment and shame and scolding whenever we try to sit quietly. How hard we are on ourselves. We were not born being hard on ourselves; we learned it from parents and at school. "You can't draw well," many of us were told. And we stopped doing the beautiful drawing that every child knows how to do, and we haven't drawn a picture since third grade. How sad it is when instead of receiving loving-kindness, a child is berated or shamed.

We live in a society that in many ways has forgotten how to love and support our children, that has lost the fundamental values of parenting. As the wisest traditional cultures remind us, we don't need more day care centers or more money, we need to regain respect and care and love for parenting. We all long to feel loving and to feel loved. We want to be the woman under the tree listening for the song of her child or the father making love and singing. We want to feel connectedness and community, to touch one another and to be held by one another, to feel that the child in each one of us is honored and respected.

Parenting gives us the chance to astonish ourselves with love. We've all heard stories of mothers and fathers doing superhuman deeds to rescue their children. I read in the newspaper about a paraplegic mother whose youngest daughter fell into a swimming pool. The mother rolled her wheelchair into the pool, and, somehow, grabbed her child, dragged her over to the side of the pool, and held on for hours until someone came to get them out.

Children can bring out this kind of love in us. They teach us that what really matters in life is love itself. As Mother Teresa said, "We cannot do great things in this life, we can only do small things with great love." It is through our parenting of our own children and the children around us and it is in supporting other parents and supporting our schools that we can reclaim or restore this love. The Buddha taught us that the only way we can begin to repay our own parents and all the generations before us is by bringing the dharma—which means respect, integrity, awareness, truth, and loving-kindness—to our parents, to our children, to all of life.

If we are to be a humane society, we must feed the children who are hungry, clothe the children who are cold, and care for all our children with respect, loving-kindness, and integrity. We must care for every child as if he or she were the Buddha. Ralph Waldo Emerson explains:

> To leave the world a bit better,
> Whether by a healthy child,
> A garden patch,
> A redeemed social condition,
> To know even one life has breathed easier
> Because you have lived,
> This is to have succeeded.

7

The Art of Forgiveness

TRADITIONALLY THE WORK of the heart begins with forgiveness. Forgiveness is the necessary ground for any healing. To begin with, we need a wise understanding of forgiveness. Then we can learn how it is practiced, how we may forgive both ourselves and others.

Forgiveness is a letting go of past suffering and betrayal, a release of the burden of pain and hate that we carry. Forgiveness honors the heart's greatest dignity. Whenever we are lost, it brings us back to the ground of love. With forgiveness we become unwilling to attack or wish harm to another. Whenever we forgive, in small ways at home, or in great ways between nations, we free ourselves from the past.

It is hard to imagine a world without forgiveness. Without forgiveness life would be unbearable. Without forgiveness our lives are chained, forced to carry the sufferings of the past and repeat them with no release.

Consider the dialogue between two former prisoners of war:

"Have you forgiven your captors yet?"
"No, never!"
"Well, then, they still have you in prison, don't they?"

We begin the work of forgiveness primarily for ourselves. We may still be suffering terribly from the past while those who betrayed us are on vacation. It is painful to hate. Without forgiveness we continue to perpetuate the illusion that hate can heal our pain and the pain of others. In forgiveness we let go and find relief in our heart.

Even those in the worst situations, the conflicts and tragedies of Bosnia, Cambodia, Rwanda, Northern Ireland, or South Africa, have had to find a path to reconciliation. This is true in America as well. It is the only way to heal.

Sometimes this means finding the courage to forgive the unforgivable, to consciously release the heart from the clutches of another's terrible acts.

We must discover a way to move on from the past, no matter what traumas it held. The past is over: forgiveness means giving up all hope of a better past.

Remember these truths:

Forgiveness is not weak or naive. Forgiveness requires courage and clarity; it is not naive. Mistakenly people believe that to forgive is to simply "forgive and forget," once and for all. This is not the wisdom of forgiveness.

Forgiveness does not happen quickly. For great injustice, coming to forgiveness may include a long process of grief, outrage, sadness, loss, and pain. True forgiveness does not paper over what has happened in a superficial way. It is not a misguided effort to suppress or ignore our pain. It cannot be hurried. It is a deep process, repeated over and over in our heart, that honors the grief and betrayal, and in its own time ripens into the freedom to truly forgive.

Forgiveness does not forget, nor does it condone the past. Forgiveness sees wisely. It willingly acknowledges what is unjust, harmful, and wrong. It bravely recognizes the sufferings of the past, and understands the conditions that brought them about. There is a strength to forgiveness. When we forgive, we can also say, "Never again will I allow these things to happen." We may resolve to never again permit such harm to come to ourselves or another.

Forgiveness does not mean that we have to continue to relate to those who have done us harm. In some cases the best practice may be to end our connection, to never speak to or be with a harmful person again. Sometimes in the process of forgiveness a person who hurt or betrayed us may wish to make amends, but even this does not require us to put ourselves in the way of further harm. In the end, forgiveness simply means never putting another person out of our heart.

FORGIVING OURSELVES

Finding a way to extend forgiveness to ourselves is one of our most essential tasks. Just as others have been caught in suffering, so have we. If we look honestly at our life, we can see the sorrows and pain that have led to our own wrongdoing. In this we can finally extend forgiveness to ourselves; we can hold the pain we have caused in compassion. Without such mercy, we will live our own life in exile.

We have all been blinded, we have all suffered. Pema Chödrön tells this story:

> A young woman wrote about finding herself in a small town in the Middle East surrounded by people jeering, yelling, and threatening to throw stones at her and her friends because they were Americans.
>
> Of course she was terrified, and what happened to her is important. Suddenly she identified with every person throughout history who had ever been scorned and hated. She understood what it was like to be despised for any reason: ethnic group, racial background, sexual preference, gender. Something cracked wide open and she stood in the shoes of millions of oppressed people and saw with a new perspective. She even understood her shared humanity with those who hated her. This sense of deep connection, of belonging to the same family, is the awakening of the great heart of compassion.

Alan Wallace illustrates this truth from the Tibetan teachings:

> Imagine walking along a sidewalk with your arms full of groceries, and someone roughly bumps into you so that you fall and your groceries are strewn over the ground. As you rise up from the puddle of broken eggs and tomato juice, you are ready to shout out, "You idiot! What's wrong with you? Are you blind?" But just before you can catch your breath to speak, you see that the person who bumped into you actually is blind. He, too, is sprawled in the spilled groceries, and your anger vanishes in an instant, to be replaced by sympathetic concern: "Are you hurt? Can I help you up?" Our situation is like that. When

we clearly realize that the source of disharmony and misery in the world is ignorance, we can open the door of wisdom and compassion.

IN THE TEMPLE OF FORGIVENESS

No matter what has happened, we can always return to the greatness of the heart.

We have all heard stories about the mysterious power of compassion and forgiveness in the lives of others. Each time we are inspired by these accounts, we remember that we, too, can forgive.

Roberto De Vicenzo, the famous Argentine golfer, once won a tournament, and after receiving the check and smiling for the cameras, he went to the clubhouse and prepared to leave. Sometime later he walked alone to his car in the parking lot and was approached by a young woman. She congratulated him on his victory and then told him that her child was seriously ill and near death.

De Vicenzo was touched by her story and took out a pen and endorsed his winning check for payment to the woman. "Make some good days for the baby," he said as he pressed the check into her hand.

The next week he was having lunch in a country club when a PGA official came to his table. "Some of the guys in the parking lot last week told me you met a young woman there after you won the tournament." De Vicenzo nodded. "Well," said the official, "I have news for you. She's a phony. She's not married. She has no sick baby. She fleeced you, my friend."

"You mean there is no baby who is dying?" asked De Vicenzo.

"That's right."

"That's the best news I've heard all week," said De Vicenzo.

The heart is released whenever we forgive or are forgiven, even in the most painful circumstances. In ancient Hawaii, if a person had broken a terrible taboo or was accused of a crime, there was always a way out. No matter what he had done, if he could get himself inside the lava rock walls of Pu'uhonua, the ocean-side Temple of Refuge, the priests would offer a ritual of purification and forgiveness. Then he was allowed to return home unharmed.

In the temple of forgiveness, we are reminded of our own goodness. If only we could help each other build temples of forgiveness instead of prisons.

We can. In our own hearts. No matter how extreme the circumstances, a transformation of the heart is possible.

Once, on the train from Washington to Philadelphia, I found myself seated next to an African-American man who had worked for the State Department in India but had quit to run a rehabilitation program for juvenile offenders in the District of Columbia. Most of the youths he worked with were gang members who had committed homicide.

One fourteen-year-old boy in his program had shot and killed an innocent teenager to prove himself to his gang. At the trial, the victim's mother sat impassively silent until the end, when the youth was convicted of the killing. After the verdict was announced, she stood up slowly and stared directly at him and stated, "I'm going to kill you." Then the youth was taken away to serve several years in the juvenile facility.

After the first half year the mother of the slain child went to visit his killer. He had been living on the streets before the killing, and she was the only visitor he'd had. For a time they talked, and when she left, she gave him some money for cigarettes. Then she started step-by-step to visit him more regularly, bringing food and small gifts. Near the end of his three-year sentence she asked him what he would be doing when he got out. He was confused and very uncertain, so she offered to set him up with a job at a friend's company. Then she inquired about where he would live, and since he had no family to return to, she offered him temporary use of the spare room in her home.

For eight months he lived there, ate her food, and worked at the job. Then one evening she called him into the living room to talk. She sat down opposite him and waited. Then she started,

"Do you remember in the courtroom when I said I was going to kill you?"

"I sure do, ma'am," he replied.

"Well, I did," she went on. "I did not want the boy who could kill my son for no reason to remain alive on this earth. I wanted him to die. That's why I started to visit you and bring you things. That's why I got you the job and let you live here in my house. That's how I set about changing you. And that old boy, he's gone. So now I want to ask you, since my son is gone, and that killer is gone, if you'll stay here. I've got room, and I'd like to adopt you if you let me." And she became the mother of her son's killer, the mother he never had.

Our own story may not be so dramatic, yet we have all been betrayed.

We must each start where we are. In large and small ways, in our own family and community, we will be offered the dignity and freedom that learns to patiently forgive over and over.

PART TWO

Taking Up the Spiritual Path

8

Spiritual Initiation

Monastic Rites of Wholeness and Commitment

IN THIS CHAPTER I would like to describe the centuries-old traditional initiation of entering a Buddhist monastery, a rite of passage that until recently was required of most young men and some young women in Southeast Asian society. As a former Buddhist monk, I had the privilege of participating in this training in the 1960s, beginning when I was twenty-three years old.

After graduating from Dartmouth College in Asian Studies, I joined the Peace Corps and asked them to send me to a Buddhist country. As a young man with a painful family history, I was looking for a teacher who could help me learn to understand how to work with my own mind. I had read stories about old Zen masters, and when the Peace Corps sent me to the Mekong River valley along the border of Thailand and Laos, I began to look for a place to learn. I was drawn to visit and then live at several of the strictest ascetic forest monasteries as a result of this longing for traditional Buddhist training. When I first visited these temples, I met a number of truly wise elders who seemed to "know," to hold in their bones a wisdom about life and death that I sought. Somehow I realized I would have to undergo an initiation, a difficult and potentially painful training to begin to discover what they knew.

Let me first speak about initiation in a general way. To awaken our innate spiritual authority, an inner sense of knowing, always involves a shift of identity, a rebirth, a recovering of our undying spirit. In the Buddhist tradition we speak of this as finding our True Nature. When we go through times of great difficulty, it is this alone that carries us through.

To find such authority requires a shift from our ordinary and limited sense of self, what's called "the body of fear," to a deeper knowing within us. At times this shift may happen in an abrupt, radical way through intensive meditation, ritual, initiation, or ceremony. At other times this shift happens slowly through repetitive practice. The Buddha likened this gradual process to the great oceans, which descend little by little to the floor of the sea; similarly, the heart gradually deepens in knowing, compassion, and trust.

The Japanese Zen master Katagiri Roshi was once asked by a student about the beautiful faith and warmth he radiated. "This is what I want to learn from you. How do I learn that?" Katagiri Roshi answered, "When people see me today, they don't see the years I spent just being with my teacher!" He described how he practiced year after year, living simply, hearing the same dharma teachings over and over, sitting in the cold temple every morning no matter what, doing the rituals of the temple. This is the slow way of initiation, putting yourself into the rituals of attention and respect, baking yourself in the oven until your whole being is cooked, matured, transformed.

The second common form of initiation is more intense and rapid. This is the sudden radical transformation brought about by powerful initiation and rites of passage. For modern young men and women this is a desperate need. If nothing is offered by the culture in the way of initiation to prove one's entry into the world of men and women, it will be done unguided, in the road or in the street, with cars at high speed, with drugs, with knives and guns.

Even those not seeking rites of passage will find initiations arising spontaneously, through unexpected loss, an accident, or a near-death experience. Sometimes initiation comes through travel, bringing a sudden maturation when one encounters danger, disease, and difficulty traveling in remote or Third World countries. Initiation is a rite of passage described as a forced journey through a rocky canyon so hard and narrow that you can't take your baggage with you. Initiation usually involves a brush with death in order to find what one truly knows.

In the Buddhist tradition, initiation is designed to awaken our buddha nature, the great fearless heart of a buddha within us. This is one reason people bow when they meet a master or spiritual teacher. They bow not only to that person but to the lineage of fearlessness that is carried in his or her presence.

To seek initiation in a Buddhist monastery, you must first find a mentor, someone who will be your preceptor, your guide. In Thailand, begin by visiting a forest or jungle monastery to meet with the master, listening to see if this is someone you would entrust yourself to. When you decide to take them as your mentor, you bow to them, you agree to be with them, to listen to their teachings, to follow their teachings, and to serve them. When they come back from collecting alms food, you make their seat, you bring them water, you do the kind of service to a teacher that offers them respect and sets your heart in line with theirs. In this you demonstrate an openness to listen and follow what they have to offer you.

Once you have entrusted yourself to a certain master and the community of elders who practice with him, you must surrender. Yet your surrender is not blind. You both know that it has a conscious purpose. My teacher Ajahn Chah always said, "I'm always asking my students to do difficult things. The food is unpredictable and poor; we sit up all night; it's freezing cold, and you only have these simple cotton robes. It's boring here; it's demanding; it's lonely; and you do things that are fearsome, like sitting alone all night in the forest. Yet all of it has the purpose of leading you to a freedom in yourself, to something greater than that which you know to be true."

The Buddhist ordination practices at the monastery I chose, led by Venerable Ajahn Chah, were offered in a Buddhist communal form that has carried this universal message of wisdom and freedom for twenty-five hundred years. Buddhist and Jain monks are the oldest existing monastic order on the face of the earth.

In Thailand or Laos or Cambodia, where I had gone to work, young men, and in some cases women, generally enter a monastery when they reach the age of nineteen or twenty. Until one enters a monastery and goes through the training of a monk or a nun, one is considered an unripe person, not ready to live in that society. You enter the monastery in order to know yourself, for your spirit to mature. Until recently, each young man, and certain young women, would go into a monastery for a year. Modern life has shortened this considerably, but hundreds of thousands still enter the monastic order.

The outer form of ordination mirrors the ancient story of the life of the Buddha. In preparation for the ordination of a man or a woman, the family and village hold a ritualized celebration. It begins with feasts and banquets for all to join. Various priests attend to officiate with blessings and offerings. The person to be ordained takes off their ordinary clothes and is dressed as a prince or princess, as a noble person, in white silk and beautiful jewelry. If they come from a family that can afford it, they may go in procession to the monastery riding on the back of an elephant.

The procession, whether by elephant, ox cart, or even bicycle, then arrives at the gates of the temple and reenacts the leave-taking of Sakyamuni Buddha, who renounced his kingdom and all the pleasures and possibilities of his worldly life to seek inner freedom and awakening, the sure heart's release. When you arrive at the gate, your head is shaved, all your jewelry and silken clothes are left behind. The gate marks the boundary of a great forest where the monks live. Here you are met by the elders of that forest, the abbot and the senior monks.

Sometimes the temple gates will have sculptures of huge guardian demons on either side. These demons symbolize the powerful forces one must pass through to enter the realm of the spirit. In the Zen tradition, when a young man or woman comes to enter a monastery, the encounter with the demons at the gate is formalized in a ritual called *tanga-ryō*. The postulants must sit unwaveringly outside the gates of the monastery for several days, even in the winter snow, to demonstrate their sincerity in wanting to receive the teachings and undertake the training. After one sits for three or more days, finally the gates are opened and the monks say, "Come in. What brings you here?"

In the forest monasteries, having left clothing, jewelry, and all the things of the world at the gate, and wearing only a simple white sarong, you are received by a group of twenty elders. They take you from your family and lead you into the forest. You realize that this is a place unlike other places in the world, a place of wonder, of peace, and of a sacred connection with nature. The elders lead you to a place deep in the forest that is a consecrated ground called a *sima*. Sometimes the sima includes a small temple building. Sometimes it is just a circle of rocks in the forest, sometimes it is surrounded by water. To properly consecrate the ground of a sima, one of the elders must offer prayers in every spot of it. Every square yard is marked off and sat in, and a series of blessings and ceremonies are performed in each square. When this ground is consecrated, the only ones who are allowed to enter during ceremonies are the fully ordained members of the monastic order. In a traditional forest monastery, the consecrated ground is a place of peace, refuge, forgiveness, and truth. You can feel it.

Once you are led to the consecrated ground, the elders sit and chant together. After you bow to them, they address you respectfully. The Buddha spoke of ordination as an invitation to the sons and daughters of noble families. You are received respectfully as if you were nobly born. Traditionally, membership in the nobility, which was so important in ancient India, was determined by what caste or class or race you were born into. The Buddha turned this upside down and said, "Nobility has nothing to do with being born into any caste or class or race, whether the priestly class, warrior class, lower class, or untouchables." He was adamantly opposed to class-structured society and racism, and spoke of those things as madness. He said, "On this earth the only true nobility is the nobility of heart and spirit that a human being brings to their life. The absence of greed, the absence of hatred, the absence of delusion, and a wise and loving heart, this is what makes a noble being."

So when you arrive, you are greeted by the elders, who address the intention in you that is most noble. Then you take refuge in the path of the elders by making three bows. The first constitutes a vow to follow the inspiration of the Buddha. The second bow is to the dharma, the truth, the law, expressed by the way of practice. The third bow is to the *sangha*, the lineage of the elders who for generations have carried the awakened heart and offered practices to bestow it in each generation.

They don't just accept you automatically. After receiving your bows and homage, the elders ask you some questions: "Are you free from debt? Are you free from disease? Are you free from obligation? Are you running away? Are you coming of your own volition? Why do you come? What brings you to practice in this sacred forest?"

When you answer and demonstrate your own sincerity, you are given teachings and practices that speak of the great cycles of birth and death and the possibility of discovering nirvana, freedom that is timeless and deathless in the midst of all things. You are also given to understand that this task will not be easy.

I remember when I first arrived at my teacher Ajahn Chah's monastery, he looked at me and said, "I hope you're not afraid of suffering." I replied, "What do you mean? I came here to meditate and find inner peace and happiness." He explained, "There are two kinds of suffering, the suffering that we run from because we are unwilling to face the truth of life, and the suffering that comes when we're willing to stop running from the sorrows and difficulties of the world. The second kind of suffering will lead you to freedom."

In bowing, you commit yourself in body, speech, heart, and mind to join the elders. You bow again and again in different parts of the ceremony. You are asked, in joining this community, to devote your life to awakening compassion, truthfulness, and freedom. Then, after your commitment is made, you are given a new name. It's as if you are born anew as you enter into this community. Out of respect for your inner nobility and buddha nature, your new name, given in Pali, the ancient language of the elders, might be "Luminous Virtue," "Aspires to Peace," "The Birth of Patience," or "Guardian of Wisdom."

Then, among the trees in the deep forest, the first meditation instruction is given. This meditation is an inquiry into the mystery of birth and death itself. You are asked to meditate on the question "Who am I?" To do this, you are instructed how to examine your own body to see that it is made up of earth, water, fire, and air, and how these form into disparate body parts: skin, hair, nails, teeth, fluid, blood, heart, lungs, and kidneys. You are asked to examine deeply the makeup of your human body and mind to see its true nature.

Then the elders begin a series of teachings on how to live as a monk. The first is the teaching of dignity. You are shown how to treat everything in your life with respect and dignity. It is beautiful. You're given a patchwork robe and a bowl. You're shown how to carefully fold your robe and how to mindfully carry your bowl. For each item you are given there are chants to recite several times daily in order to remember your true purpose. "I carry this bowl with great respect for what is offered. I receive this food with great sincerity. I wear this robe out of respect for a life devoted to awakening." Everything you do serves the purpose of mindfulness, awareness, and compassion.

Following these offerings, the elders give you further teachings to calm your heart, because if you want to investigate "Who Am I?" there must be an inner silence that allows such a question to drop to the depths of your being. You are given breath practices to deepen your concentration and walking practices to stabilize mindfulness throughout the day. From this day on, you are enjoined to live according to the principles of mindfulness. Your outer life is one of respect and your inner life is one of attention. In this way you enter the community.

After the ordination ceremony you take up the daily meditations of a monk. Every morning before dawn, you join the monks' recitations that reflect on the truth of impermanence and death. You begin a process of daily meditation on change, slowly sitting and walking, examining the nature of all perceptions as they come and go, being mindful without being entangled with them. You learn to notice the movement of thoughts and feelings, to see impermanence, to study the changing show of body and mind, in order to find an equanimity in the midst of it all. It is explained that you never possess anything for very long. You can love and care for people and things in your life but you do not own them. Your children, the things around you, your ideas, even your own body, are not yours. You are instructed to find freedom and compassion in renunciation. You chant the Buddha's words, "'Look how he abused me, how he threw me down and robbed me.' Live with such thoughts and you continue the cycle of hatred. You too shall pass away. Knowing this, how can you quarrel?"

Following the practices of dignity, respect, and renunciation, the monks undertake a series of practices of surrender. You wear one set of robes stitched together from discarded cloth. You eat one meal a day, only what is given. Through these practices of surrender there grows a ripening of trust as the heart learns to face the mystery of life with patience, faith, and compassion.

Monks must go out each morning with a bowl for alms rounds. This is not like street-corner begging. For me, it was one of the most beautiful experiences of my life. Just as the sun rises, you walk across the green rice paddies to small villages with packed earthen lanes. Those who wish to offer alms wait for the monks to come and bow before they offer their food. Even the poorest villages will offer part of their food to make merit and as if to say, "Even though we are poor, we so value what you represent that we give of what little we have so that your spirit may be here in our village, in our community, and in our society."

Alms rounds are done completely in silence. When you receive the food, you can't say, "Thank you; I appreciate the mango you gave me," or "Thanks for the fish this morning; it looks really good." The only response you can make is the sincerity of your heart. After you receive this food, you take it back to support and inspire your practice. When the villagers value the monk's life and give of the little they have, you must take that. The extraordinary generosity of the village brings a powerful motivation in a monastery.

The rules about alms food govern monastic life. Monks are not allowed to keep food overnight or eat anything that's not put into their hands each morning by a layperson. This means that monks can't live as hermits up in the mountains far from the world. They must live where people can feed them. This immediately establishes a powerful relationship. You must do something of enough value that they want to feed you. Your presence, your meditation, your dignity, has to be vivid enough so that when you bring your bowl, people want to offer food because that's the only way you can eat! This creates an ongoing dynamic of offering that goes both ways, from those who are in the process of being initiated in the monastery, and those of the community whom it benefits.

The process of surrender builds as you live in the community. You begin the early-morning chant and meditation at three thirty in the morning, complete it in two hours, and then repeat it again at night. You hear the dharma talks over and over. You must sit in meditation all night long at least one night a week. You do long alms rounds barefoot in the morning before the sun comes up, walking five, ten, or more miles before you eat anything.

When your practice becomes more deeply established, the elders give you ways to more directly face death. You will already have done regular contemplations on the brevity of life and the certainty of death. You will have done days of visualization of the decomposition of your body, and have meditated on the movement of consciousness in the process of death and rebirth. You may then be instructed, as I was, to sit all night in the charnel grounds in the forest. There villagers will bring, in a procession, the body of one who has died, and the monks recite the funeral prayers. The body is placed on the burning grounds, and you sit with it through the night while you meditate on your own body and the inevitable death that will come to everyone you know.

"Without an understanding of death," taught Ajahn Chah, "life is confusing." In his monastery, the traditional funeral meditation led to one further practice. When any of the monks died, rather than burn his body, it was set on a platform in the Buddha Hall for the monks to contemplate. The body was left out for ten days to bloat and decompose as would happen to any meat left out in the sun for this period of time. We sat, meditated, and chanted in front of the body. It brought a vividness to our meditations on death.

Initially the training in Ajahn Chah's tradition requires long periods of communal walking and sitting practice, and frequent all-night sittings in the Buddha Hall. After training together with the collective of monks, you may then be directed to a period of practice in solitude for some months. For this part of the training, monks live in isolated caves or in more distant parts of jungles and mountains, a long morning's walk from the last remote village. Or, in certain retreat centers, small huts are provided for solitary intensive meditation. My own training included a solitary retreat for one year and three months. I didn't leave my room, just meditated fifteen to eighteen hours a day, sitting for an hour, walking for an hour, then sitting again. I'd see my teacher every two days for a fifteen-minute interview. You don't have to be in solitude very long before any pride you have goes away. It is quite humbling. Your mind will do anything. Every past thing you've ever done or imagined comes back. Every mood, every fear, every longing, your loneliness, your pain, your love, creativity, and boredom appear with great intensity.

Gradually these are followed by visionary states, and by powerful releases of the energy system, which dissolve the body into light. Then there are ecstatic states, samadhi states, and techniques for entering profound states of emptiness and silence. Throughout this meditative process, your teacher gives instructions on how to understand and skillfully use these forces to transform yourself. Finally you are taught how to rest in the archetype of a Buddha, with great compassion and emptiness, containing all things, yet not limited by them.

Your wisdom and spiritual maturity deepen through these many forms of practice, augmented by the communal life of the monks. The community practices include regular council meetings, practices for conflict resolution, vow renewals, and practices of mutual respect. The repetition and surrender of this life guided by a community of elders is consciously intended to bring a deep trust of ourselves and the ground of our being.

Throughout the whole duration of the monastic training, you are also guided to hold all experiences in a great heart of loving-kindness for yourself and all beings. Formal instructions for developing practices of loving-kindness, compassion, and forgiveness are offered to all members of the community. These include visualizations and recitations that are first directed toward yourself through repeated phrases such as "May I be well, may I have ease of body and mind, may I be filled with compassion and forgiveness." You are taught to direct the phrases of loving-kindness and forgiveness to yourself over and over because loving-kindness is the basis of true respect. Then you gradually extend it to others, to the members of your community, the villagers nearby, the beings in the forest, the whole of the world. As you repeat these practices a thousand times, you notice the barriers of the heart that interfere with your openness. In the spirit of this practice you're given the traditional story of Angulimala, a mass murderer who went through a profound process of forgiveness and healing as a monk. You are asked to study in your own heart how each of us contains the source of all suffering and the source of all freedom. You are directed to see how conflict, fear, hatred, and attachment, all of the afflictions of the heart, are cured by true generosity and respect.

Finally, like the Buddha, you are invited to sit and find an unshakable knowing in yourself. In your meditation you become a yogi sitting like the Buddha in the unmovable spot under the Bodhi tree, seeking the knowledge of the deathless. Sometimes your teacher will pose a question: "What is our true self?" "What was your true nature before you were born?" To discover your true nature, you meditate on sights and sounds, smells and tastes, thoughts and feelings, until you see how ephemeral all sense perceptions are. Relinquishing the senses, you are directed to meditate and enter a deep stillness. From the silence you must find that which is beyond your usual "small self," your ordinary identity. Your task is to awaken within to "the one who knows" and come to rest in the timeless, unconditional, or eternal.

Ajahn Chah put it this way:

When you can rest in the original heart and mind, it shines like pure clear water. This is the Buddha. But what is the Buddha? When we see with the eyes of wisdom, we know that the Buddha is timeless, unborn, unrelated to any body or history or image. Buddha is the ground of all being, the truth of the unmoving mind. So the Buddha was not enlightened in India. In fact, he was never enlightened, he was never born and never died. When we take refuge in the Buddha, the dharma, the sangha, all things in the world are free for us; they become our teacher moment after moment, proclaiming the one true nature of life.

Over initial months and years you continue to practice in these ways, combining periods in community with periods of solitude. You learn to cultivate wisdom, fearlessness, and compassion, studying death and surrendering to the rhythms of nature, always guided in these rhythms by the elders. After a suitable period of practice, when you have integrated and stabilized these teachings, you may choose to remain in the monastery to teach others or you may find that you are called to return to the world to integrate and manifest your newfound maturity there.

As monks prepare to leave, they gather for a last time with the elders in the sacred grove. They are ritually released from their vows of renunciation, return their robes, and are given a set of new clothing. They bow three times, retake the refuges (of buddha, dharma, and sangha), and vow to follow the five precepts of nonharming that are the ground of practice for all Buddhist laypeople.

After their time in the monastery, most young men and women will return to their villages, having completed their training with the elders. They are now accepted as "ripe," as initiated men and women, respected in their community. Outwardly they will have learned the religious forms and sacred rituals of the Buddhist community. Inwardly, these ancient forms are intended to awaken an unshakable virtue and inner respect, fearlessness in the face of death, self-reliance, wisdom, and profound compassion. These qualities give one who leaves the monastery the hallmark of a mature man or woman.

Perhaps as you read about this ordination process, its beauty will strike a chord in you that intuitively knows about the need for initiations. This does not mean that you have to enter a monastery to seek this remarkable and wonderful training. By reading about this tradition, you may simply awaken that place in yourself, which exists in each of us, that longs for wholeness and integrity, because the awakening that comes through initiation is a universal story. In our time we need to reclaim rites of passage, we need to honor elders, we need to find ways to remind our young people and the whole of our communities of the sacredness of life, of who we really are.

Remember, too, that initiation comes in many forms. I have a friend who has three children under the age of five. This is a retreat as intensive as any other, including sitting up all night in the charnel grounds. Marriage and family are a kind of initiation. As Gary Snyder says,

All of us are apprentices to the same teacher that all masters have worked with—reality. Reality says: Master the twenty-four hours. Do it well without self-pity. It is as hard to get children herded into the car pool and down the road to the bus as it is to chant sutras in the Buddha Hall on a cold morning. One is not better than the other. Each can be quite boring. They both have the virtuous quality of repetition. Repetition and ritual and their good results come in many forms: changing the car filters, wiping noses, going to meetings, sitting in meditation, picking up around the house, washing dishes, checking the dipstick. Don't let yourself think that one or more of these distracts you from the serious pursuits. Such a round of chores is not a set of difficulties to escape so that we may do our practice that will put us on the path. It IS our path.

What gives a spiritual initiation or a rite of passage its great blessing, whether it is marriage or child rearing or entering the monastery, is that it is held in a sacred context. The difficulties one goes through are conscious and purposefully used to find freedom. They are witnessed and blessed by those who have gone before you. Without the conscious purpose and witnessing, you will have an incomplete initiation in which you won't know what you have learned; you will have simply suffered. True initiation is done deliberately and consciously. In traditional Buddhist societies it is repeated again and again through prayer, discipline, meditation, surrender, and ritual, lifelong practices that are held by the elders. The elders are there to teach the practices that have transformed generations before you. They offer each participant a way to step outside of their small sense of self, their worries and their past, and awaken the "one who knows," the elder within.

To awaken this understanding in yourself is the blessing of spiritual life. To offer the energy of wisdom, fearlessness, and compassion to the society around you is the gift that your spiritual life brings to this world.

9

Perils, Promises, and Spiritual Emergency on the Path

IN THIS CHAPTER I would like to explore the kinds of difficulties that can arise in intensive meditation, especially for those undertaking a deep and committed practice or long retreats as part of their spiritual discipline. To be involved in such intensive practice is one of the most exciting, arduous, wonderful, and difficult adventures that we can take as human beings. It is a journey in which we can explore the farthest inner realms of consciousness, awaken to the myriad parts of ourselves, and bring mind and heart as far as they can reach into our deep connection with the whole of the universe.

However, it is not necessarily an easy or gentle journey. Tibetan meditation master Chögyam Trungpa spoke about this. In a talk he gave in Berkeley, California, he sat up in front of a large hall filled with people who had paid to see him. He began his talk by asking, "How many of you are just beginning a spiritual practice?" A number of people raised their hands. He said, "Fine. My suggestion is that you go home." He continued, "It is a lot more difficult than you know when you begin. Once you start, it is also difficult to stop. So my suggestion to you is not to begin. Best not to start at all. But if you do start, then it is best to finish."

No matter what form of mediation we practice, sooner or later obstacles arise. The first arise because when we stop our distractions and bring meditative attention to our inner experience, we will encounter the unfinished business we carry, the untended longings, loves, fears, and hurts. And as we get even quieter and more vulnerable, we will face the mystery of our own mortality, of living and dying. In all of the great spiritual traditions, attention is given to these problems and pitfalls in spiritual practice, for it is through these that the path often unfolds. In the Christian mystical tradition one of the great texts is *Dark Night of the Soul* by Saint John of the Cross, in which he talks about the periods of loneliness, fear, and doubt that one goes through after the initial awakenings into the light. Evagrius, a fourth-century Christian monk who lived in the Egyptian desert with the Christian desert fathers, wrote a text on the demons that come to people who go into the desert as hermits and undertake a meditation practice. These include the demons of pride, the demons of fear, the demons of lust, and the noonday demon (the demon of sleep).

In Buddhist traditions there are descriptions of similar kinds of obstacles. In Zen, practitioners might experience *makyo* ("diabolic or disturbing phenomena") during meditation. These are hallucinations involving vision, hearing, smell, or other senses. Though everyday life is often referred to as illusory or dreamlike in Zen, makyo are a kind of superillusion, above and beyond ordinary illusion.

How does one begin to understand and work with the pitfalls and the difficulties that arise on the path of awakening? The basic Buddhist teachings begin by addressing how to approach the common hindrances, such as physical pain and restlessness. Then the instructions move on to explore the more extreme, delightful, and terrifying kinds of visions, mental states, and difficulties that can arise for people in more intensive or advanced spiritual practice.

Buddhist meditation and other systematic disciplines train awareness and concentration, which bring us into the present. This is the first task of the spiritual path, to focus and steady the fluctuating, frenetic mind. The present moment is the entry into spiritual realms, because the past is just memory and the future is just imagination. The present moment provides the gateway to enter into all the realms of consciousness that are beyond the everyday level. To be here fully requires a steadying of the mind, concentration, and attention. It is like that sign in a Las Vegas casino, "You must be present to win." You have to be present to awaken.

To do so, one undertakes a discipline: following the breath, doing a visualization, doing a loving-kindness meditation—employing one of many practices that focus and develop our attention. Then the trouble

starts. In meditation, as we become more fully present, physical difficulties often arise. There are several categories of pain that we might
experience. There are the physical pains that signal that you are doing
something that is not good for your body, so you have to find a way to sit
and be more respectful of your capacities. Then there are the physical
pains that arise out of a new but unaccustomed posture. A steady posture has to be carefully tended and borne with, allowed, until the knees
and the body and the back get used to meditating in a way that is still,
where we can allow the body energies to open without too much movement. This is a steadying and bringing together of the body and mind.

Then the most interesting kind of pain that arises is the pain of
various patterns of tension and holding. Each of us has areas of tension:
it could be our jaws, our neck, our shoulders—whichever part of our
body it is that becomes tight and accumulates tension when we meet
stressful situations. Through the stillness of meditation, these patterns
of holding come into awareness or consciousness. As they release, they
can bring pain, vibration, and sometimes also powerful images from
the past. These may be traumatic images of accidents or medical proce-
dures we've endured, or they could be images of times that we got angry
and squashed it inside, of past emotional wounds, or even past lives. All
kinds of past situations will arise and manifest themselves during the
physical opening of the body.

Most people who have sat for even a single day experience these various kinds of physical pains. One of the tasks of meditation practice is to
learn how to sit comfortably still and be steady with these physical openings. We need to train our mindfulness and compassion to hold the pain
fearlessly and graciously, the way we would hold a crying child. Then
with further investigation we can see what elements comprise the physical pain, such as throbbing, burning, twisting, tension, or ache. As we
sense the pain clearly, we can also notice our reactions to it. With mindfulness we can notice our contraction, fear, aversion, or desires. We can
see the stories the mind tells and adds to this pain. And we can learn to
hold all this with a spacious and kind attention, where even the most
intense pain will release, or change, or we will have somehow made our
peace with it. Pain turns into an intense but workable experience.

As we start to concentrate, along with powerful physical openings
there will arise difficult states of mind. As we begin to collect or steady
the mind, it is initially like a fish out of water, flopping around on dry

land. We give it a very simple task: "Mind, please follow the breath." Does it listen? For about two seconds. The process of beginning to steady the mind is an arduous one. It requires overcoming our habit of being lost in the past and future. It requires a repeated willingness to be present with experiences from which we usually run away.

THE FIVE HINDRANCES

As we try to steady the mind, the most common difficulties that arise in practice are called by the Buddha the five hindrances. These hindrances are familiar to all those who meditate, and the wisest approach to them is illustrated in the story about the spiritual teacher Gurdjieff. There was an old man in Gurdjieff's community who was difficult for everyone to live with. He was argumentative, obnoxious, noisy, and smelly, an all-around troublemaker. After many months of conflict with the other community members, this old man gave up. He decided to leave and return to Paris. When Gurdjieff heard about this, he was upset. He went directly to Paris, found the man, and with great effort convinced him to come back, but only by offering him a big monthly stipend. Everyone else paid to study with Gurdjieff, but this man was *getting paid*. When the other students saw him return and found out he was being paid to be there, they became quite upset. When they complained to Gurdjieff, he explained, "This man is like yeast for bread. Without him here you would not really understand the meaning of patience, the meaning of loving-kindness or compassion. You would not learn how to deal with your own anger and irritation. So I bring him here. You pay me to teach and I pay him to assist."

The practice of developing patience and compassion with the hindrances and blockages means allowing them to arise and observing them with awareness. We use them as an opportunity to learn directly about anger, fear, and desire. We can learn how to relate to them without being so identified with them, without being caught up in them, and without resisting them. This takes practice.

In order to work with these common hindrances, we must learn to identify them clearly. The first is desire, the wanting mind. The second is its opposite which is aversion—dislike, resistance, judgment, anger, and fear; all those mental states in which we push away or reject our experience. The next is sleepiness, dullness, and lethargy (also forms of resistance to experience); and the fourth is its opposite: agitation and restlessness of mind. The fifth is doubt, the voice in the mind that says, "This breath practice is boring and dull. What good is it?" Or "I can't do it. It is too hard, I am too restless, it is the wrong day to meditate. I should wait until tomorrow. Maybe I should do something a little more entertaining like Sufi dancing."

To work with the hindrances, we must study them, observing and allowing them to be incorporated into our meditation practice. When desire arises, we begin to examine the desiring mind with mindfulness. We acknowledge it when it arises, labeling it "desire" and feeling its quality. To look at desire is to experience the part of ourselves that is never content, that always says, "If only I had something else, something different from this, then I would be happy. If only I had some other relationship, some other job, some more comfortable cushion, less noise, cooler temperature, warmer temperature, another meditation shawl, a little more sleep last night, then I could sit well."

The mindful way of working with desire is not to condemn it but to turn our attention to the state of desire, to experience it in the body and mind, and to stay with it and gently name it "wanting . . . wanting." In this way we learn to be fully aware of states like desire without being so caught up by them. Then we can consciously choose which way to go, which impulses to follow. Desire is rampant in the modern world. Mindfulness brings real understanding and freedom.

The same approach of mindfulness is used when working with aversion, anger, or fear. We may have to acknowledge fear eighty times before it becomes familiar to us. But if we sit unmoving, and every time fear comes we note, "fear . . . fear," and let ourselves be mindful of the trembling and the coolness and the breath stopping and the stories and images, if we just stick with it, one day fear will arise and we will say, "Fear—oh, I know you. You are very familiar." Our whole relationship to the fear will have changed and we will see it as an impersonal state, like a program that comes on the radio for a while and passes away, and we will be freer and wiser in our relationship to it.

This may sound easy, to be present with a balanced and soft attention, but it is not always so. There were several therapists at one long retreat I taught who were schooled in the Primal Scream tradition.

Their practice was one that emphasized release and catharsis through screaming, and they normally set aside a period of time each morning to do this. After doing sitting meditation for a few days they said, "This mindfulness is not working." I asked, "Why not?" They replied, "It is building up inner energy and anger and we need a place to express it. Could we use the meditation hall at a certain hour of the day to scream and release? Otherwise it gets toxic when we hold it in." I suggested that they go back and sit with it anyway, suggesting that it would not kill them to stay with the energies that were building up. I asked them to sit and see what happens, since they were there to learn something new. They did. And after a few days they came back and said, "Amazing. It changed!" They became free in a new way.

Anger, fear, desire—all these states can be a source of wisdom when they are acknowledged and felt fully. As we become more present for them, we see how they arise according to certain conditions and affect the body and mind in certain ways. If we are mindful and not caught up in them, we can observe them like a storm. They are experienced for a time and then they pass away.

When we become skillful at being mindful of these hindrances and look carefully and closely, we find that no state of mind, no feeling, no emotion actually lasts more than fifteen or thirty seconds before it is replaced by some other one. But we must look really closely to see this. We might be angry, and then, if we name it—"angry . . . angry"—and observe this state with patient attention, then we soon discover it is no longer anger, it has now turned into resentment. The resentment is there for a little while and then it turns into self-pity. Then we observe the self-pity and it turns into grief or despair and we observe the despair for a little while and it turns into self-justification, and then that turns back into anger. If we look, we see that the mind is constantly changing. Mindfulness teaches us about impermanence, movement, and how there's no need to identify with any emotional or mental state.

In the same way, when sleepiness and restlessness arise, we can observe them with the eye of awareness and the heart of tenderness instead of with judgment. Sometimes our body is simply tired. In one monastery sleepiness is called "the poor man's nirvana." It is important to allow each state to arise, to see sleepiness, to discover its nature. If our sleepiness is related to resisting our experience, we can just sit and say,

"What is going on here that makes me want to put myself to sleep?" See if you can wake yourself up to it.

The same with restlessness and boredom. If you are restless, you can note, "restless . . . restless," feel it, without fear. If it is very strong, you must allow yourself to surrender. You can say, "All right, I will be the first meditator ever to die of restlessness," and let it take you over and see what happens. Of course, as you stop resisting, it loses its power over you.

Finally, you can also apply mindfulness when doubt arises. Thoughts like "This isn't working," or "I'm no good at this" are just the doubting mind. You can learn to name doubt and let it come and go without identification or concern. Through systematic training with these hindrances, you discover a way of relating to them wisely. You can experience them without getting caught up in them.

ANTIDOTES

The Buddhist tradition also tells us that when these hindrances are strong, there are specific antidotes. For desire, there is the antidote of reflecting on impermanence and death. For anger, there is the antidote of loving-kindness and forgiveness. For sleepiness, the antidote is to arouse energy through changing posture, visualization, or summoning courage. For restlessness, the antidote is to bring calm or concentration through inner techniques of steadying and relaxing. And for doubt, the antidote is faith or inspiration through reading or speaking with someone wise or finding some way to inspire oneself.

If you do not have the training and skills to help you work with the hindrances, they can seem overwhelming and you may want to give up on your spiritual practice. This is why you need a teacher and systematic training to begin to work with your mind: your mind and the forces you encounter there can be very confusing.

Buddhist teachings point to the basic roots of human suffering as "greed, hatred, and delusion." These are what get us into trouble. The hindrances grow from these roots. We may not be worried by this: "Oh, just desire and aversion, our dislikes and ignorance, and a little bit of unclarity of mind. We can work with this. That is not too bad." But after we have meditated for a while, we discover that greed means

confronting attachment in the deepest sense, that our desire is a powerful and primal kind of force, and that hatred means discovering a rage
within us like Attila the Hun or Hitler. All of these are found in each
person's mind. Greed is the deepest kind of hunger, and it drives the
world. Delusion includes the darkest kind of confusion and ignorance.

These states are powerful. They are the forces that create violence
and war. They are the forces that create poverty and starvation in one
country and abundance in another. They are the forces that cause what
Buddhist tradition calls "samsara," an endless cycle of confusion and
suffering that continues through countless moments of birth and death
until we awaken. We will all encounter the seeds of hatred, greed, and
delusion when we practice living in the present moment with steady,
concentrated attention. This is not easy. At times it seems too much for
us, too difficult. Yet here is where we learn. Thomas Merton said, "True
prayer and love are learned in that hour when prayer becomes impossible and the heart has turned to stone." In facing the most difficult of
your hindrances honorably, if you let yourself sit with them, there will
come a real opening of the heart. An opening of the heart, body, and
mind takes place when we finally stop running away from our boredom
or our fear, our anger or our pain.

In addition to mindfulness, Buddhist teachings also offer many
other systematic ways of working with difficult energies when they
arise. Here are five of them:

1. When strong desire, fear, or anger arise, just let it go. Or if you
cannot let it go, let it be. To "let it be" is a better expression of letting go
anyway, because usually when we hear "let go of it" we think of getting
rid of it, but we cannot really just get rid of it. To do so is adding more
desire, fear, or anger; it is saying in effect, "I don't like this, so I'm going
to stop it." But that is like trying to get rid of your own arm; this feeling
is a part of us in some way. So instead of "letting go," *letting be* means
"to see it as it is," seeing clearly. There is fear, there is anger, there is joy,
there is love, there is depression, there is hatred, there is jealousy. Let it
be. There is embarrassment. Let it be. There is self-judgment. Let it be.
Then there is self-pity, then there is delight. They are just different states
of mind. The human mind has all of these states, and our task is to let
them be, to learn to relate to the mind in a compassionate and wise way.

2. If we are unable to let it be, we can sublimate it. This means to

take the energy of our difficulty and transform it outwardly or inwardly. For example, in working with anger outwardly we might go out and chop the winter's wood as a way to transform and use the angry energy. Similarly, for inward transformation there are exercises for moving energy within the body, from a place where it is caught to a more useful expression. For example, the energy of lust and of obsessive sexual desire can be moved up into the heart, where it becomes an energy of desire for connection through compassion or caring. The inner transformation is more difficult than the outer.

3. Another way of approaching difficulties is the appropriate use of suppression. This is tricky, but can be important at certain times. For example, suppose a woman who is a surgeon is having a fight with her husband when her beeper goes off. She knows it is time to go directly to the hospital operating room. She is needed to do emergency cardiac surgery. This is not the time for her to continue thinking about what is going on with her husband. It is a time to put that aside and do her surgery. Later on, when the circumstances are suitable, she can go home and work toward a resolution.

Similarly, in our spiritual practice there are times when it's probably best to put aside very difficult energies and wait for a circumstance that is more still and supportive. We might seek out a quiet period of personal reflection or meditation later, a dialogue with a spiritual teacher or a therapy session—whatever can help us to deal with it in a more skillful or wise way.

4. Another approach is to explore the hindrance by acting it out fully in our imaginations. This method and the next one (acting it out externally, with mindfulness) are more difficult and more "tantric," because if they are not done with careful attention, it is possible to reinforce the desire or give more power to the anger. Acting out a hindrance in your imagination means that you deliberately allow yourself to envision acting out the energy to its fullest with all its consequences. For example, with anger, you would see yourself hitting or even shooting someone. With greed you would visualize yourself completely fulfilling that desire, whether it is for sex, food, love, or whatever. Envision the abundance of it, imagine what it is like, and then see how you feel after you have had your fill. By following through and even exaggerating these feelings you can then learn what it means to be released from them.

5. A more tantric approach would be to deliberately act out the

mind state. In a way, that's what we do most of the time, without noticing it. But that's unconscious acting out. Here we act it out with awareness, with attention, with mindfulness. If there is a strong desire or feeling that needs to be expressed, we do so, as long as it does not cause harm. One of my Indian teachers had an unceasing craving for sweets. Finally he took himself to the local sweet shop and ordered two pounds of his favorites. He sat down and deliberately ate all of it with exquisite mindfulness until he was ready to throw up. Sweets never had the same hold on him after that.

When I was dealing with a lot of anger, my teacher Ajahn Chah told me to just stay with it and be angry. I was instructed to put on all of my robes during the hot season and sit with my anger all day long, allowing the full force of the fire, the hurt, the aggression, and the self-justification to manifest until I was thoroughly familiar with the power of this energy. Then later, as I practiced, I learned to express it with some mindfulness and not do destructive harm. Through this process, I found that I shed some of my fear of anger.

The energies and states we encounter in the journey become workable when we engage them fully with mindfulness. But if we don't pay attention, our practice can become unconsciously superficial. We can become comfortable with the outer forms, but not use them for genuine change. Instead of facing the depth of our vulnerability and fear and humanity with courage, we use our practice to carefully smooth things over and hide from reality. This is another common pitfall.

A brilliant exposition of how spiritual practice can be misused to bolster our ego or to create a new, improved self-image is spelled out in the book *Cutting through Spiritual Materialism* by Chögyam Trungpa. We can become attached to noble views and ideals, and unconsciously do an imitation of spirituality, using its forms and meditations and beliefs as a place to hide or seek security from the ever-changing world.

As we mature in our practice, we have to bring to consciousness the ways in which we have tried to escape or hide—if we wish to come to a fuller sense of freedom. Those who do not look into this after some period of practice can become stuck. There are committed meditators who are chronically slightly depressed because their real growth process has stopped, yet on the outside they follow the forms and ideals of practice and pretend to be fulfilled in it. These issues need investigation and heartfelt integrity to bring us again to the growth of real spiritual opening.

Additionally, as we look at the mystery of our human incarnation with mindfulness, we will come to see more clearly the patterns of identity we call our personality. With mindfulness, we will see how our personality is constructed out of thoughts and feelings, styles of relating to life, attachments and fears. Each person will see their personality and neurotic style more vividly. There are systems in Western psychology for describing personality patterns, such as introversion or extroversion, timid or novelty seeking, thinking or feeling types. Theravada Buddhist psychology describes undeveloped personality styles based on the three root causes of suffering: greed, hatred, and confusion. We must become aware of the undeveloped aspects of our basic personality style so that it does not become the basis for misusing our practice. Otherwise, those who are prone to greed will find themselves being greedy for spiritual experiences, spiritual knowledge, spiritual friends, and not see the neurotic aspect of their grasping. And those prone to aversion, who ordinarily dislike or reject experience, may use practice to condemn samsara and try to escape from life or use their spiritual teachings as a justification to judge others. And those whose personality tends toward confusion have a danger of getting stuck in doubt or getting lost in its opposite, blind faith, which brings temporary relief but does not serve true illumination.

Yet the point is not to get rid of the personality, but to see it clearly. It is a pitfall to simply judge the fears and neurotic patterns of personality. We should also understand that every unconscious personality style can be transformed into useful positive qualities through the development of our awareness. Greed can become appreciation, hatred can become clarity, doubt and confusion can become open-mindedness. As our journey progresses, we learn to employ and honor the personality without being lost in it.

GOING DEEPER

So far we've encountered some of the common, preliminary difficulties as we pursue mediation practice. Through mindfulness and loving-kindness we have learned how to deal with pain, the five hindrances, and the patterns of personality. They have not gone away, mind you;

they are there for a very long time. So when a group of advanced students is asked, "What are the difficulties you are working with?" their answers inevitably include laziness, fear, greed, anger, delusion, self-judgment—the same old stuff. Advanced students and beginners, it seems, are much the same. But when you have developed your practice, you learn how to relate to these difficulties more wisely. It can take a long time before they stop being a problem, yet after a while the heart and mind are calmer and better able to relate wisely and mindfully to what arises in the present. Then you may decide to do further practice.

A Foundation of Virtue

To continue this journey requires reinforcing the necessary foundation of virtue. By establishing a practice of basic morality, of nonharming, virtue becomes a safeguard on the path, guiding and protecting us and all we touch from harm. In the simplest fashion these safeguards are spelled out in the five traditional Buddhist precepts: (1) not killing, (2) not stealing, (3) not speaking falsely or with words that are undermining or untrue, (4) refraining from sexual misconduct and sexual activity that causes suffering or harm to another person, and (5) refraining from intoxicants that lead to the point of heedlessness or loss of awareness.

These basic precepts offer us a powerful means of establishing our life in harmony with the world around us. Without them our minds will be filled with conflict, guilt, remorse, and complexity. Some of the pioneer teachers in Western spiritual practice got into trouble because they did not develop the ground of virtue and nonharming. They became intoxicated with their practice or inflated, and then created suffering through hurtful speech or unskillful action or the misuse of sexuality and intoxicants. Following the precepts is a way of stabilizing the heart. By committing to not harming ourselves and not harming others, we develop a reverent relation to life.

These ways of conduct become the basis for quieting the mind, for living a life that is in harmony with the plants, the animals, and the earth around us. They become the basis for disconnecting ourselves from the most strident powers of greed, hatred, and delusion. On almost every occasion where we would break a precept, the mind has become filled with one of these unhealthy forces. Keeping these precepts functions as a protection and a source of consciousness; whenever difficulty arises, they steady our journey.

Letting Go of the Search for Comfort and Happiness

With virtue established, the next step in deepening practice is to move beyond the search for pleasure and happiness. Initially in spiritual practice we try to quiet ourselves and enhance our well-being. We may do some yoga to open the body, do a few breathing exercises, offer a prayer before dinner, hold hands with people, and follow a simpler, more moral life. These practices of developing virtue and loving-kindness, living a moral life, tending the body, and quieting the mind will lead us to experience more delight and joy, more harmony in our lives. These are important preliminary benefits of undertaking spiritual practice.

But to go further, the next level of spiritual practice must be undertaken for the sake of finding the deepest freedom possible for a human being. This level of practice has nothing whatsoever to do with happiness or comfort in the normal sense. This requires a willingness to face pleasure and pain equally, to open to what Zorba called "the whole catastrophe," to look directly into the light and the shadow of the heart and the mind.

We have established virtue and learned to quiet the mind and not be so caught up in restlessness, fear, desire. We have learned to pay increasing attention and be more fully in the present moment. What happens next?

Concentration and Its Side Effects

What often happens next is that as we give ourselves more fully to meditation practice, the power of our concentration will really start to deepen, and with further training the mind begins to get steadier on the meditation object—the breath, the visualization, the prayer, the light, or whatever is the inner focus. This steadiness of mind becomes a gateway to other spiritual realms. As concentration develops, a great variety of so-called spiritual experiences will begin to happen. Many are side effects of the meditation, and the better we understand them, the less likely we are to get stuck in them or confuse them with the goal. Let us consider what may arise with the development of stronger concentration.

Rapture is one of the first states to arise. Rapture arises most commonly on intensive and long retreats, although for some people it comes in their daily practice as well. Rapture is not necessary to develop wisdom. But at certain points in many people's practice, rapture will appear. Many types of rapture can arise, such as pleasant thrills in the body, waves of delight, lightness and expansion, pulsing and trembling with energy, and ecstatic pleasure, sometimes almost painful in its intensity. There are many other forms of bodily rapture, which can include vibrations, tingling, or prickles. Sometimes it feels as if ants or some other kind of bugs were crawling all over you; at other times you can feel very hot, as if your spine were on fire. This can alternate with feelings of cold, beginning as a little bit of chill and turning into very profound, deep states of cold.

With bodily rapture also arises various colored lights; on occasion these are blues, greens, or purples. More commonly as concentration gets stronger, there arise golden and white kinds of light and finally very powerful white light. In meditation it can seem like you are looking into the headlamp of an oncoming train, or as if the whole sky were illuminated by a brilliant white sun. Or your entire body can dissolve into light.

With concentration there can also arise a whole series of altered bodily perceptions. The body may seem very tall or very short. You may feel that you are heavy like a stone or being squashed under a wheel. Or you may feel so light that you believe you are floating and you have to open your eyes and peek to make sure that you are still actually on the ground.

These experiences can also arise during walking meditation. You can walk and be so concentrated on the steps that it appears that the whole room begins to sway as if you were on a ship in a storm; you put your foot down and you feel like you are drunk or the earth is moving. Or as your walk, everything starts to sparkle and turns into light.

Your sense of your body can change in unusual ways. As mentioned, you can feel small or large. Sometimes it feels as if your nose (where the sensation of the breath is often strongest) is located in your heart or outside your body, as if your breath is four feet away from you, or your head is twisted on backward. There can be spontaneous releases of physical energies in the body, which can be scary. These can come in many different forms. Sometimes they appear as a single, involuntary movement, or as a release of a knot or tension. At other times, they can take the form of dramatic, complex movements that can last for days or weeks. During a one-year retreat as a monk, I experienced weeks of a very powerful release of energy in the form of shaking, flapping, and other spontaneous movements. I tried to stop these movements but couldn't. The body can tremble, shake, twist, lean, in spontaneous ways. There are can be profound physical releases and openings that take place over months and years for some, like a form of bodywork that takes place as we sit silently and the energy of our body system opens and balances itself. Along with these unusual physical sensations, you can hear powerful inner sounds—bells, musical notes, high-pitched tones, voices, celestial-sounding music, or choruses.

The opening of the senses can become incredibly refined. You can hear or smell or see in a way that is by far superior to your everyday perception. I remember walking outdoors during a long retreat, and my usually dull sense of smell opened as if I were the most sensitive dog. As I walked, every foot or two there was a different smell—something cooking, the dirt on the sidewalk, the fertilizer over there, the new paint on part of a building that I went by, or someone lighting a fire at a distance. It was an extraordinary experience to go through the world primarily attuned to smell. I hardly saw or heard anything because the smells were so powerful. The same can happen with the ears or the eyes. The eyes can become opened to inner or outer revelation. There can be visions of past lives, great temples, scenes from other cultures, or images of things that you have never seen, in addition to colors and lights. These visions tap into the collective unconscious, the storehouse of human experience. Beyond this there can come psychic openings where one can see visions and experiences beyond the present moment, including visions of future events.

There can also be powerful releases on the emotional level. As one goes deeper in practice, there can arise the strongest kinds of emotions—despair, delight, rapture, profound grief, and many kinds of fear. There can also be worry, remorse, and guilt from things in the past and anxiety about the future. As the primary emotional storehouse opens, often with very great swings in emotions, it helps to have the guidance of a skilled teacher to offer a sense of balance.

This great variety of unusual experiences creates an obstacle course of repeated difficulties and pitfalls on the spiritual journey. The main difficulties arise when people get frightened by these unusual experiences or resist and judge them: "My body is dissolving and it's terrifying. I have got prickles, I am burning up, I am too cold, the sounds are too loud, there are too many inner sounds and they are bothering me." Aversion, contraction, and fright can arise toward these experiences. Each time we resist them, we get trapped by them, and through fear and misunderstanding we can struggle with them for a long time.

Some people are not afraid of these unusual experiences and find that they enjoy them. However, they can get trapped in the opposite response: developing a powerful attachment to these experiences, these side effects of practice. The perception of light or feelings of rapture can be very pleasant and can seem important, even revelatory, so some meditators become deeply attached to them, trying to hold on to these experiences or repeat them.

If you have a delicious experience of rapture, then in the next meditation period you might try to re-create it. You try to hold your body at what you found was the right angle and breathe exactly the way you did the last time. If you fail to experience rapture this time, you might try over and over. Even if you succeed, you end up stuck where you have already been. Seeking to repeat these special, pleasant experiences is a danger. Attachment does not allow you to open to the next experience, and your meditation cannot deepen.

Over time you learn that meditation will naturally produce a wide range of experiences including profound calm, rapture, inner light, and other more unusual phenomena. While in themselves these experiences can be beneficial and healing, they must actually be considered side effects on the path. These states are sometimes called "the corruptions of insight," because even though they are positive results of meditation, when they arise, our tendency is to get identified with them, to cling to them. Then we end up stuck there and do not learn what real freedom means.

So there is a radical shift necessary if we are to move beyond the sticking point of pleasure in meditation. This is the profound realization that freedom comes only from fully experiencing and releasing whatever is present, no matter how beautiful or how painful. The true path is one of letting go and allowing the process of awakening to open us to every moment without attachment. As we stay present with mindful and wise attention, we notice three things will happen to our experience: it will go away, it will stay the same for a while, or it will get more intense. Which of these occurs is none our business! Our job is to allow the experience of the phenomenal world to unfold in all its infinite richness—to see, hear, smell, taste, touch, and think, to rest in mindfulness and freedom at the center of it all.

When we have learned to be mindful without getting entangled in the positive and seductive states of the corruptions of insight, then there arise deeper levels of experience and insight, and with them come new difficulties. Here are some examples of some of these experiences, which though not necessary, can occur for many practitioners. There can arise at this point in practice, or even earlier for some meditators, a series of powerful energetic phenomena, sometimes called the awakening of the kundalini. What this means is simply a profound opening of the energy centers of the body, or the chakras, and a simultaneous opening of the energy channels, or *nadis,* in the body. While there is a basic pattern to this opening, it can happen in different ways.

Sometimes as one meditates and gets more concentrated, the body will begin to burn or there will be a feeling of heat in the spine, vibrations, and tingling. At times, one can actually feel energy move physically in the body as if fire, pulsations, or vibrations are pushing and moving spontaneously through blocked energy channels as a way to open and free them. Sometimes this inner release is combined with spontaneous movement and the forms of rapture we have described. These energetic openings up the spine and throughout the body can take hours, or months, or years. They are all a part of the process of psychophysical opening and purification.

As inner energy moves, the different chakras open and bring with them a whole variety of unusual physical phenomena. With the lowest chakras, the initial opening while bringing a profound sense of grounding can also include a release of fear that can take the form of nausea and vomiting. With the opening of the sexual chakra, there can be waves of powerful lust and rapture, including visions of every kind of sexual encounter. Openings of the chakra at the sternum can include releases of the energies of anger and aggression, and a strong awakening of inner sense of power.

When the heart chakra opens, there is an enormous release of compassion and love, but this is often preceded by a great deal of grief and physical pain because most of us have bands of tension around our heart. During retreats many students (often physicians and nurses) have come to me saying, "I think you need to call an ambulance. I think I'm having a heart attack." When I inquire further, almost always what's causing these sensations is the opening of the heart chakra. Sometimes I joke, "What better place to die than at a retreat? We have not lost anybody yet. It is worth it to have one's heart opened. So go back and sit."

The opening of the throat chakra can release a full range of expression, sounds of truth telling, of voice and song. But it can be accompanied by coughs, tension, days of swallowing, and at times a need for screaming or shouting to bring release.

The opening of brow and crown chakras can reveal visionary states, insight, even psychic clarity. There can be a sense of resting in perfect harmony at the center of the universe, the crown of the head like a lotus opening a radiant awareness amid all time and space. But the opening of energetic centers in the head can also involve experiencing bands of tension and pressure, long-lasting headaches, tears, and burning of the eyes and ringing of the ears.

Energy released through the spine and chakras can become very powerful, to the point where there is so much energy coursing through the body that one cannot sleep for a number of nights. The entire body will vibrate. This process can go on for days or even months.

Spiritual Emergency

If this process of opening is especially strong and unstoppable, even when the student is not meditating, then it can be experienced as a spiritual emergency. *Spiritual emergency* is a term coined by Christina and Stanislav Grof (two leaders in the field of transpersonal psychology) to describe overwhelming spiritual experiences that can take over our life for a time. These experiences are generally not well understood in our culture, so people find them confusing or frightening. The sense of spiritual emergency can arise earlier on the path of practice, when raptures, body distortions, lights, or inner sounds and voices arise. These become emergencies because they frighten uninformed people, who become distressed and fear they are losing their grip on reality, going crazy. If a person experiencing these states consults a doctor, they might be given tranquilizers, antipsychotic medication, or even sent to a mental hospital.

Spiritual emergencies are not only brought about through intensive spiritual practice, they can also be triggered by powerful life events, such as the death of a loved one, divorce, childbirth, transcendent sexual experience, taking psychedelics, or having a near-death experience.

Whatever their causes, what is needed for most spiritual emergencies is normalization. When a practitioner or student hears from a trusted and experienced source that these altered perceptions are normal, and that they are only a phase that will pass in time, the fear and sense of emergency vanishes. Then the process can be seen as interesting and informative as it continues.

Sometimes, especially when practitioners make enormous effort, these experiences can get extraordinarily powerful. There was a young, overzealous martial arts student who sat for a three-month retreat at our center in Massachusetts. Contrary to our instructions to practice with balance, he decided to sit for twenty-four hours straight without moving. He sat all day and night, through increasingly intense sensations of fire and intense pain, until his consciousness became wrenched away from its identification with his physical body. He became filled with enormous energy and felt propelled into our silent dining hall, where he began shouting and wildly doing karate moves at three times normal speed. You could not get near him. He shouted that he could see a whole string of past lives for each person that he looked at. He was living in a very different realm of consciousness, which he had attained through pushing his body and mind to that limit. But he could not stand still or focus. There was a strong fear in his agitation and a manic state as if he had gone temporarily crazy.

Our response was to get him to do some running. Since he was an athlete, we got him to run ten or more miles a day. We also changed his diet; while everyone else was eating vegetarian food, we got him meat loaf and hamburgers. We made him take long, frequent hot baths and showers. We had him walk and work and dig in the garden. These were methods for helping him recover a sense of grounding. We also had someone stay with him all the time. In about three days he came down. While his energetic experiences and psychic openings were genuine, they were not brought about in a natural way, so he could not integrate them or benefit from them in an ongoing way.

Beyond this, there are states resembling psychosis that arise at certain points in meditation. We have had many thousands of people at our retreats over the years. Out of these, about a dozen have had true psychotic breaks. For the most part these were people who had been previously hospitalized for mental illness. When people who have had serious mental illness come to do meditation practice, sometimes they find themselves reliving their mental crises. Whatever we are most afraid of will eventually come up. Many of these people are successfully able to reexperience these past crises and traumas in the context of the safety and balance of the retreat. The meditation provides enough support that they can remember and touch the places of fear again and see that they are just another part of the mind. But for a few people intensive meditation can reactivate psychosis.

As teachers, we become concerned and respond immediately when persistent auditory and visual hallucinations overwhelm a student. While ordinarily students are encouraged to sit through whatever experience presents itself, the persistence and seeming reality of inner voices can indicate problems. Added to this, we become especially concerned when a student stops eating or cannot sleep, or when they become overtaken by obsessions, paranoia, and fear. When overwhelming visions and fears are combined with a lack of sleep and food, we immediately respond. We have students limit their meditation and shift to grounding and calming practices. As we did with the young martial arts student, we focus on stabilizing and releasing through walking, running, physical work, engaging with others. We implement a heavier diet, use massage, acupuncture, and other calming and grounding practices. We find that providing food and sleep are especially important in these situations.

We have also found that those who experience a spiritual emergency often have a background of serious trauma that initiates or further potentiates this process. For this we use and recommend body-based trauma work such as the somatic-experience work of Peter Levine. In a few extreme cases we have brought in a psychiatrist to evaluate the student and prescribe a dose of a tranquilizer or antipsychotic to help stabilize them. Occasionally meditators are hospitalized for a few days, because we do not have adequate staff or resources to give them the level of support they need.

In a centuries-old Zen text called "The Tiger's Cave," a famous Japanese Zen master named Hakuin describes his own spiritual emergency. It came after arduous practice pursuing awakening, when finally great joy and liberation arose and Hakuin's teacher declared that Hakuin had tasted enlightenment. But several months later the joy and harmony disappeared. Hakuin was beset by a wild, racing mind accompanied by freezing-cold legs and a sensation of burning in his mouth. He heard a torrent of rushing inner sounds, sweated profusely, and was in tears night and day. He sought out masters and healers for help, but to no avail. Finally he visited a Taoist hermit, who gave him two practices: to breathe so as to draw down energy from the head into the belly, and to do visualizations that circulate and balance energy in the body. Hakuin regained his balance and became a great teacher. Accounts like those of Hakuin and Saint John of the Cross show that spiritual emergencies do not happen only in modern times; there are descriptions of practitioners encountering them in all ages and major methods of practice.

The Transcendence and Dissolution of Self

Spiritual emergencies happen to a small percentage of those who go on retreat. But they should not be confused with the powerful process of inner deconstruction that is a normal, though difficult passage in the deeper levels of meditation. The transcendence and dissolution of the self is experienced in a sequence of states naturally arising in advanced Buddhist practice. These states begin after one has stabilized the mind and developed a concentration powerful enough to pass through the initial difficulties and hindrances. Then you reach a steady level called access concentration, meaning you have access to deeper realms of insight.

At this point, you can direct consciousness into different realms of absorption up to the level of cosmic consciousness. These *jhana* states, or absorption levels, begin when the mind becomes so fully absorbed in the meditation object—whether the breath, a mantra, or the feeling of love—that all other sense experience begins to drop away. With this steady concentration, consciousness fills with rapture and light, and most thoughts and outer perceptions disappear. From here it is possible to direct consciousness to enter the many stable states of jhana samadhi, which are characterized by vastness, luminosity, and refined happiness. The shift into these states feels like diving from the wave and windswept surface of the ocean to the peaceful underwater realm of silence and beauty. The jhana states transcend our ordinary sense of self. Some are characterized by boundless joy or happiness. Others are even more refined, opening us to states of limitless space, boundless consciousness, or silence beyond perception. In Buddhist training, attaining the transcendent stillness of the jhana states helps in understanding the nature of self. This refined and stable attention can be turned toward insight. With it you can investigate the workings of consciousness and intimately realize the transient or empty nature of body and mind.

But attaining the level of jhana concentration is difficult for many meditators and is not necessary for profound inner exploration. Prior to jhana states, when a meditator reaches the level of access concentration there is already great stability. Here the mind is quite unmoving and there is very little thought. With access concentration, awareness rests stably and fully in the present moment. Then instead of being turned toward jhana states, this concentrated attention can be directed to changing sensory experiences. Close attention to the breath, or the body, begins to reveal deep levels of insight. As concentration and an increasingly steady power of mindfulness are directed to each moment's experience, a spontaneous process of deconstruction of experience brings penetrating insight. As if it were a microscope, this concentrated mindfulness notices how each sense experience arises and passes ceaselessly. Continuous microscopic mindfulness over days and weeks reveals a constantly changing experience of the physical senses and rapidly cycling mental events, arising and interacting in an almost mechanical way. We see how the movement of the body is conditioned by mental states and how every mental state is conditioned by sensory input. Experiences appear and disappear quickly in an increasingly impermanent and selfless process.

When insight into this moment-to-moment, ever-changing body and mind becomes stabilized, a great sense of freedom and joy arises. There arises joy, balance, strong faith, concentration, and mindfulness. It is as if the solid sense of body and mind has become a river of sensations and perceptions, and we have learned to joyfully float in it. Our meditation has never felt better. Yet these positive states, which are important fruits of the meditation, can become corruptions of insight. On experiencing them, we are delighted and grasp them, identifying them as the goal of meditation. They become a new sticking point. After a time, we realize that the path to liberation requires us to let go of clinging to even the most beautiful states and fruits of practice. Only then can we open to that which is beyond this limited body and mind.

When we have abandoned clinging to pleasant states, our letting go begins a profound series of new perceptions. We now go into the insight levels of the dark night. Our level of concentration and attention now becomes even more refined, so that we actually see and feel the entire world begin to dissolve in front of us. Wherever we focus, our sensory world of seeing, hearing, smelling, tasting, or touching starts to dissolve. Wherever we look, we see sights arise and pass away. If we see a person, we look away from that image and we see it dissolve, and the next thing appears, and we look away and we notice the next dissolution after that. Our attention becomes like a magnifying glass revealing the tiny evanescent pulses and pixels that make up what we took to be a solid sense of form. With hearing, when sounds come, we feel them as tiny pulses tinkling on the ear and dissolving one moment after another. Body sensations, smells, tastes, images, and feelings are the same: wherever we turn our attention; the solid world becomes seen as momentary particles.

From this experience of arising and vanishing at the sense doors, there begins spontaneously a series of meditative states Buddhist texts refer to as the stages of fear and dissolution. Just when the outer world dissolves when we observe lights, colors, and other sense objects, the inner world of thoughts and perceptions starts to dissolve as well, and we lose our entire point of reference. Everything becomes shaky, unstable. Our sense of our self and the world becomes progressively insecure and fleeting, yet we keep paying attention because mindfulness is now riveted by the process. It is all dissolving, and there is a stage of unease that gradually becomes a sense of terror. Nothing lasts. Impermanence and dissolution is so apparent that we come to a deep realization of the inevitability of suffering. We perceive the suffering of the loss of all that is created or loved by us. Everything in the world—family members, loved ones, our own body—all of it will be lost. Tremendous sympathy for the sorrow of the world arises. Whether pleasant or painful, experiences all dissolve, so we cannot hold on to them.

In this stage of fear, there are periods of paranoia. Wherever we look, the world is fearsome. If we walk out of the door, something could run us over. If we take a drink of water, there could be harmful bacteria in it, and we could die. Everything becomes a source of potential death or destruction in this stage of the dark night of the soul. Powerful visions of loss can also arise. These can be spontaneous visions of a hundred forms of one's own death, or the death of other people, wars, dying armies, or charnel grounds. Sometimes we look down and see pieces of our body appear to melt away and decay as if we were a corpse. In the shamanic traditions these are called "the experiences of dismemberment," while the Tibetans describe them as a process of "ego death." These are very compelling visions. We see how all we hold dear in the world arises tentatively into being and how it inexorably passes away.

States of claustrophobia and oppression can arise as well. With the dissolution of the body and all experience, a sense of world weariness and the inevitability of suffering are common experiences. But paradoxically there may also arise a sense of how hard it is to let go of attachments and continue this process. We feel that we cannot do it, seeking liberation is too hard, the world is too difficult, and the tangle of being identified with all these things is too deep. It seems beyond us to find a way out. We wish only to roll up our mat, to quit and go home. Yet we know there is nowhere to run. Out of this arises a deep desire for deliverance. We long for freedom where consciousness is not bound up in ever-changing seeing, hearing, smelling, tasting, and touching. We no longer want to be caught in the fear of being a separate self, body, and mind. Step by step, we have to gradually detach and disidentify from everything but awareness itself.

The stages of fear, dissolution, and wanting to just roll up the mat are hard to go through. It is important to have support; otherwise we get lost, overwhelmed, or we quit. And if we stop in the middle of this process, the stages of dissolution, fear, or claustrophobia can become the undercurrents in our unconscious and can last for months or years until we do deep practice to return to that level and resolve them.

It is critical to work with a teacher who understands how to go through these levels. We must get to the place where we can look these difficult states straight in the eye and know they are aspects of life to be accepted with unshakable mindfulness. When we look at the horrors and the joys with an unbiased heart and an open mind, neither resisting nor grasping them, we open the gate to freedom.

When we finally can do this, there arises the most beautiful and profound equanimity, in which everything that appears is singing one song, the song of emptiness. It says, "Experience arises by itself, it is ungraspable, none of it is 'me' or 'mine.' It is just a world of phenomena, of consciousness, and of light and dark playing out." In this equanimity there is no sense of separation, no sense of self. There are simply moments of seeing, hearing, smelling, tasting, touching, and mental events, all seen with luminous clarity as impermanent, insecure, ungraspable. We cannot hold them and say, "Here is happiness." From this vantage point any grasping of body and mind has an inherent unreality and unsatisfactoriness to it.

Letting go into equanimity brings profound relief and rest. The mind becomes clear and shining like a crystal goblet, open like the sky, in which all things are balanced. We become completely transparent, and every phenomenon just passes through the mind and body, which has now become simply space.

This spiritual process of dissolution and opening takes us to what is called in the Christian mystical tradition "divine apathy." It is not a lack of caring, but pure consciousness, which, like the eye of God, can see creation and destruction, light and dark, with a heart that embraces it all, because it is all of that. We see that we are nothing and we are everything. We taste what it is like to be in the world, but not caught by a single thing in it. From this vast, open balance there arise other extraordinary states of mind. There is a realization of the inherent completion and perfection in all things. Through direct experience we know what it means to be free of greed, hatred, delusion, fear, and identification. We discover the art of balance. We can enter the void and the fabric of existence just disappears and then reappears all by itself.

Liberation opens us to our own timeless, true nature. We know firsthand the greatness that it is possible to uncover within the human heart. And even though we will not remain in this state, like climbing to the top of a mountain, we have glimpsed what liberation really means, and it informs and affects our whole life thereafter. We cannot ever again believe that we are separate. We cannot ever really be afraid to die, because we have died already. This is called "dying before death," and it brings the most wonderful kind of detachment and equanimity.

We see for ourselves the Buddha's Noble Truths: that there is suffering in life, and that the cause of it is our grasping, our identification. We learn what it means to be free of clinging, free in a way that nothing can touch us. We discover the liberation that is possible for every human being, and realize the greatness of the heart where the ten thousand joys and the ten thousand sorrows can dance within pure consciousness, now awakened and clear.

Finally we see that spiritual practice is simple; it is the path of opening and letting go, of being aware and not attaching to a single thing. As my teacher Ajahn Chah explained, "The Middle Path is simple. When I see someone getting lost in the sidetrack on the right side of the road or going off in a ditch, I yell, 'Go left.' When that same person is about to get lost in a sidetrack on the left or they fall off in the ditch, I yell, 'Go right.' That is all I do. Wherever you get attached, let go and come back to the center." With balanced awareness, you can be here now, gracious, awake, present, and free.

For meditators who have come through the stages of dissolution and discovered this inner freedom, there arises joy and boundless gratitude. But this tremendous and enlightening phase of the journey will end, and we will inevitably come down. In coming back from this intensive process, like a descent from a mountain, we may reencounter in reverse some of the difficult stages of the journey, but now we can bring to these challenges a sense of balance and disidentification, a quality of ease and tenderness with all that arises.

You might imagine that a practitioner who has reached this stage now lives happily ever after, or at least has an easy time when they return home. But because the process of disidentification has been so profound, and the concentrated stilling of the mind so deep, new dimensions of difficulties and experiences of spiritual emergency can arise.

Reentering Ordinary Life

We may continue to experience detachment and depersonalization as we reenter our work and family life. This can make us feel like an alien, a zombie. We might feel confused or depressed. We can also feel bombarded and oversensitive, and we might begin to doubt that our journey was of value. Because our mind has become so still, and the thoughts that create our sense of self and our plans are gone, it is hard to think in ordinary ways. We can be unable to make decisions or take action.

Our time in retreat has given us an alternative set of values. It has focused us on a reality outside of our ordinary obligations, beyond our career goals, our marriage, and so forth. The detachment that arises in mediation practice can undermine our worldly interests, our ambition and motivation. We become interested primarily in silence, love, and living in the moment.

After an intensive meditation retreat or spiritual experience, we need to allow for a process of reentry into the rhythms of ordinary daily life. Commonly this reentry process will take as long as the time we spent in retreat. If we are guided to relax and accept the inevitable process of depersonalization, indecisiveness, and identity confusion, we will slowly become able to function well in our old life.

But if we are not helped, or the process of reentry is unusually intense and difficult, this can turn into a period of spiritual emergency. When this happens, as we return to our ordinary lives, our fears, inability to make decisions, and sense of alienation can become frightening and painful. This can be compounded by tremendous sensitivity, spontaneous movements, energy release, and disorientation—the common features of other forms of spiritual emergency. We may need weeks or months of quiet to protect ourselves, to slow down the reentry process and focus on getting grounded. Again hot baths, jogging, walking, tai chi, and working in the garden can help us to find grounding. Inwardly, we can bring attention downward through the body, visualizing our connection to the earth. We can also use bodywork (such as massage), *chi gung,* and other forms of movement to help us release energy. Acupuncture can be helpful in correcting intense imbalances of energy, and because past trauma is so often intertwined with spiritual emergency, body-based trauma work such as Somatic Experiencing is almost a necessity. Sexual release is helpful, too, as are active forms of therapy, such as Gestalt work, Reichian work, Jungian sand play, or movement therapy. These therapies can help us to find release, balance, and understanding. To further ground ourselves, we can also change our diet to heavy foods, such as grains and meats. Overall, the goal is to seek out the kinds of activities that release tension and fear and gently bring us back down to earth.

After an intensive retreat, we may also discover that certain difficulties have waited for our return, especially if we have used practice as a way of trying to escape from life, as a method of denial or suppression of what we couldn't deal with. When we are afraid of the world, afraid of living fully, afraid of relationships, afraid of work, or afraid of some aspect of what it means to be alive in the physical body, we may run away to meditation. Whoever has practiced for a while will probably have seen some element of this in his or her own heart and mind.

Meditation, like any discipline, can be used in skillful ways—for freedom, for liberation, for opening the heart. It can also be used in defensive and unskillful ways—in service of the ego and of our fears. We might sit quietly so that we do not have to deal with difficulties, follow our breath to avoid feeling certain difficult emotions, pay attention to the light so that we can avoid our shadow side. To return we have to include these too in our practice.

All of these reentry difficulties need to be respected in the process of mindful descent. For some, this return can be as arduous as the deconstruction process. To reintegrate ourselves into our lives, we must start our thinking mechanism going again. We must reflect on our life, looking freshly at the question of right livelihood, the needs of our society and of our loved ones, reenvisioning how we are going to live in the world. We need to look with wisdom at our roles and deliberately choose how to fully engage with this messy human realm with clear vision and compassion.

When the mind is quiet, the prospect of dealing with these areas may seem quite painful. Reentry can be tough, moving us through dizziness and suffering, not wanting to accept that we are limited beings in a physical reality that must be embraced. And yet when we do reintegrate, the blessings of our journey, the wise heart and tender kindness we have awakened, become gifts we can bestow on the world and all we touch. This will have made the whole journey worth our while.

This sacred cycle is illustrated by a story of an old Chinese monk who was determined to go practice on top of a mountain and either get enlightened or die. He had sat in a monastery and had many years of peaceful meditation, but he was never enlightened. So he went to the master and said, "Please, may I just go up into the mountains and finish this practice? That is all I want from life now, to see what this enlightenment is about." The master, knowing the monk was ripe, gave permission.

Partway up the mountain path he met an old man walking down carrying a big bundle. The old man was really the bodhisattva Manjushri, who is said to appear to people when they are ready for enlightenment. Usually he is depicted carrying a sword that cuts through all illusions. But on this day he had a great bundle, and as he came down the mountain, he asked, "Where are you going, monk?" The monk replied, "I am going up to the top of the mountain with my bowl and a few belongings. I am going to sit there and either get enlightened or die. That is all I want. I have been a monk for a long time, and now I must know liberation for myself."

Since the old man looked very wise, the monk then asked, "Tell me, old man, do you know anything about enlightenment?" The old man looked him in the eyes, smiled, let go of the bundle, and it dropped to the ground. In that moment the monk became enlightened. "You mean it is that simple, just let go and don't grasp anything?" Yes. But this truth is hard for us to realize, because our attachments are so strong. We take our body, feelings, and beliefs to be ourselves—as "me" and "mine"—and the deep process of dissolution that I have described can be required to untangle these attachments. For most people a period of systematic and disciplined practice is needed to do this.

In this process of finding freedom we will pass through temptations, hindrances, and difficulties, through storms of emotion, through realms of fire and dissolution. In the end, whatever level of freedom we find, we must return. In this same Zen story the newly enlightened monk looks back at the old man and asks, "So now what?" In answer, the old man smiled again, reached down to pick up the bundle, and walked off toward town.

The story illustrates the full cycle of practice. Meditation teaches us to let go, to relinquish our grasping, our fears, our identification with all things. We learn to see that we are not this body, we are not these feelings, we are not these thoughts, that we just rent this house for a while. And once we have let go and realized freedom, this story teaches us that we must reenter the world—this time with a caring heart, with universal compassion, and with a great deal of balance and wisdom. We must pick up our bundle and take it back into the realms of ordinary life. But now we can travel as a bodhisattva, as one who has traversed the terrain of life and death and understands it deeply enough to be free in a whole new way. With this freedom, we bring a heart of understanding and compassion to a world that needs it so much.

10

The Near Enemies
of Awakening

Nonattachment Is Not Indifference

ONE OF THE MOST IMPORTANT questions we come to in spiritual practice is how to reconcile service and responsible action with a meditative life that fosters nonattachment, letting go, and shows the emptiness of all conditioned things. Do the values that lead us to actively give, serve, and care for one another differ from the values that lead us on a journey of liberation and awakening?

To consider this question, we must learn to distinguish between the radiant abodes (the description of the awakened heart—love, compassion, sympathetic joy, and equanimity) and what might be called their "near enemies." Near enemies may seem to be like these qualities and may even be mistaken for them, but they are not fundamentally alike. The near enemies depict how spirituality can be misunderstood or misused to separate us from life.

LOVE VS. ATTACHMENT

The near enemy of love is attachment. Attachment masquerades as love. It says, "I will love this person because I need them." Or, "I'll love you if you'll love me back. I'll love you, but only if you will be the way I want." This isn't love at all—it is attachment—and attachment is rigid, it is very different from love. When there is attachment, there is clinging and fear. Love allows, honors, and appreciates; attachment grasps, demands, needs, and aims to possess. Attachment is conditional, offers love only to certain people in certain ways; it is exclusive. Love, in the sense of *metta*, used by the Buddha, is a universal, nondiscriminating feeling of caring and connectedness. We may even love those whom we may not approve of or like. We may not condone their behavior, but we cultivate forgiveness. Love is a powerful force that transforms any situation. It is not passive acquiescence. As the Buddha said, "Hatred never ceases through hatred. Hatred only ceases through love." Love embraces all beings without exception, and discards ill will.

COMPASSION VS. PITY AND DESPAIR

The near enemy of compassion is pity. Instead of feeling the openness of compassion, pity says, "Oh, that poor person. I feel sorry for people like that." Pity sees them as different from ourselves. It sets up a separation between ourselves and others, a sense of distance and remoteness from the suffering of others that is affirming and gratifying to the self. Compassion, on the other hand, recognizes the suffering of another as a reflection of our own pain: "I understand this; I suffer in the same way." It is empathetic, a mutual connection with the pain and sorrow of life. Compassion is shared suffering.

Another enemy of compassion is despair. Compassion does not mean immersing ourselves in the suffering of others to the point of anguish. Compassion is the tender readiness of the heart to respond to one's own or another's pain without despair, resentment, or aversion. It is the wish to dissipate suffering. Compassion embraces those experiencing sorrow, and eliminates cruelty from the mind.

JOY VS. COMPARISON

The third quality, sympathetic joy, is the ability to feel joy in the happiness of others. The enemy of shared joy is comparison and jealousy. Jealousy compares our joy to that of another. It separates us and believes that joy is limited. If others have it, there will not be enough for us. True shared joy is joy in being, in aliveness, it is an openhearted celebrating of our life with one another. Shared joy takes delight in the success and happiness of all. It wishes that their and our happiness may increase.

EQUANIMITY VS. INDIFFERENCE

The near enemy of equanimity is indifference or callousness. We may appear serene if we say, "I'm not attached. It doesn't matter what happens anyway, because it's all transitory." We feel a certain peaceful relief because we withdraw from experience and from the energies of life. But indifference is based on fear. True equanimity is not a withdrawal; it is a balanced engagement with all aspects of life. It is opening to the whole of life with composure and ease of mind, accepting the beautiful and terrifying nature of all things. Equanimity embraces the loved and the unloved, the agreeable and the disagreeable, the pleasure and pain. It eliminates clinging and aversion.

Although everything is temporary and dreamlike, with equanimity we nevertheless honor the reality of form. As Zen master Dogen says, "Flowers fall with our attachment, and weeds spring up with our aversion." Knowing that all will change and that the world of conditioned phenomena is insubstantial, with equanimity we are able to be fully present and in harmony with it.

WISE AND ENGAGED

In the eightfold path, the Buddha talks about right intention, which engages the world wisely in three ways. First, we cultivate a mind free from unhealthy desire by developing a sense of inner contentment. Second, we free ourselves from ill will and resentment by cultivating thoughts of compassion and gentleness. Third, we develop a mind that is free from cruelty by nourishing the forces of kindness and love within us. With right intention, we can engage all of life and the different situations we face as stepping-stones for awakening.

Attachment, pity, comparison, and indifference are all ways of disengaging, of separating ourselves from life out of fear. True spirituality is not a removal or escape from life. It allows us to enter the world with a deeper vision that is not self-centered or dualistic, that sees the interconnectedness of all of life. It is the discovery that freedom lies in the midst of our own bodies and minds.

Years ago in India, I asked a meditation teacher named Vimala Thaker about the question of meditation and activity in the world. Vimala had worked with the followers of Gandhi for many years in rural development and land redistribution projects when, as a result of her studies with Krishnamurti, she began to teach meditation and devoted many years to this. Then later she returned to development work and to helping the hungry and homeless, teaching meditation less than she once had. I asked her why she decided to go back to the service work she had been doing years before. She replied, "Sir, I am a lover of life, and as a lover of life, I cannot keep out of any activity of life. If there are people who are hungry for food, my response is to help feed them. If there are people who are hungry for truth, my response is to help them discover it. I make no distinction."

The Sufis have a simple saying that articulates this paradox: "Praise Allah, and tie your camel to the post." Pray, but also make sure you do what is necessary in the world. Meditate, but manifest your understanding of this spiritual experience. Balance your realization of emptiness with a sense of compassion and care in order to guide your life impeccably.

Seeing emptiness means seeing that all of life is like a bubble in a rushing stream, a play of light and shadow, a dream. It means understanding that this tiny planet hangs in the immensity of space amid billions of stars and galaxies—that all of human history is like one second compared to the billions of years of the earth's history, and that it will all be over very soon and no one is really going anywhere. This context helps us to let go amid the seeming seriousness of our problems, to enter life with a sense of lightness and ease.

Care and compassion mean realizing how precious life is, even though it is transient and ephemeral, and how each of our actions and words affect all beings around us in a most profound way. There is nothing inconsequential in this universe, and we need to respect this fact personally and act responsibly in accordance with it.

How do we put emptiness and care together? One could make a very convincing case for simply devoting oneself to meditation. Does the world need more medicine and energy and buildings and food? Not really. There are grain elevators full of food while elsewhere people starve. There are millions of people sick with diseases we have medicine to cure. There are enough resources for all of us. There is starvation and poverty and disease because of ignorance, prejudice, and fear, because we hoard materials and create wars over imaginary geographic boundaries and act as if one group of people is truly different from us. What the world needs is not more oil or food, but more love and generosity, less greed and more kindness and understanding. The most fundamental thing we can do to help this war-torn and suffering world is to free ourselves from fear and the divisive views in our own minds, and then help others to do the same. Thus, spiritual practice is not a privilege; it is a necessity, a basic responsibility.

But there is an equally convincing argument for devoting oneself entirely to service in the world. I have only to mention the horrors of Darfur, the ongoing violence in the Middle East, the devastation in Haiti—situations in which the enormity of suffering is almost beyond comprehension. In India alone, three hundred million people live in such poverty that one day's work pays for only one meal. I once met a man in Calcutta who was sixty-four years old and pulled a rickshaw for a living. He had been doing it for forty years and had ten people dependent on him for income. He had gotten sick the year before for ten days. Within a week money ran out and they had nothing to eat. How can we let this happen? Dozens of children per minute die from starvation while twenty-five million dollars per minute are spent on arms. We must respond. We cannot hold back or look away.

We have painful dilemmas to face. Where should we put our energy? Which should we do first? Should we meditate? No amount of service will be enough unless we also change the consciousness of the world. We need to learn that we are interconnected. We need ways to find contentment and inner peace, to meditate and simplify. Yet we also need to serve those in immediate distress. We need to do both. Only our heart can tell us what is the right balance and rhythm to follow. To serve wisely and not burn out we will need our meditation and our courage.

SPIRITUAL LIFE TAKES COURAGE

Equanimity is not indifference, and compassion is not pity. True spirituality requires us to be fully present for life. For us to begin to look directly at the world situation is not a question of ceremony or of religion. Meditation helps us to look deeply at the sorrow that exists now in our world, and to look at our individual and collective relationship to it, to bear witness to it, to acknowledge it instead of running away. Without mindfulness and compassion the suffering is too great to bear. We close our minds. We close our eyes and hearts.

Yet opening ourselves to all aspects of experience is necessary if we want to make a difference. To look at the world honestly, unflinchingly, and directly requires us to also look at ourselves. We discover that sorrow and pain are not just out there, external, but are also within ourselves. We have our own fear, prejudice, hatred, desire, neurosis, and anxiety. It is our own sorrow. In opening ourselves to suffering, we discover the great heart of compassion.

In the heart of each of us, a potential exists for experiencing this compassion and wholeness. The problem is that we become so busy and lost in our own thinking that we lose connection with our true nature. When we reconnect with our wholeness, our being naturally expresses itself both in meditation and through sharing ourselves with others.

I spend most of my time teaching meditation. Years ago, when many thousands of Cambodian people were fleeing violence in their homeland only to face starvation and disease in refugee camps in Thailand, something in me said, "I've got to go there," and so I went. I knew the people and a few of the local languages. After being there trying to assist, I returned to this country to guide intensive meditation retreats. I did not deliberate much at the time about whether or not I should go to work in the refugee camps. I felt that it had to be done, and I went and did it. It was immediate and personal.

In years following I have done work in Palestine and Burma, in prisons and hospitals, and with kids in street gangs. This is what I have been called to do alongside my meditation teaching. This has been my way. But it is not right for everyone. Some monks spend their lives in caves in the Himalayas ceaselessly radiating compassion for the world. Others run orphanages for children whose parents have died of AIDS. Which is the right way? The spiritual path does not present us with a prescribed, pat formula for everyone to follow. It is not a matter of imitation. We cannot be Mother Teresa or Gandhi or the Buddha. We have to be ourselves. We must discover and connect with our unique expression of the truth. We must learn to listen to and trust ourselves.

THE TWO GREAT FORCES IN THE WORLD

There are two great forces in the world. One is the force of killing. People who are not afraid to kill make wars, govern nations, and control much of the activity of our world. There is great strength in not being afraid to kill. The other source of strength in the world—the real strength—is in people who are not afraid to die. These are people who have touched the very source of their being, who have looked into themselves in such a deep way that they understand and acknowledge and accept death and, in a way, have already died. They have seen beyond the separateness of the ego's shell, and they bring to life the fearlessness and the caring born of love and truth. This is the only force that can match someone who is not afraid to kill.

This is the power of Nelson Mandela and Aung San Suu Kyi. Gandhi called it "satyagraha," the force of truth, and the force that he demonstrated in his own life. When India was partitioned, millions of people became refugees—Muslims and Hindus fled from one country to another. There was horrible violence and rioting. Tens of thousands of troops were sent to West Pakistan to try to quell the terrible violence, while Gandhi went to what was then East Pakistan. He walked from village to village asking people to stop the bloodshed. Then he fasted. He said he would take no more food until the violence and insanity stopped, even if it meant his own death. And the riots stopped. They stopped because of the power of his love, because Gandhi cared about something—call it truth or life or whatever you wish, that was something much greater than Gandhi the person. This is the genuine power of spiritual practice, whatever form it may take. Living aligned with truth becomes more important than either living or dying. This understanding is the source of incredible strength and energy, and will be manifested through love, compassion, sympathetic joy, and equanimity.

One of the exquisite experiences of my travels in India was going to the holy city of Benares by the Ganges River. Along the river bank are ghats where people bathe as a purification, and there are also ghats where people bring corpses to be cremated. I had heard about the burning ghats for years and had always thought that being there would be a heavy experience. I was rowed downriver in a little boat, and up to the ghats where there were twelve fires going. Every half hour or so, a new body would be carried down to the fires as people chanted "*Rama nama satya hei* (the only truth is the name of God)." I was surprised. It was not dreadful at all; it was peaceful, quiet, and very sane. There was a recognition that birth and death are part of the same process, and therefore death need not be feared.

There is a deep joy that comes when we stop denying the painful aspects of life, and instead allow our hearts to open to and accept the full range of human experience: life and death, pleasure and pain, darkness and light. Even in the face of the tremendous suffering in the world, there can be a joy, which comes not from rejecting pain and seeking pleasure but rather from our ability to meditate and open ourselves to the truth. Spiritual practice begins by allowing ourselves to face our own sadness, fear, anxiety, desperation—to die to the ego's ideas about how things should be, and to love and accept the truth of things as they are.

With this as our foundation, we can see the source of suffering in our lives and in the world around us. We can see the factors of greed, hatred, and ignorance that produce a sense of separation. We can also see the end of suffering, an acknowledgment of the oneness of light and dark, up and down, sorrow and joy. We can see all these things without attachment and without separation.

We must look at how we have created and enforced separation. How have we made this a world of "I want this; I want to become that; this will make me safe; this will make me powerful." Race, nationality, age, and religion all enforce separation. Look into yourself and see what is "us" and what is "them" for you. When there is a sense of "us," then there is a sense of "other." When we can give this up, then we can give up the idea that strength comes from having more than others or from having the power to kill others. When we give this up, we give up the stereotype of love as a weakness.

That is our aspiration and our task—to drop our clinging, condemning, identifying, our opinions, and our sense of I, me, mine. We have to see that we are all woven together. Then we can act effectively, even dramatically, without bitterness or self-righteousness. We can be motivated by a genuine sense of caring and of forgiveness, and a determination to live our lives well.

A number of years ago I attended a conference at which Mad Bear, an Iroquois medicine man, was invited to give a lecture. He said, "For my presentation I'd like us to begin by going outside," and we all went out. He led us to an open field and then asked us to stand silently in a circle. We stood for a while in silence under a wide-open sky, surrounded by fields of grain stretching to the horizon. Then Mad Bear began to speak, offering a prayer of gratitude. He began by thanking the earthworms for aerating the soil so that plants can grow. He thanked the grasses that cover the earth for keeping the dust from blowing, for cushioning our steps, and for showing our eyes the greenness and beauty of their life. He thanked the wind for bringing rain, for cleaning the air, for giving us the life breath that connects us with all beings. He thanked the sun and the moon and the rivers and stones. He spoke in this way for nearly an hour, and as we listened, we felt the wind on our faces and the earth beneath our feet, and we saw the grass and clouds, all with a sense of connectedness, gratitude, and love.

This is the spirit of mindfulness. Love (rather than attachment), compassion (rather than pity), joy (rather than jealousy), and equanimity (rather than indifference) infuse our awareness. They enable us to open to and accept the truth of each moment, to feel our intimate connectedness with all things, and to see the wholeness of life. Whether we are sitting in meditation or sitting somewhere in protest, that is our spiritual practice in every moment.

11

The Bodhisattva Way

Tending to the Suffering of All Beings

The Buddha's teaching arose in India as a spiritual force against social injustice, against degrading superstitious rites, ceremonies, and sacrifices; it denounced the tyranny of the caste system and advocated the equality of all men; it emancipated women and gave them spiritual freedom.
　—WALPOLA RAHULA, *WHAT THE BUDDHA TAUGHT*

Those who say that spirituality has nothing to do with politics do not know what spirituality really means.
　—MAHATMA GANDHI

LAUREN CAME TO BUDDHIST MEDITATION to relieve the overwhelming stress of her eight years of intense work in international women's rights. But she also wanted a child, and she knew she needed more balance in her life. She struggled with whether to go back to Indonesia, where she'd been working, or to make a home in San Francisco. The outer needs of the world seemed so pressing. Lauren was concerned about the safety of her young feminist Muslim partners. But her commitment to them conflicted with her increased longing to become a mother.

During a ten-day retreat, the power of these two polarities became like a pressing koan for Lauren. A genuine koan cannot be solved by the thinking mind. In the words of one Zen saying, it's like having a hot iron ball caught in your throat, too hot to swallow, too hot to spit up. What do you do? Lauren sat and walked with her dilemma for days, sometimes frustrated, sometimes in tears. Gradually her mind quieted, her boundaries began to loosen, her drivenness melted. Then early one evening she came to see me, quietly excited. "I've been caught up thinking about this all wrong. I'm not separate from the world I want to help. We're the same thing!"

Lauren had a tender smile on her face. She explained how at first, having a child felt selfish. She always felt she was a failure, that she hadn't done enough. Waves of pain and old family shame and unworthiness flooded her. Then she realized she was trying to save the world primarily as a way to feel better about herself. This was an embarrassing insight, but her loving-kindness practice softened the self-condemnation. Gradually her body and senses opened to the Spanish moss on the trees, the rain-drenched mulch, the spring frogs, the oak forest, the newborn fawns, the generations of children born of all mothers. She knew she could have a family and also contribute to the world. This was a radical, true, unshakable knowing—she experienced her interconnection with life and the koan fell away. Caring for her own life, she could care for the world; caring for the world, she could care for herself.

Like Lauren, many of us wrestle with our response to the sufferings of the world. What can we do in the face of poverty, disease, war, injustice, and environmental devastation? With the torrent of world news, it is easy to despair, to become cynical or numb. Our psychologies tend to treat this as a personal problem, but it is not. We are all affected by the suffering of the world and need to find a way to work with it. This is a pressing problem for psychology. The Buddhist approach to this collective suffering is to turn toward it. We understand that genuine happiness and meaning will come through tending to suffering. We overcome our own despair by helping others to overcome theirs.

We might hear this and become afraid of being overwhelmed. Or, like Lauren, our response might be confused with guilt, unworthiness, and our need for personal healing. Still, even though our motivation is mixed, we have to respond. And we can. It is simple. Each of us can contribute to the sanity of the world. We can tend to ourselves and we can tend to others. In doing so, we discover the role of the bodhisattva.

THE BODHISATTVA

The problem with the world is that we draw our family circle too small.
—MOTHER TERESA

Bodhisattva is the Sanskrit word for a being who vows to save all beings from suffering. The way of the bodhisattva is one of the most radical and powerful of all Buddhist forms of practice. It is radical because it states that the fulfillment of our happiness comes only from serving the welfare of others as well as ourselves. Our highest happiness is connected with the well-being of others.

The bodhisattva's path is a striking contrast with the common Western modes of therapy that so often reflect the excessive individualism of our culture. Everything can get focused around "me": my fears, my neurosis, my happiness, my needs, my boundaries. We can get so caught up in our own drama that we stop our own growth. Reflective self-absorption can be valuable for a time, but we don't want to stop there. Therapists talk about how clients eventually become sick of listening to themselves, which is actually a good sign. It means we are moving beyond the identification with our personal suffering. We are ready to care for a world larger than our own.

Every wisdom tradition tells us that human meaning and happiness cannot be found in isolation but comes about through generosity, love, and understanding. The bodhisattva, knowing this, appears in a thousand forms, from a caring grandmother to the global citizen. In certain Buddhist traditions, individuals regularly recite the bodhisattva vows when they do sitting meditation, "Sentient beings are numberless; I vow to bring liberation to them all." Like the ancient Hippocratic oath, the vow to serve the sick taken by every physician, the bodhisattva vows to serve the welfare of all.

In a more poetic fashion, the Dalai Lama takes bodhisattva vows based on the words of the beloved sixth-century sage Shantideva:

May I be a guard for those who need protection
A guide for those on the path
A boat, a raft, a bridge for those who wish to cross the flood
May I be a lamp in the darkness

A resting place for the weary
A healing medicine for all who are sick
A vase of plenty, a tree of miracles
And for the boundless multitudes of living beings
May I bring sustenance and awakening
Enduring like the earth and sky
Until all beings are freed from sorrow
And all are awakened.

Psychologically this is an astonishing thing to say. Does this mean that I am going to run around and save seven billion humans and trillions of other beings? How can I do so? When we think about it from our limited sense of self, it is impossible. But when we make it an intention of the heart, we understand. To take such a vow is a direction, a sacred purpose, a statement of wisdom, an offering, a blessing. When the world is seen with the eyes of a bodhisattva, there is no "I" and no "other," there is just us.

The Dalai Lama serves as a source of love and strength to millions of oppressed Tibetans. His picture is secretly carried and hidden among sacred altars and he blesses and encourages them from afar. But it is not just the Dalai Lama who supports others with his bodhisattva vows. All those who care about us sustain us in ways that transcend time and space. James Hillman, the Jungian analyst, has described the plight of the Chinese dissident Liu Qing, who was arrested as an activist for democracy and held in prison for eleven years, forced by the guards to remain in silence all that time. If he moved or talked, he was beaten. To be released, he did not have to implicate others; he only had to sign a statement saying that he had made "errors in his thinking," to offer a simple admission of wrong ideas. Remarkably, Liu would not sign. He later explained that over the eleven years, whenever he wavered, he could see the faces of his family and friends before him and he knew he could not betray their trust. He was sustained by his visions of those who cared for him.

"We are not separate, we are interdependent," declares the Buddha. Even the most independent human being was once a helpless infant cared for by others. The Thai monk Ajahn Buddhadasa instructed all those in his forest temple to do a daily contemplation of interdependence. With each breath we interbreathe carbon dioxide and oxygen with the maple and oak, the dogwood and redwood trees of our biosphere. Our daily nourishment joins us with the rhythms of bees, caterpillars, and earthworms; it connects our body with the collaborative dance of myriad species of plants and animals. Nothing is separate. Biologist Lewis Thomas explains, "The driving force in nature, on this kind of planet with this sort of biosphere, is cooperation . . . . The most inventive and novel of all schemes in nature, and perhaps the most significant in determining the great landmark events in evolution, is symbiosis, which is simply cooperative behavior carried to its extreme."

Unless we understand this, we are split between caring for ourselves and caring for the troubles of the world. "I arise in the morning," wrote essayist E. B. White, "torn between a desire to save the world and an inclination to savor it." A psychology of interdependence helps to solve this dilemma. Through meditation we discover that the duality of inner and outer is false. Thus when Gandhi was lauded for all his work in India, he demurred, saying, "I do not do this for India, I do this for myself."

There is no separation between inner and outer, self and other. Tending ourselves, we tend the world. Tending the world, we tend ourselves.

A LIFE OF BALANCE: TURN OFF THE NEWS

In some form, the vision of the bodhisattva is celebrated in every culture. We revere the figures of Saint Francis and Kwan Yin and we take public inspiration from the medical mission of Albert Schweitzer in Africa and Dorothy Day, the founder of the Catholic Worker Movement. But following the bodhisattva way does not require us to become a monk like Saint Francis or to work in Central Africa like Albert Schweitzer. It is based on the truth that we can transform our own circumstances into a life of inner and outer service. To do this without being overwhelmed, the bodhisattva creates a life of balance.

This is eminently practical. If we want to act wisely in the world, the first step is to learn to quiet the mind. If our actions are born from anger, grasping, fear, and aggression, they will perpetuate the problems. How many revolutions have overthrown oppressive regimes, to then turn around and become the new oppressors? Only when our own minds and hearts are peaceful can we expect peace to come through the actions we take.

To understand this integration of inner and outer, we can again look at the life of Gandhi. Even during the most turbulent years, when he was dismantling the British Empire's control of India, Gandhi spent one day a week in silence. He meditated so that he could act from the principles of interdependence, not bringing harm to himself nor another. No matter how pressing and urgent the political situation, the day he spent in silence allowed him to quiet his mind and listen to the purest intentions of his heart.

If you want to live a life of balance, start now. Turn off the news, meditate, turn on Mozart, walk through the forest or the mountains, and begin to make yourself a zone of peace. When I return from a long retreat or from traveling for months, I'm amazed that the news is pretty much the same as when I left. We already know the plot, we know the problems. Let go of the latest story. Listen more deeply.

Remember the story Zen master Thich Nhat Hanh told of the crowded refugee boats. "If even one person on the boat stayed calm, it was enough. It showed the way for everyone to survive." When we react to terrorism with fear, we worsen the problem, we create a frightened, barricaded society—a fortress America. Instead, we can use courage and compassion to respond calmly, with both prudent action and a fearless heart.

The quieting of our mind is a political act. The world does not really need more oil or energy or food. It needs less greed, less hatred, less ignorance. If we have inadvertently taken on the political bitterness or cynicism that exists externally, we can stop and begin to heal our own suffering, our own fear, with compassion. Through meditation and inner transformation, we can learn to make our own hearts a place of peace and integrity. Each of us knows how to do this. As Gandhi acknowledged, "I have nothing new to teach the world. Truth and nonviolence are as old as the hills." It is our inner nobility and steadiness that we must call upon in our personal and collective difficulties.

FACING THE TRUTH

Once we learn to quiet our mind, the second step for the bodhisattva is seeing the truth. We deliberately turn toward the difficulties of the world and shine the light of true understanding on them. "The enemy," said Ajahn Chah, "is delusion." Delusion blames others, creates enemies, and fosters separation. The truth is that we are not separate. War, economic injustice, racism, and environmental destruction stem from the illusion of separateness. It is delusion that separates us from other human tribes and from the forests and the oceans on this increasingly small planet. When we look honestly, we can also see that scientific and material advancement cannot solve our problems alone. New computer networks, innovative fuels, and biological advances can just as easily be diverted to create new weapons, exacerbate conflicts, and speed environmental degradation. Economic and political change will fail unless we also find a way to transform our consciousness. It is a delusion that endless greed and profit, hatred and war, will somehow protect us and bring us happiness.

More than half a century ago, President Dwight Eisenhower, who had been Supreme Allied Commander during World War II, gave a remarkable address just before he left office. Eisenhower, the world's most respected military man, spoke out against the madness and unchecked growth of the defense industry worldwide. "Every gun that is made, every warship launched, every rocket fired signifies, in the final sense, a theft from those who hunger and are not fed, those who are cold and are not clothed. This world in arms is not spending money alone. It is spending the sweat of its laborers, the genius of its scientists, the hopes of its children . . . . This is not a way of life at all, in any true sense. Under the cloud of threatening war, it is humanity hanging from a cross of iron."

President Eisenhower also spoke of the immense cost of the military-industrial complex, which, like the prison-industrial complex and the foreign-policy-power complex, chooses power and profit instead of compassion. We must learn that this will not make us safe. Collective well-being arises when we govern by wisdom and loving-kindness instead of fear. "Human beings should refrain from causing harm to one another and not allow their actions to be based on hatred and greed," said the Buddha, in words that speak directly to modern times. "They should refrain from killing, from stealing. They should refrain from occupations that bring suffering, from weapons trade, from any actions that bring the enslavement of others." Through these words, he was not proclaiming a religious code. He was providing a social psychology for the happiness of individuals and the collective.

In facing the truth, the bodhisattva deliberately bears witness to our personal and collective suffering with compassion. The power of such witness was revealed to an amazed world by the Truth and Reconciliation Commission in South Africa, which for years broadcast accounts of perpetrators and victims alike. The truth telling and revelation of so many destructive acts committed during the apartheid era did not stir hatred and retaliation, but somehow brought healing and calm to the suffering of the nation. It is a testament to the power of truth to allow a community to rebuild itself after so much devastation. The Reverend Bongani Finca was one of the fifteen commissioners who conducted the South African hearings. He describes how, in spite of the past atrocities and cruelty, victims and survivors wanted to find reconciliation: "I remember hearing the testimony of the daughter of one of the four gentlemen killed in Cradock, a girl who was sixteen years old. She said, 'I want to forgive. But I do not know whom to forgive. If only I could know who did what to my father, I would like to forgive.' This was such a moving testimony by a young person who, at that age, we would expect to be so bitter. But there was no bitterness. Often the attitudes and responses of the victims to the Truth Commission were just amazing. It was an indication of the fact that the people who have suffered most become so generous in spirit, for some strange reason."

In the end, the unarmed truth will come out. It will be whispered in the alleyways, canonized by our poets, held in the hearts of all those who care. Martin Luther King, Jr., said, "I still believe that standing up for the unarmed truth is the greatest thing in the world. This is the end of life. The end of life is not to achieve pleasure and avoid pain. The end of life is to do the will of God, come what may." These words describe the moral and psychological power when we step out of delusion and tell us the truth.

ENVISION LIBERATION AND JUSTICE

After we quiet the mind and face what is true, the next step of the bodhisattva's way is to envision liberation from suffering for ourselves, our community, and the world. Envisioning has enormous power. With our vision and imagination we can help create the future. Envisioning sets our direction, marshals our resources, makes the unmanifest possible. A bodhisattva's vision is the necessary step toward transformation of the world. We must courageously envision a world where all children have proper care and food, where instead of an arms race our creative efforts are put into conflict resolution. We must see how individuals of all castes, tribes, races, and orientations can be treated with equal respect and opportunity.

In the Buddhist texts, the bodhisattva Vimalakirti is a wild figure who exemplifies this courage. Among the wisest of beings, he deliberately seeks out the worst difficulties of the world and magically transforms himself to help teach there. Vimalakirti makes himself sick in order to teach the healers in the hospitals how to practice the path of awakening as they work. He enters the crowded markets as a businessman, and the taverns to be with those who drink. As he tends to others, he demonstrates that happiness and freedom are possible for all he meets. He uses each circumstance as the perfect place to teach the path of awakening.

Do not confuse Buddhism with withdrawal from the world. The Buddhist teachings about wise society and wise leadership are taught from earliest childhood throughout the Buddhist world. In hundreds of popular tales, the Buddha-to-be appears as a prince or an animal. In one story, the Buddha-to-be is born as a banyan deer king who nobly offers his life to a human king in place of that of a pregnant doe that has been caught. His gesture so inspires the human king that the hunting of deer and other forest animals is forbidden throughout the kingdom. In another story, the buddha-to-be is born as a small parrot, who tries to save the animals around him from a forest fire. Repeatedly dousing his wings with river water, he flies into the great flames to find and wet down his frightened friends. His bravery touches the heart of the rain god, whose tears fall, quenching the flames and rescuing all the creatures from a fiery death. For those who grow up in a Buddhist culture these beloved tales of wise leadership are recounted a thousand times.

At a more sophisticated level, Buddhist psychology shows how training in mindfulness, integrity, generosity, and respect can create a healthy society. Buddhist practices of right speech, right action, and right livelihood foster moral character and the creation of harmony in village schools and community meetings.

Buddhist temples model this psychology. They are among the oldest formal social institutions in the world. For over two thousand years, temples have served as seats of education and service, offering help with community government, community projects, social organization, and the mediation of disputes. Villagers go to the monasteries to be reminded of this healthy way to live, and the whole society is nurtured and bene- fited by the examples set by the monks and nuns. Today the Southeast Asian environmental crisis has led Burmese and Thai monks to turn their forest monasteries into wild-animal sanctuaries to help preserve the remaining tigers. In Cambodia, monks and nuns run addiction treatment centers and AIDS hospitals. In Thailand, monks wrap robes around the most ancient trees to "ordain them" and save thousands of acres of disappearing forest.

Even when there is conflict in the monastery, it is dealt with as a practice. There are councils of reconciliation, vows of nonharming, trainings in mindful listening, and formal methods of confession, re- pentance, and release. The work of both Gandhi and Martin Luther King, Jr., was founded on ahimsa, on the principles of nonharming as a path to happiness.

The Buddha applied these principles quite directly. Denouncing the caste system, he created an alternative society based on equal respect for every human being. Once, a local king sent his chief minister to seek the Buddha's advice about starting a war with a people called the Vajjians. The Buddha responded with a series of questions. "Do the Vajjians come together in regular and frequent assembly?" "They do, sir." "Do they honor their elders and the wise ways they have established?" "They do, sir." "Do they care for their most vulnerable members—women and children?" "They do, sir." "Do they respect the nature shrines and holy places and listen respectfully to their citizens and neighbors?" "They do, sir." "Then the Vajjians can be expected to prosper and not decline. Any society that does so," explained the Buddha, "can be expected to prosper and not decline." The minister returned with these words and the king decided to abandon his plans for war.

There is much for us to learn from these words. If we meet together in harmony and respect, care for the vulnerable among us, tend to the environment, and respect our citizens and neighbors, we will thrive and prosper. A strong and stable society arises through mutual generosity, not gross inequity. These teachings are surprisingly modern. In his Long Discourses, the Buddha explains that poverty gives rise to theft, violence, and other crimes. He states that simple punishment alone cannot suppress crime. Instead he teaches us to transform the causes. "The economic conditions of the people should be improved: seed grain and help should be available to farmers, support provided for business-people, adequate wages paid to workers. When the people are thus provided for, there will be contentment, and the country will be peaceful and free from crime." This is not just an idealistic vision. It is a practical way for happiness to prevail.

TENDING THE WORLD

Somewhere I have saved an old photo from the front page of *The Manila Times* in 1967. I was doing my Peace Corps training at San Lazaro Hospital in the Philippines. In the photo I stand alone in front of the U.S. embassy, holding a big peace sign in a one-man demonstration against the war in Vietnam. It was the day of a huge antiwar rally in Washington and I wanted to be part of it. I thought I knew enough about Vietnam to see that we were wrong to intervene, that we were simply perpetuating the mistakes of the French colonialists before us. My first years of traveling in Thailand, Laos, and Vietnam reinforced this view, as did many of the soldiers I talked to.

Of course, the reality turned out to be more complex than I could have known. I later met people who had suffered horribly under the North Vietnamese Communists, people who were beaten in dismal camps and tortured for ideological retaliation. Similarly, I met many who had lost family members and suffered terribly under the South Vietnamese Diem regime. Up close, everyone had a compelling story. They wanted you to understand and take their side. What is certain is that there are no smug answers. Now I approach activism with a wholly different understanding. I try to bring respect to everyone involved. I'm not so stuck on my position. Instead of creating scapegoats, instead of seeing some people as all wrong and others as all right, I see suffering growing out of the powerful energies of delusion and ignorance. When I take action, I do not want to add my own arrogance or aggression to our conflicts.

When Zen master Thich Nhat Hanh took a stand for peace in the 1960s in Vietnam, he understood that true peace would grow from building schools and hospitals, not from taking sides. His book *Lotus in a Sea of Fire* described how the Young Buddhist service movement, which he helped to found, chose to support everyone, regardless of their politics. Martin Luther King, Jr., was so inspired by this work that he nominated Thich Nhat Hanh for the Nobel Peace Prize. But back in Vietnam, because the Young Buddhists refused to swear allegiance to either the northern or the southern faction, they were considered a threat by both. "If you're not with us, you must be with the enemy." Many of the Young Buddhists were killed by both sides. In spite of these deaths, Thich Nhat Hanh and his colleagues continued their work. A bodhisattva commits to heal suffering undaunted by outward periods of failure and success.

One of the stories from the Buddha's own life concerns the hostilities between the neighboring countries of Magadha and Kapilavastu, where the Buddha's own Shakya clan lived. When the Shakya people realized that the king of Magadha was planning to attack, they implored the Buddha to step forward and make peace. The Buddha agreed. But although he offered many proposals for peace, the king of Magadha would not hear them. His mind would not stop burning, and finally he decided to attack.

So the Buddha went out by himself and sat in meditation under a dead tree by the side of the road leading to Kapilavastu. The king of Magadha passed along the road with his army and saw the Buddha sitting under the dead tree in the full blast of the sun. So the king asked, "Why do you sit under this dead tree?" The Buddha answered the king, "I feel cool, even under this dead tree, because it is growing in my beautiful native country." This answer pierced the heart of the king. Recognizing the commitment and dedication the Shakyas felt for their land, he returned to his country with his army. Later, however, this same king was again incited to war. This time, Shakyamuni Buddha could not stop the conflict, and the Magadhan army destroyed Kapilavastu.

We cannot control the outcome of our actions. Still, we can turn toward the world, plant good seeds, and trust that they will eventually bear fruit. Whenever a few people are committed to the vision of a free and just humanity, transformation can happen, despite the greatest odds. The story of one such amazing transformation is told in *Bury the Chains*, by Adam Hochschild. Hochschild's account begins in 1787, with the meeting of just a dozen men in a London printer's shop, gathered to consider the evils of slavery. The Caribbean slave trade was the economic underpinning of the entire British Empire, but these men chose to envision an empire without slavery. The key protagonist was Thomas Clarkson, who joined together with a small group of other dedicated abolitionists, especially Quakers, to change the society's views on slavery.

These few men began a long, deliberate campaign. Clarkson himself rode on horseback thirty thousand miles around England over several decades in service of this vision. He brought a few ex-slaves who were well educated and articulate and spoke of the horror of their experiences in the parlors and the meeting houses of British folk. By 1833, this small group had succeeded in getting Parliament to pass a law outlawing slavery in the British Empire, which in turn catalyzed the process of ending slavery around the world!

Hochschild tells us that the Quakers of the time refused to take their hats off to King George or to any king other than God. But when Clarkson died, even the Quakers took their hats off to honor what he had done for humanity.

We are limited only by our imagination. Yes, there will always be suffering. Yes, greed and fear and ignorance will be part of our psychology. But there are ways we can live wisely. For the bodhisattva, raising a family, running a conscious business, and righting an injustice can all contribute to the fabric of the whole. Every one of us can sense this potential. We human beings can live with more compassion, with more care for one another, with less prejudice and racism and fear. There are wise ways of solving conflict that await our hands and hearts.

BODHISATTVA VOWS

Consider undertaking the vows and practice of a bodhisattva. In taking these vows you will join with the millions of Buddhists who have done so. As is traditional, you might seek out a Buddhist center or temple and take the bodhisattva vows in the presence of a teacher. Or, if you choose, you can take them at home. Create a sacred space and place there the images of bodhisattvas or Buddhas who have gone before you. If you wish, invite a friend or friends to be your witness. Sit quietly for a time and reflect on the beauty and value of a life dedicated to the benefit of all. When you are ready, add any meaningful ritual, such as the lighting of candles or the taking of refuge. Then recite your vows. Here is one traditional version, but there are many others:

> Suffering beings are numberless, I vow to liberate them all.
> Attachment is inexhaustible, I vow to release it all.
> The gates to truth are numberless, I vow to master them all.
> The ways of awakening are supreme, I vow to realize them all.

You can change the wording of these vows so that they speak your deepest dedication. Then you can repeat them every time you sit in meditation, to direct and dedicate your practice.

12

Samadhi

Developing a Steady, Concentrated Mind

IN THE EARLY 1970S I collected teachings from twelve of the most
highly regarded meditation masters in Thailand and Burma who were
teaching various forms of insight meditation or vipassana practice. This
material became my first book, *Living Buddhist Masters.* The twelve
styles in this book represented just a fraction of the fifty or a hundred
ways that I know of to do vipassana. In many cases these masters did not
agree with one another on the best way to practice. Sometimes the styles
were diametrically opposed to one another. In laying out *Living Buddhist Masters,* I deliberately contrasted the teachings, so that the chapter
of one great master, who emphasized meditation on the body as the best
way to attain enlightenment, was next to that of another enlightened
master, who said the only way to get liberated is to meditate on the
mind. I did this so people would understand that there are different
skillful means for cultivating the factors of enlightenment and coming
to liberation. Any practice that cultivates mindfulness, wise effort, investigation, joy, concentration, calm, equanimity, and compassion will
bring one to liberation, and there are many ways to do that. They are
each part of a mandala, a sacred wheel that contains distinct segments
all leading to the center, all contributing to the whole.

This understanding of the mandala of skillful means is enormously
helpful for us as we bring all the Buddhist traditions together in America.
We are learning about Theravada, Mahayana, and Vajrayana understandings of samadhi—they are all being presented to the same greater community of practitioners in America. If we don't have the understanding

of the mandala of skillful means, then we get fixated on one view, we believe we have the right way, and we lose wisdom. The maturity and wisdom of a human being comes when we can see multiplicity and appreciate paradox and complementary differences with a spacious mind and an open heart.

In the same way there are many approaches to samadhi and to jhana practice, the practice of concentrated absorption. Pa Auk Sayadaw, of Burma, follows the depth practices of the great commentary known as the Visudhimagga. To start, he requires students to sit for months and be able to meditate for two hours with a stable inner light and no thoughts before they can begin to explore the jhana states. This great depth is then developed further into profound unmoving stillness and later used for awakening insight. In the tradition of Ayya Khema, Leigh Brasington uses a much lighter approach in which the tastes of concentration come easily to students in ten days and background thoughts and sounds are still part of the experience. U Pandita and Ajahn Brahm take a middle-level approach that uses the breath or metta to foster clear development of concentration factors such as one-pointedness and joy, but to a level that can be developed in weeks. All of these approaches have value, all are means for stabilizing the mind and opening the doorway to new understanding. Throughout Buddhist Asia, people are often opinionated about their views on jhana (meditative absorption), and vipassana, and what creates true insight. This is unfortunate. In the Sutta Nipata, the Buddha explained that those who cling to views annoy other people and cause themselves to suffer as well. Fortunately there is generally a much more open-minded and less dogmatic approach in the United States and in the West than I found among students and teachers in Buddhist Asia. This has come about because we have had access to the dharma of many traditions that make up this entire mandala. We get to see great teachers and masters who clearly have different perspectives, who offer profound wisdom and thoroughly different sets of skillful means.

My two root meditation masters, Ajahn Chah and Mahasi Sayadaw, did so. They had different approaches to meditation practice, and strikingly different approaches to enlightenment. They fundamentally disagreed on what brought one to enlightenment and on the nature of enlightenment, even though they would agree that enlightenment meant the freeing of oneself from greed, hatred, and delusion. For Mahasi Say-adaw the way to enlightenment was through the progress of insight gained by very deep, sustained, profound mindfulness and concentration. For Ajahn Chah, enlightenment was attained by letting go. With Ajahn Chah, meditation was simply a way to get quiet enough to see clinging in the mind and to learn how to release it. This is similar to the approach of U Tejaniya Sayadaw. For Ajahn Chah, any attainment in meditation, whether jhana or any deep insight alone is not the source of enlightenment. Enlightenment comes from letting go. I learned a great deal from the perspectives of both Mahasi Sayadaw and Ajahn Chah.

Different approaches to practice were argued about from the moment the Buddha died, according to the stories in the texts. There were those who wanted to conserve things exactly as they were when the Buddha lived, and then there were those who wanted to adapt them and change them in different ways. The disagreements that started at the death of the Buddha continue to this day. We benefit from them all. We need those who conserve the tradition of the texts and commentary and the classical lineages within Theravada or Mahayana. And we also need those who can adapt the language and the skillful means to a new culture. While the Buddha consistently kept to his core teachings, he also added new skillful means as his life went on. It is not that one form of skillful means is right and the other wrong. They're all part of the mandala of dharma, in which every element complements the others. When we understand this, then we can appreciate the people who are deeply tied to a particular historical tradition. They carry the wisdom of that perspective for all the rest of us. And those who are willing to expand that with new ways and bring that new language and skillful means into the mandala also contribute to the whole.

I have heard many Asian masters say, "I teach the true way, right from the *suttas,* from the original texts. This is the real way the Buddha taught." And yet their teachings are contradicted by those of other teachers, who also claim to be offering the original teachings. So don't buy into only one side or the other. That's called "ignorance." The real freedom is what Ajahn Chah understood: using all as skillful means to foster the freedom of letting go. This means not clinging to one way that is said to be historically true, because what is historically true is this mandala of many ways to practice. With this perspective, let us consider different approaches to concentration, one-pointedness, or steadiness of mind, also called samadhi.

When my colleagues Joseph Goldstein and Sharon Salzberg and I were teaching retreats in the early years, we used the practice of mental noting in the style of Mahasi Sayadaw. Sharon observed that people were not getting as deep, on the whole, as they did when they sat with Goenka doing three days of *anapanasati* (mindfulness of the breath) and then seven days of nonstop body scan practice. Goenka offers a wonderful form of body-focused vipassana practice that fosters profound concentration, and the concentration was accentuated in those days by people doing "long vow sittings," during which they sat for hours without any movement.

But then Sharon and I considered the quality of wisdom. We acknowledged that people could get more deeply concentrated doing body scan, but they weren't necessarily wiser. Some had deep insights into *anicca, dukkha,* and *anatta* (impermanence, suffering, and no-self). But many other people had more wisdom arise through the Mahasi practice without that deeper level of concentration. Because Mahasi's approach focused more on mindfulness of body, feelings, mind, and dharma, they could see their own mental states and the clinging to them, their emotions and the clinging to them, and release them. For many, wisdom grew with mindfulness more than if they had focused only on concentration and body sensation.

So, there is a spectrum in practice, from concentration to mindfulness, and at each end there is a trade-off. If you focus a great deal on concentration, wisdom doesn't grow as quickly. It can grow very deep later on, when concentration is turned toward insight. But first it brings the states of calm and concentration. If you are looking for understanding to grow quickly, such as on a short three- or four-day retreat, then you might need to emphasize mindfulness.

As you mature and become a dedicated practitioner over a number of years, you find it skillful to practice at both ends of that spectrum. It is valuable to train yourself in concentration in order to learn skillful means and ways of deepening your concentration. This powerful concentration can steady the mind and heal the body. It can calm and integrate the psyche and, when used properly, open us to profound wisdom. It can be used for the dissolution of the self, the illumination of emptiness, and the understanding of selflessness and impermanence. At the same time it is equally important to develop a balanced mindfulness. You need to be able to be mindful as you move about, to let go of changing conditions and rest in unconditioned awareness, to notice all states of mind, notice the reactivity, notice the clinging, and be able to release it all. Otherwise, any attainments of concentration won't really serve you to live as a liberated being in the world. Both of these, concentration and mindfulness, are important during retreat practice and afterward. And, of course, people have different propensities and temperaments, which makes concentration easy for some, hard for others.

In my own teaching, I take the middle path. I emphasize mindfulness in the very beginning, because people have so much difficulty when they try to simply concentrate and without also practicing mindfulness they suffer a lot. Mindfulness makes space to hold the initial difficulties and understand them with some wisdom. But I also value concentration and make its practice a part of every retreat. When students settle down and their concentration deepens, I encourage them to practice concentration. I work individually with people, especially on longer retreats. If someone has the propensity or capacity for deep concentration, I will direct them to use skillful means to cultivate the jhana factors so they can mature into jhana practice. Other students may not have the ability to concentrate very easily, or concentration will not arise because they are dealing with trauma and difficulties. When trauma is present, to skip over it would either be impossible or would do them a disservice in their practice. For those for whom trauma is present, concentration will come at a later stage of practice.

As a practitioner's capacity to concentrate well emerges, I will lead them to cultivate and deepen the jhana factors by dwelling in these states. The language of dwelling is terribly important. There are many approaches to developing concentration in the Buddhist tradition, from those that stress profound effort and depth to those that are more relaxed. When I learned jhana, I learned in monasteries where there was a great deal of effort and striving involved, and I found that forcing concentration didn't help me so much. While I could make a great effort and get quite concentrated, it was exhausting. This kind of striving is not a good path for most people in the West, unless they are young men looking for initiation, looking to go through the hardest thing they can find. What I found instead is that wise concentration is better cultivated through relaxed dedication and sustained focus, and this relaxed dedication leads to learning to dwell in the jhana factors as they begin to arise. Dwelling and relaxing allows one to embody, feel, and deepen the jhana factors and fill the mind with increasing pleasure, delight, calm, and happiness. Dwelling naturally deepens concentration. With time, wise effort brings a shift of consciousness, from the effort to get somewhere to dwelling in well-being. Once that happens, meditation seems to take on its own momentum. You start to enter a stream of concentration quite naturally.

Then, if the jhana factors become strong, I teach people to use inner resolutions or intentions that direct consciousness to open in a particular way. When the conditions are developed, they can resolve for jhana factors, asking, "May joy or happiness arise." Doing so they can become spontaneously filled with joy or happiness. After they learn to resolve for each of the jhana factors to arise, and once the jhana factors are strong and somewhat balanced, they make resolutions to enter first, second, third jhana, and so forth. Initially they resolve for short periods of time and then longer, and then learn to move easily between jhanas. Jhanas are discreet, stable states of consciousness with little or no thought and they are pervaded by the qualities of steadiness, joy, happiness, and one-pointedness. Entering jhana is like slipping from the windswept waves of the ocean surface to the silent, tranquil depths below. Each level of jhana is more refined and silent than the one before it. With deep concentration we can enter jhanas for hours at a time, states filled with boundless light and luminous rapture or vast silence and profound peace.

Once people have developed a stable capacity to enter and rest in jhana samadhi, they use concentration for wisdom. Traditionally, as meditators come out of the jhanas, they are directed to notice the impermanence of the states, which is one way for wisdom to arise. Or they become mindful of the elements that make up the body, or of selflessness and emptiness. They come out of jhana and shift from concentration to a deep mindfulness practice.

Along with this, I find wisdom resolutions to be strikingly helpful. This comes out of my own experience with the other kind of resolutions that U Pandita and Mahasi Sayadaw taught. The root source of these resolutions are the kind of determinations that one finds in the suttas, where a monk turns their mind toward, or determines that they will enter, this jhana or that jhana. Those determinations are resolutions.

They work to resolve for wisdom as well. The kind of wisdom resolutions I use invite a deep understanding of the key dharma teachings, key elements of wisdom to arise. I will instruct someone like this: "When you come out of second, third, or fourth jhana, make the resolution 'May a deep insight into anicca (impermanence) arise.'" In the same way, you can resolve, "May a deep insight into anatta (no-self) arise" or "May a deep insight into emptiness arise." "May a deep insight into compassion arise." It can be any of the key dharma qualities. Then sometimes, but not always, depending on the depth of that person's practice and the particular karmic conditions, wonderful displays of wisdom will arise.

For example, I made the resolution for myself coming out of jhana, "May a deep understanding of emptiness arise," and all of a sudden I felt as if I were falling backward into vast galaxies of space. My body and mind dropped away, differently than in the jhanas, and there arose a sense that intergalactic space and I are exactly the same thing, and the stars and the luminosity are the forms that shine out of it. I had no idea that was going to happen. I had no idea what would come of it.

On another occasion I made a resolution to myself, "May a deep understanding of anicca (impermanence) arise." And all of a sudden my attention went to the bald top of my head. I thought, "This is odd." What came into consciousness is all the hair that I'm losing. I thought, This is a funny response to this resolution. And spontaneously my attention slowly scanned down to my ears, where I'm losing hearing, and then it went to my nose, and started sweeping down through my body. As it went to my nose, I could feel my history of years of allergies and nasal surgery. And then it went to the fillings in my teeth, and then it went to a bad vertebra in my neck, and then down to my lungs, where I've had pneumonia. Then it went to where I had had an appendectomy and some lower-back problems, and it scanned down through my old runner's knees, and by the time it was done, the falling apart of my body was palpable throughout it. I had no idea this undeniable insight into impermanence was going to come in this form.

Wisdom resolutions allow for a profound intelligence of wisdom to display itself. Setting the intention of a wisdom resolution opens a doorway for deep wisdom, just as setting a concentration intention opens a doorway for jhana. With wisdom resolutions when the mind is concentrated, malleable, pliable, luminous, clear with deep concentration, and is directed toward understanding—as it says in the texts—a dimension of wisdom, the *paramita* of understanding, displays itself, in the same way that jhana states arise and display themselves. It's a beautiful thing to experience. Wisdom resolutions can include understanding of anicca, dukkha, anatta, emptiness, or compassion. Or it might be a deep understanding into dependent origination or interdependence. You could make a resolution for a deep understanding of letting go or of selflessness. You can explore the dharma in many ways. That's the power of a luminous and malleable concentrated mind.

One of the Spirit Rock/Insight Meditation Society teachers tells a wonderful story about when he was a young student in practice and first being taught jhanas. He worked with Joseph and Sharon in U Pandita's system, which included resolution practice. After his concentration had gotten strong, he was given the resolution for the jhana factor called *piti* (joy or rapture) to arise. But he didn't know Pali and he had the meaning of this word confused in his mind. Then the most magical thing happened. He thought he was making a resolution for calm concentration, and yet when he said, "piti," his body became filled with joy and rapture. He didn't know this Pali word given by his teacher, he thought it meant something else, but the joy arose anyway. There is something mysterious in the psyche, in consciousness, that knows these states and this terrain. When the mind is deeply concentrated and open, and resolutions are made, magic happens. And of course, this can lead to the highest magic of all, as the Buddha said, the magic of the wisdom that liberates the heart.

13

Spiritual Maturity

FRUIT FALLS FROM A TREE naturally when ripe. After due time in spiritual life, the heart, like fruit, begins to mature and sweeten. Our practice shifts from the green hard growth of seeking, developing, and improving ourselves to a resting in mystery. It shifts from reliance on form to a resting in the heart. One young woman who had struggled greatly in the early years of her practice in the face of family difficulties and the fundamentalist church to which her parents belonged wrote, "My parents hate me when I'm a Buddhist, but they love me when I'm a buddha."

To mature spiritually is to let go of rigid and idealistic ways of being and discover a flexibility and joy in our life. One becomes more comfortable with paradox, more appreciative of life's ambiguities, its many levels and inherent conflicts. We develop a sense of life's irony, metaphors, and humor, and gain a capacity to embrace the whole, with its beauty and outrageousness, in the graciousness of the heart. Ease and compassion become our natural movement. The Taoist Lao Tzu celebrated this spirit when he wrote,

> She who is centered in the Tao can go where she wishes without danger.
> She perceives the universal harmony, even amid great pain, because she has found peace in her heart.

When Eastern spirituality began to be popular in America in the 1960s and 1970s, its practice was initially idealistic and romantic. People tried to use spirituality to "get high" and to experience extraordinary states of consciousness. There was a belief in perfect gurus and complete and wonderful teachings that, if followed, would lead to our full enlightenment and would change the world. These were the imitative and self-absorbed approaches that the Tibetan meditation master Chögyam Trungpa called "spiritual materialism." By taking on the rituals, the costumes, and the philosophy of spiritual traditions, people tried to escape their ordinary lives and become more spiritual beings.

After a few years it became clear to most people that being high would not last forever and that spirituality was not about leaving our life to find existence on an exalted, light-filled plane. We discovered that transformation of consciousness required a great deal more practice and discipline than we initially imagined. We began to see that the spiritual path asked more of us than it appeared to offer. From romantic visions of practice, people began to wake up and realize that spirituality required an honest, courageous look into our real-life situations, our family of origin, our place in the society around us. Individually and in communities, through growing wisdom and disillusioning experience, we began to give up the idealistic notion of spiritual life and community as a way to escape from the world or save ourselves.

For many of us this shift has become the foundation of a more deeply integrated and wiser spiritual work, a work that includes right relationships, right livelihood, right speech, and the ethical dimensions of the spiritual life. This work has required the end of compartmentalization, an understanding that whatever we seek to push into the shadow or avoid must eventually be included in our spiritual life, that nothing can be left behind. Spirituality has become more about who we are than what ideal we pursue. Spirituality has shifted from going to India or Tibet or Machu Picchu to coming home.

This kind of spirituality is filled with joy and integrity; it is both ordinary and awakened. This spirituality allows us to rest in the wonder of life. This mature spirituality allows the light of the divine to shine through us.

Let us look at the qualities of spiritual maturity.

NONIDEALISM

The mature heart is not perfectionistic: it rests in compassion for our being instead of in ideals of the mind. Nonidealistic spirituality does not seek a perfect world; it does not seek to perfect ourselves, our bodies, our personalities. It is not romantic about teachers or enlightenment-clinging images of the immense purity of some special being out there. Thus, it does not seek to gain or attain in spiritual life, but only to love and be free.

The frustration of seeking perfection is illustrated by a story of the holy fool Mullah Nasrudin. One day in the marketplace he encountered an old friend who was about to get married. This friend asked the Mullah whether he had ever considered marriage. Nasrudin replied that years ago he had wanted to marry and had set out to find the perfect woman. First he traveled to Damascus, where he found a perfectly gracious and beautiful woman but discovered she was lacking a spiritual side. Then his travels took him farther to Esfahān, where he met a woman who was deeply spiritual yet comfortable in the world and beautiful as well, but unfortunately they did not communicate well together. "Finally in Cairo I found her," he said, "she was the ideal woman, spiritual, gracious, and beautiful, at ease in the world, perfect in every way." "Well," asked the friend, "did you then marry her?" "No," answered the Mullah wryly, "unfortunately, she was looking for the perfect man."

Mature spirituality is not based on seeking perfection, on achieving some imaginary sense of purity. It is based on the capacity to let go and to love, to open the heart to all that is. Without ideals, the heart can turn the suffering and imperfections we encounter into the path of compassion. In this nonidealistic practice, the divine can shine through even in acts of ignorance and fear, inviting us to wonder at the mystery of all that is. We can protect one another, yet in this there is no judgment and no blame, for we seek not to perfect the world but to perfect our love for what is on this earth. Thomas Merton saw it this way:

> Then it was as if I suddenly saw the secret beauty of their hearts, the depths where neither sin nor desire can reach, the person that each one is in God's eyes. If only they could see themselves as they really are. If only we could see each other that way there would be no reason for war, for hatred, for cruelty.... I suppose the big problem would be that we would fall down and worship each other.

KINDNESS

Another quality of mature spirituality is kindness. It is based on a fundamental sense of self-acceptance, rather than guilt, blame, or shame, for the ignorant acts we've committed or the fears that still remain within us. It understands that inner opening requires the warm sun of loving-kindness. It is all too easy to turn spirituality and religion into what Alan Watts called "a grim duty." Poet Mary Oliver writes in one her poems that we do not have to "walk on our knees" repenting. Our great spiritual task is not the perfection of ourselves, but the perfection of our kindness—toward ourselves and all others.

In deep self-acceptance grows a compassionate understanding. As one Zen master said when asked if he ever gets angry, "Of course I get angry, but then a few minutes later I say to myself, 'What's the use of this?' and I let it go." This self-acceptance is at least half of our spiritual practice. We are asked to touch with mercy the parts of ourselves that we have denied, cut off, or isolated. Mature spirituality is a reflection of our deep gratitude and capacity for forgiveness. As the Zen poet Edward Espe Brown writes in *The Tassajara Recipe Book,*

Any moment, preparing this meal,
we could be gas thirty thousand
feet in the air soon
to fall out poisonous on leaf,
frond and fur. Everything
in sight would cease.

And still we cook,
putting a thousand cherished
dreams on the table, to nourish
and reassure those close and dear.

In this act of cooking, I bid farewell.
Always I insisted you alone were to blame.
This last instant my eyes open
and I regard you with all
the tenderness and forgiveness
I withheld for so long.

With no future
we have nothing
To fight about.

PATIENCE

Another quality or sign of spiritual maturity, is patience, which allows us to live in harmony with the dharma, the Tao. As Chuang Tzu states,

> The true men of old
> Had no mind to fight Tao
> They did not try by their own contriving
> To help Tao along.

Zorba the Greek tells of his own lesson in patience:

> I remember one morning when I discovered a cocoon in the bark of a tree just as the butterfly was making a hole in its case and preparing to come out. I waited awhile but it was too long appearing and I was impatient. I bent over it and breathed on it to warm it. I warmed it as quickly as I could and the miracle began to happen before my eyes, faster than life. The case opened, the butterfly started slowly crawling out, and I shall never forget my horror when I saw how its wings were folded back and crumpled; the wretched butterfly tried with its whole trembling body to unfold them. Bending over it, I tried to help it with my breath. In vain. It needed to be hatched out patiently and the unfolding of the wings needed to be a gradual process in the sun. Now it was too late. My breath had forced the butterfly to appear, all crumpled, before its time. It struggled desperately and, a few seconds later, died in the palm of my hand.

Spiritual maturity understands that the process of awakening goes through many seasons and cycles. It asks for steady commitment, that we "take the one seat" in our heart and willingly open to the unfolding of life.

True patience is not about gaining or grasping, it does not seek any accomplishment. Patience allows us to open to that which is beyond time. When Einstein was illustrating the nature of time, he explained, "When you sit with a pretty girl for two hours, it seems like a minute, and when you sit on a hot stove for a minute, it seems like two hours. That's relativity." When the Buddha spoke of practicing for one hundred thousand *mahakalpas* (billions of years), he did not mean that it takes forever to awaken but that awakening is timeless. It is not a matter of weeks or years or lifetimes, but a loving and patient unfolding into the mystery just now.

"The problem with the word *patience*," said Zen master Suzuki Roshi, "is that it implies we are waiting for something to get better, we are waiting for something good that will come. A more accurate word for this quality is *constancy*, a capacity to be with what is true moment after moment, to discover enlightenment one moment after another." Patience means understanding that what we seek is always here. It is what we are. The great Indian teacher Ramana Maharshi said to students who were weeping as he died, "Where do you think I could go?" Maturity of spiritual life allows us to rest just here in the truth that has always been and always will be.

IMMEDIACY

Spiritual awakening is found in the here and now. In the Zen tradition they say, "After the ecstasy, the laundry." Spiritual maturity manifests itself in the immanent as well as in the transcendent. It seeks to allow the divine to shine through our every action. Altered states, extraordinary experiences of the mind, great openings of consciousness are valued, not for their own sake, but only to the extent that they return us to our human incarnation to inform our wisdom and deepen our capacity for compassion. As Ajahn Chah said, "Even the extraordinary experiences are of no use, only something to let go of, unless they are connected with this moment here and now." Spiritual states are honored when they clear the vision and open the body and mind, but only as a passage to return to the timeless present. As the mystic Kabir says of whatever we seek, "What is found then is found now."

In the immediate present, mature spirituality invites us to "walk our talk," to act and speak and touch one another as a reflection of our deepest understanding. We become more alive and more present. We discover that our very breath and body and human limitations are a part of the divine. This maturity listens to our body and loves it all, the body of joy and of grief; it listens to the heart and loves the heart's capacity to feel. This immediacy is the true source of compassion and understanding. "Only within our own body, this heart and mind," said the Buddha, "can bondage and suffering be found, and only here can we find true liberation."

INTEGRATED AND PERSONAL

With spiritual maturity also comes a sense of the sacred that is integrated and personal. "Integrated" means that spirituality does not create separate compartments of our life, dividing that which is sacred from that which is not. "Personal" means that we honor spirituality through our own words and actions. Otherwise our spirituality is not of any true value. Integrated and personal spiritual practice includes our work, our love, our families, and our creativity. It understands that the personal and the universal are inextricably connected, that the universal truths of spiritual life can come alive only in each particular and personal circumstance. How we live is our spiritual life. As one wise student remarked, "If you really want to know about a Zen master, talk to their spouse."

An integrated sense of spirituality understands that if we are to bring light and compassion into the world, we must begin with our own lives. Our personal life becomes more genuinely our spiritual practice than any set of experiences we have had or philosophy we espouse. This personal approach to practice honors both the individual and the universal in our life, respecting life as a tentative dance between birth and death, yet also honoring our unique body, our particular family and community, and the personal history and joys and sorrows that have been given to us. In this way, our personal awakening is a matter that affects all other creatures.

In the Amazon jungle there are nine hundred different species of wasps, each of which pollinates a different shape and species of fig tree. These fig trees are the main source of nutrition for all the smaller mammals of the rain forest, and these smaller mammals in turn provide the basis of life for jaguars, monkeys, peccaries, and others. Each species of wasp keeps a chain of other animals alive. In the same way, every individual in the world has a unique contribution. Fulfilling spiritual life can never come through imitation; it must shine through our particular gifts and capacities as a man or a woman on this earth. This is the pearl of great price. In honoring our own unique destiny, we allow our most personal life to become an expression of the Buddha in a new form.

OPEN-MINDEDNESS

Rather than adopting a philosophy or blindly following a great teacher or compelling path, as we mature we come to recognize that we must see for ourselves. This quality of open-minded questioning is called by the Buddha Dhamma-vicaya our own investigation into the truth. It is a willingness to discover what is so, without limitation and without following the wisdom of others. Someone once told Picasso that he ought to make pictures of things the way they are—objective pictures. When Picasso said he did not understand, the man produced a picture of his wife from his wallet and said, "There, you see, that is a picture of how she really is." Picasso looked at it and said, "She's rather small, isn't she? And flat?" Like Picasso, we must see things for ourselves. In spiritual maturity we find a great sense of autonomy, not as a reaction to authority, but based on a heartfelt recognition that we, too, like the Buddha can awaken. Mature spirituality has a democratic quality in which all individuals are empowered to discover that which is sacred and liberating for themselves.

This questioning combines an open-mindedness, the "don't know" mind of Zen, with a "discriminating wisdom" that can separate what is useful from what is not, that keeps the eyes open to learning. With an open mind we are always learning.

Our questioning allows us to use the great wisdom of traditions, to learn from teachers and to be part of communities, yet to stay in touch with ourselves. We can seek the truth with a great respect for our own integrity and our own awakening. This investigation may not bring us blind certainty, but it allows us to be more honest with ourselves, and in this, our spiritual practice becomes filled with interest and aliveness. The Dalai Lama, referring to his life in exile, said, "Sometimes I think this Dalai Lama has the hardest life of all—but of course it is the most interesting."

FLEXIBILITY

Spiritual maturity allows us, like bamboo, to move in the wind, to respond to the world with our understanding and our hearts, to respect the changing circumstances around us. The spiritually mature person has learned the great arts of staying present and letting go. Their flexibility understands that there is not just one way of practicing or one good spiritual tradition, but that there are many ways. It understands that spiritual life is not about adopting any one particular philosophy or set of beliefs or teachings, that it is not a cause for taking a stand in opposition to someone else or something else. It is an easiness of heart that understands that all of the spiritual vehicles are rafts for crossing the stream to freedom.

In his earliest dialogue, the Buddha cautioned against confusing the raft with the shore and against adopting any rigid opinion or view. He went on, "How could anything in this world be in conflict to a wise person who has not adopted any view?" In place of arrogance, the Buddha recommends freedom, and reminds his followers that those who grasp at philosophies and views simply wander around the world annoying people. The flexibility of heart brings a humor to spiritual practice. It allows us to see that there are a thousand skillful approaches to awakening, that there are times for formal and systematic ways and times for spur-of-the-moment, unusual, and outrageous ones. It allows us to be playful and responsive wherever we are.

A would-be high school basketball coach named Ron Jones learned this lesson when taking over the San Francisco Recreation Center for the Handicapped. He intended to coach his team to great victories, only to discover on the first day that there were just four players who came for training, one of whom was in a wheelchair. This initial problem was solved when a six-foot-tall black woman came striding out of the men's bathroom demanding to be included on the team as well. The coach describes throwing out his first lesson plan when he found it took forty-five minutes simply to get all five players lined up along one side of the court facing in the same direction. But as he threw his plans away, the basketball team grew. They had practices and cheerleaders and hot dogs, although often they had seven or twelve people on the team instead of five. Sometimes they would stop the game in the middle to play music and invite everyone down to dance. And in the end, they became the only basketball team in history to win a game by over a million points, when one of their members, who was scorekeeper, found joy in pressing the point button on the scoreboard to ring in new baskets.

Easy come, easy go. There is a great freedom that comes in this flexibility. My teacher Ajahn Chah spoke of himself as resting like a tree, bearing fruit, giving room for the birds to nest, moving in the wind. The dharma of flexibility is joyful and restful.

EMBRACING OPPOSITES

When we are young children, we see our parents as either all good or all bad. When they provide us with what we want, they are all good, and when they frustrate our desires and do not act as we wish them to, they are all bad. A great development of the consciousness of children eventually lets them see their parents clearly and understand that within the same person there is both good and bad, love and anger, generosity and fear. A similar development occurs as we mature in spiritual practice. We no longer seek perfect parents, perfectly wise teachers or gurus; we stop trying to find that which is all good as opposed to that which is all bad; we cease trying to separate the victim from the abuser. We begin to understand that each part of any duality contains its opposite.

One young woman who had been the victim of abuse in her own family spent much of her early spiritual practice healing this pain. As part of her healing, she became a counselor for other victims of abuse and finally began to work with offenders and perpetrators themselves. In the first year of working with this latter group, almost all men, she thought she was clear about what was right and what was wrong, what was unacceptable and who had committed the crimes. However, as her work continued and she listened more deeply to the stories of the perpetrators of abuse, she discovered that almost every one of them had themselves been abused in their own childhood. Here she sat in a room surrounded by men, forty, fifty, sixty years old, yet under the surface was a roomful of abused children. To her shock, she found that many of them had been abused by their mothers and, as she learned their stories further, that their mothers had been abused by their grandfathers and great-uncles, and in that way sorrowful patterns of abuse were revealed that stretched back generation after generation. What was she to do?

Who was she to blame now? All that she had left was to say with all her strength, "No, these actions must not continue," and then to hold them all in her heart of compassion, abuser and abused in one person.

As we've seen in spiritual life, we develop a sense of comfort with life's paradox, we embrace the whole, with its beauty and outrageousness, in the graciousness of the heart.

This paradox is always here in front of us. In a well-known story of a Zen master, a disciple asked him, "Please, master, speak to me of enlightenment." As they walked through the pine forest, the Zen master responded by pointing to a tree. "See how tall that tree is?" "Yes," answered the student. Then the master pointed to another. "See how short that other tree is?" "Yes," answered the student. "There," said the master, "is enlightenment."

When we embrace life's opposites, we hold our own birth and death, our own joy and suffering, as inseparable. We honor the sacred in both emptiness and form. We learn to allow the opposites of our practice—the need for a teacher and the need to take responsibility for our own spiritual practice; the experience of transcendent states of consciousness and the necessity to fulfill them in a personal way; the power of our karmic conditioning and the capacity for full human freedom—to be part of the dance of our spirit, to hold it all with ease and humor, to be at peace with it all.

RELATEDNESS

We are always in relationship to something. It is in discovering a wise and compassionate relationship to all things that we find a capacity to honor them all. While we have little control over much of what happens in our life, we can choose how we relate to our experiences. Mature spirituality is an acceptance of life in relationship. With a willingness to relate to all things in life, we enter into a spirit of practice that regards all as sacred. Our family life, our sexuality, our community, the earth's ecology, politics, money—our relationship to each being and action becomes a gracious expression of the Tao, the dharma. Zen master Thich Nhat Hanh is fond of reminding us of how we wash the dishes. "Can we wash each cup or bowl," he asks, "as if we were bathing a newborn baby buddha?" Each act has meaning, and all our encounters are related to the whole of our spiritual life. In the same way, the care and compassion with which we relate to the difficulties and problems we encounter is the measure of our practice. Spiritual maturity honors our human community and interconnectedness. Nothing can be excluded from our spiritual life.

The ancient wisdom of the Tao Te Ching instructs,

> I have just three things to teach:
> simplicity, patience, compassion.
> These three are your greatest treasures.
> Simple in actions and in thoughts,
> you return to the source of being.
> Patient with both friends and enemies,
> you accord with the way things are.
> Compassionate toward yourself,
> you reconcile all beings in the world.

ORDINARINESS

The last quality of spiritual maturity is that of ordinariness. In some traditions this is called "postenlightenment practice," the ordinariness that arises after the special spiritual states and side effects have faded away. Nisargadatta, the great master of the nondual, was asked how his own consciousness differed from the seekers around him. He smiled and stated that he had stopped identifying with the seeker. Yes, he might sit and wait for his lunch, hungry and perhaps impatient like the others, but underneath and all around was an ocean of peace and understanding. He was not caught up in or identified with any of the changing conditions of his life, and so, unlike those around him, whatever happened, Nisargadatta was at rest.

Ordinariness is a simple presence in this moment that allows the mystery of life to show itself. When Thoreau warns us to "beware of any activity that requires the purchase of new clothes," he reminds us that simplicity is the way we open to everyday wonder. While consciousness can create an infinite variety of forms, ordinariness is interested in what is here and now. This is the ordinary mystery of breathing or of walking, the mystery of trees on our street or of loving someone near to us. It is not based on attaining mystical states or extraordinary powers. It does not seek to become something special, but is emptying, listening.

Walt Whitman praises this ordinariness in his poetry:

I believe a leaf of grass is no less than
the journey-work of the stars. . . .
And the running blackberry would adorn
the parlors of heaven . . .
And a mouse is miracle enough to stagger sextillions of infidels.

The ordinariness of spiritual life comes from a heart that has learned trust, from a gratitude for the gift of human life. When we are just ourselves, without pretense or artifice, we are at rest in the universe. In this ordinariness there is no higher or lower, nothing to fix, nothing to desire, simply an opening in love and understanding to the joys and sufferings of the world. This ordinary love and understanding brings an ease and peace of heart to every situation. We discover that our salvation lies in the ordinary. Like the water of the Tao, which finds its way between the stones and gradually lowers itself to return to the ocean, this ordinariness brings us to rest.

There is a power in ordinariness, a strength in spiritual maturity. There comes the power to heal ourselves naturally, and then just as naturally, our sanity and compassion extend to the world around us. The beloved Japanese Zen poet Ryokan filled his life with this spirit of ordinariness and transformed those whom he touched. It is told that Ryokan never preached to or reprimanded anyone. Once, his brother asked Ryokan to visit his house and speak to his delinquent son. Ryokan came but did not say a word of admonition to the boy. He stayed overnight and prepared to leave the next morning. As the wayward nephew was lacing Ryokan's straw sandals, he felt a drop of warm water. Glancing up, he saw Ryokan looking down at him, his eyes full of tears. Ryokan then returned home, and the nephew changed for the better.

With spiritual maturity our capacity to open, to forgive, to let go grows deeper. In this comes a natural untangling of our conflicts, a natural undoing of our struggles, a natural easing of our difficulties, and the capacity to come back to a joyful and easeful rest.

PART THREE

Lessons from Modern Masters

14

Natural Freedom
of the Heart

The Teachings of Ajahn Chah

IN THE 1960S, '70S, AND '80S, I had the privilege of practicing in several of the great temples in the Tradition of the Elders of Thailand and Burma. My home monastery was Wat Ba Pong, a forest monastery in Thailand near the border of Laos and Cambodia. Wat Ba Pong Monastery covers several hundred acres of forest with dense foliage, hanging vines, and a wildlife population that includes deer, wild fowl, snakes, birds, lizards, scorpions, and a myriad of bugs. The small huts in which monks live and practice meditation are connected by paths, but are separate enough so that you can't see from one to another. It was there that I began practice as a monk in ocher robes under the guidance of Ajahn Chah. Ajahn Chah was a meditation master in the lineage of the ancient Thai forest tradition, where a simple and austere life was stressed as a path to awakening. He carried the dharma of liberation in all he did, and he demonstrated the great heart of a buddha to all who came to join him in the forest.

In this chapter I would like to convey some of the blessings I received in this training, the inspiration and understanding that came from it, handed down through the simple monk's and nun's life since the time of the Buddha. While the stories of Ajahn Chah's monastery may at first sound like tales of a distant culture, they point to the universal principles of dharma training experienced by all who undertake a genuine path of practice. Those who enter intensive retreats in the

West also face periods of surrender and simplicity. They too must come to terms with the suffering of their own body and mind and must endeavor to find compassion and freedom in their midst. In this way modern retreat practice offers an initiation that carries some of the spirit of the ancient monasteries and forests of Asia.

Ajahn Chah described two levels of spiritual practice. On the first level, you use dharma to become comfortable. You become virtuous and kinder. You sit and quiet your mind, and you help make a harmonious community. There are genuine blessings of this comfortable level of dharma. But the second kind of dharma, he said, is to discover real freedom of mind. This level of practice has nothing whatsoever to do with comfort. Here you take every circumstance of life and work with it to learn to be free. He told us, "That is what we're dong here. If you want to come join us in the forest, that's our purpose."

Ajahn Chah spoke of the second kind of dharma the day I arrived at his monastery. He smiled and welcomed me by saying, "I hope you're not afraid of suffering." I was shocked. "What do you mean? I came here to practice meditation, to find inner peace and happiness." As I have described earlier, he explained, "There are two kinds of suffering. The first is the suffering that causes more suffering, when we run away it follows us. The second is the suffering that comes when we stop running. The second kind of suffering can lead you to freedom."

Ajahn Chah's monastery became renowned in Thailand as a center for very strict practice. This style of practice is broader than the sitting practice we do on retreats in the West. It is a year-round mindful and disciplined way of life where the monks must be attentive to everything they do. There are hundreds of monastic rules in Theravada Buddhism that demand care, and in his monastery Ajahn Chah set up an environment that challenged his monks to follow them all. A mindful presence and awareness was expected of all who lived there. Ajahn Chah would tell people when they arrived that if they were coming to simply relax, they'd come to the wrong place. Everything was disciplined, not with an external force but out of a beautiful sense of respect; when one saw everything done with such care, it was inspiring to do the same.

Within the monastery, Ajahn Chah's teaching had four levels to it, and each level included wisdom, humor, and a great sense of compassion. The first level of his teaching was surrender: the surrender of using every experience as your practice. The second level was seeing clearly:

opening up to each experience to see what is happening. The third level was releasing difficulties: overcoming each difficulty, and learning to let go of it. The last level of his teaching was the balance of the one who knows how to rest in wisdom and equanimity in the face of all things.

SURRENDER

People were invited to work hard and bring an impeccable spirit to their lives as monks. Our lifestyle was intentionally austere. In the meditation hall we sat without cushions on a platform made of stone. When I began many hours of sitting this way, it hurt. My knees were high off the floor. When I tried to lower one knee, the other would push up farther. It made for a lot of pain. Then I discovered that if I got to the meditations early, I could get a seat near one of the supporting pillars in the front of the hall. After everyone closed his eyes and started meditating, I could lean against the pillar. I did that for about two weeks until Ajahn Chah gave an evening dharma talk. Although he was speaking to the group, he smiled at me and noted that learning to practice dharma required learning how to be independent, how to not have to "lean on things." I moved my seat.

Ajahn Chah expected surrender and care from everybody, but it wasn't the surrender of blind faith. It simply meant accepting that whatever your experience was in that monastery, that was your practice. He would test us often. We would sit in meditation for long hours. Ajahn Chah used to hold what the Western monks later called "endurance sessions." He could easily sit and give a dharma talk for five hours. We'd be sitting on the stone floor waiting, thinking, "My God, when is he going to finish?" He'd go on and on, and he'd look around amused to see who was squirming; we were supposed to stay respectful and mindful until he was finished.

Ajahn Chah wanted people to take impeccable care with whatever they did. We'd be quickly sweeping the paths, and he'd come out and show us patiently, "Sweep this way." Or if we were making brooms, he'd come out and show us how to make an elegant bamboo broom that would really work. I discovered from watching him what the real teaching was. He didn't care whether the path got swept or not. After all, a day later the forest leaves would cover it up again. What he cared about was people learning to do these tasks in order to awaken. He would show you how to do something so that it was really done well, whether it was tying a broom, sweeping, or building a wall.

The spirit of meditation in the monastery was to do whatever was needed. This is surrender, and it is part of everyone's practice. For a monk it meant taking whatever came to us—the food, the weather, the tasks of the temple—and working with it, whether it was easy or hard. There were people who were difficult to live with in the monastery, and Ajahn Chah valued them as well. Remember the story of Georges Gurdjieff's community in France where an obnoxious Russian character from Paris was actually hired to stay? In the same spirit, if there weren't enough difficulties at our forest monastery, Ajahn Chah would play this role for his disciples.

On full-moon nights we would renew our vows in the ceremonial hall and then be dismissed to return to the main meditation hall and stay up all night sitting and chanting. Late in the evening the villagers would come and offer us a drink of thick, sweet coffee. Since we ate only one meal a day in the morning, that one drink was really wonderful. One night Ajahn Chah had a visitor, an older monk, one of his teachers. The two of them were having a lengthy dharma conversation, and it appeared that they had simply overlooked dismissing the monks; they sat and talked from eight o'clock until about midnight. I was restless, wanting my coffee so I could "really meditate" in the other hall. Every once in a while Ajahn Chah would look around to see how people were doing. He'd sit quietly for a moment, and then he and his teacher would start talking again. I kept thinking, "When is he going to get done? When will I get my sweet coffee?" It got to be one in the morning, then two in the morning. I got more upset as the night went on, until about three o'clock. I finally figured out that my meditation practice had better happen then and there, because it wasn't going to happen anywhere else that night.

In the morning, as he got up to leave, Ajahn Chah smiled in a kindly manner. He'd watched us through the night. I had realized that my meditation practice had to take place wherever I was sitting, not just in the meditation hall or buoyed up by sweet coffee. This was his teaching: the surrender of knowing that wherever you are is your place of practice.

As much as he demanded of his monks, he also demanded of himself. I remember being with him on the coldest morning in a remote mountain-cave monastery, when we went out for a long alms round.

There was a strong wind, and it was below forty degrees outside. I had my cotton robes on, and I also had a towel that I had managed somehow to wrap under my robes so that it came up and covered my ears a little bit, since they're a big part of my body. It was five miles each way to the village where we went for alms every morning at dawn. By the time we got there, my teeth were chattering from the cold. After the villagers put rice and whatever they could afford into our bowls, we turned to go back to the monastery. Ajahn Chah looked and me and said, "Cold?"

"Freezing!" I replied.

He laughed. "Well, don't worry, this is as cold as it gets in Thailand!"

His spirit was right there with you. He was there when it was cold, and if you had to sit a long time, he sat there, too. He was there with you in a strong and compassionate way, giving you the sense that whatever the difficulty might be, you could learn to work with it and use it.

Ten years after I left the monastery, after I had begun teaching in America, I returned and reordained for some months to continue my training. On the first full-moon night when the monks gather to recite the rules of the order, I fixed my robes in the formal fashion for this ceremony and went to the hall. Right before the ceremony was to start, Ajahn Chah looked at me and said, "You're not supposed to be here. Go back to your cottage." Usually those who were asked to leave are people who are undisciplined, visiting monks who may not be keeping their vows, who may not be upholding the standard of conduct of the order. I was upset. It seemed he wasn't aware of my considerable efforts. I was doing everything I knew to be a good monk, and he didn't believe it. He kicked me out. I heard later that as I was walking down the steps, he turned to a couple of the senior monks there and said, "Oh, he's a meditation teacher, he won't mind."

For over three months he wouldn't let me join the community in that full-moon ceremony. At first I was upset, then when I saw that I was quite attached, I let it pass away. The last day before I was leaving to go to Bangkok, I was attending Ajahn Chah at his cottage. He had just taken a bath, and I was helping to dry his feet. He looked down at me and kind of chuckled. Then he nudged me and said, "Well, how did you like being treated just like any other visiting monk?" testing to see if I was still upset.

I said, "Actually, it was appropriate since I am a visiting monk. I'm only here for a short while."

He laughed, and said, "It's wise of you to see that." He was always trying to see what you were attached to, in order to teach you to surrender and let go.

SEEING CLEARLY

After one surrendered to the reality of one's circumstance, the second step of Ajahn Chah's teaching was to open up to each experience and see it clearly. It's essential in meditation and in our dharma life, to see our situation clearly and to see what is true of our mind. Ajahn Chah called this being honest with yourself. He demonstrated this quality quite openly.

I once asked Ajahn Chah how he became a monk, what attracted him to that kind of life. He said that when he was a small boy playing games with the other village children, one of them would want to be the village headman, someone else would want to be the nurse, and someone would be the teacher. "I always wanted to be the monk," Ajahn Chah said with a laugh, "so I would seat myself in a higher place than all the other little kids, and I'd get them to bring me food and sweets."

He would talk candidly about his own years of practice. Throughout his training, he had lots of problems, doubts, difficulties, and suffering. His body hurt and his mind gave him a hard time. He talked of sitting in the forest in the dry season when unexpected rains came. The water soaked his robes, his bowl, and his few books—everything that he had. He told me, "I was sitting in the forest feeling discouraged. The rain coming down was drenching everything, and tears were streaming down my cheeks. I couldn't tell what was rain and what were my tears, but I just sat there anyway. Sometimes in practice you just weep. I sat and sat and sat, because I had a quality of daring in my practice. No matter what came, I wanted to understand, I was willing to face it." There were times he was very sick. He had malaria, like many of the old forest monks, and there was little medicine in those days. He said, "At one point people thought I was seventy years old, when I was about thirty-five. I had just wasted away, and my skin was all dry. But I kept on practicing. I just did it."

Just as Ajahn Chah spoke honestly and directly about himself and his difficulties, he was equally honest about people around him. He would tease people and laugh about their hang-ups. In the 1970s I brought a group of friends to visit him, including Joseph Goldstein and

Ram Dass. Ram Dass had just come from surfing and lying on the beach in Bali; although he was fifteen years older than the rest of our group, he was trying to look young and fit. We sat down at the teacher's cottage, and Ajahn Chah looked around and started in on Ram Dass right away. "Oh," he said, "who's the old man you brought with you?"

At times we would be sitting at his cottage when laypeople would come. He'd introduce his monks, sometimes in a very formal and respectful way, but other times he would make fun of us. He would say, "Oh, here's the monk who likes to sleep all the time. He's my sleeping monk. Whenever you look for him, he's always sleeping." He'd point to another monk: "And this one's always sick. He's got this thing about getting sick, I don't know why. And this monk is a big eater. He is our eating monk. And this one likes to sit a lot. This monk is really attached to meditation. You can't get him to move or do anything. And this old monk, would you believe it, he had two wives before he ordained—at the same time, poor guy. No wonder he looks so old!" He would go through the monks around him, teasing them, and being very accurate about what that particular person's roles and attachments were. He'd say, "Me, I like to play teacher. That's my role here." Then he'd laugh.

Once, a Western monk who had been in a Chinese temple for ten years came to visit. He requested to stay at the monastery. Ajahn Chah said he could, and then he started questioning him, because he was quite stout. "Why are you so fat? Do you really eat that much?" Finally he said, "All right, you can stay, but only under one condition. We have a cottage that's really tiny. You'll just barely fit into it now, so if you eat too much, you'll squeeze into your cottage one morning and you won't be able to get out. Then we'll just lock the door, and you'll have to stay there." The irony of this, of course, is that Ajahn Chah himself was also fat, which he readily admitted. So it was wonderful to see that, for him, there was nothing sacred. Whatever happened to be true was the place to look. "Pay attention to that."

When I translated for him, he would tease me. "I know that you translate what I say in a decent way, but I'm sure you leave out some of the biting and difficult parts. Even though I don't speak English, I can tell that you're too soft on them. You don't quite tell them all the tough dharma that I'm saying, do you?" The method of his teaching was not to be coy, but to be straightforward and honest, to look directly at our difficulties so that we too could see ourselves freshly.

I asked him once what was the biggest problem with his students. He said, "Opinions. Views and ideas about all kinds of things, about themselves, about practice, about the teachings of the Buddha. Many who come to practice have had worldly success—they're wealthy merchants, university graduates, teachers, government officials—and their minds are filled with opinions about the world. They're too clever to listen. It's like water in a cup. If the cup is filled with dirty, stale water, it's useless. Only when the old water is thrown out does the cup become useful. You must empty your minds of opinions, and then you will begin to learn." To see clearly, you must learn to be simple, to see things as they are.

Ajahn Chah also taught about seeing one's own limits clearly. Ram Dass asked him how people should teach if they hadn't finished their own practice yet. If we are still suffering, how can we teach others to be free? Ajahn Chah replied, "First of all, be very honest. Don't pretend that you are wise in ways you are not. Tell people how you are yourself. And then take the measure of things. In weight lifting, if you're strong, you know that through practice you can lift a really big weight. Maybe you've seen someone lift a weight bigger than you can. You can tell your students, 'If you practice, you can lift that big weight, but don't try it yet. I can't even do it, but I've seen people do it.' Be willing to express what is possible without trying to fool someone that you've done it. Be scrupulously honest with yourself and in your teaching, and all will be well."

In seeing clearly, Ajahn Chah stressed where it was important to look—at ourselves. I remember feeling very frustrated in my first few months at the monastery. On certain days I wanted to leave because my practice wasn't going well. I dreamed of a quieter place where I could sit eight, ten, fifteen hours a day. Instead, I had to go on alms rounds and chant and work with other monks and was only able to sit five or six hours a day. He said our practice was to live wisely, and sitting would help with that. But for Ajahn Chah, sitting was simply the support for wisdom, not our main task. I was angry at what I saw as interruptions in my meditation. I told him that I didn't like it there and that I was going to go to a Burmese monastery. I was so frustrated that I said to Ajahn Chah, "And another thing, you don't seem so enlightened to me. You often contradict yourself. One time you say one thing, one time you say another. And sometimes you don't look truly mindful to me. I see you eating, and how do I know you're mindful? You drop things on the ground like anybody else. You don't look perfect." He thought this was very funny.

He said, "It's a good thing that I don't look enlightened to you."

I said, "Well, how come?"

He said, "Because if I did, you would still be caught in looking for the Buddha outside yourself. You cannot look outside and find enlightenment. Each person is different. Freedom does not come by imitating others. If you want to know about freedom, it only comes in your heart, when you're not attached to things."

He went on, "Wisdom is for you yourself to understand and develop. Take from the teacher what's useful and be aware of your own practice. If I am resting while you all have to sit up, does this make you angry? Or if I say that the sky is red or that a man is a woman, don't follow me blindly. Look at what is true and beneficial for yourself. One of my own teachers ate very fast. He made a lot of noises as he ate, yet he told us all to eat slowly and mindfully. I used to watch him and get very upset. I suffered, but he didn't. I was only watching the outside. Later I learned how some people can drive very fast but carefully, and others drive very slowly and still have many accidents. So don't cling to rules, to outer form. If you observe others ten percent of the time and attend to yourself ninety percent, this is proper practice. Looking outside yourself is comparing, discriminating; it will bring you more suffering. You won't find happiness or peace looking for the perfect man or the perfect teacher. The Buddha taught us to look at the dharma, the truth, not to look at other people."

This was his second level of practice: to be honest. To see clearly is to look at your own mind, your fears, and your patterns with compassion. "Really look at yourself," he said. Keep the attention inside, rather than comparing yourself with others outside.

FACING DIFFICULTIES

The third level of Ajahn Chah's teaching was working directly with difficulties as they arose. To do this, he most frequently offered two skillful means. The first was overcoming the difficulties by going through them mindfully, and the second was letting go. He expected people to face their difficulties as a way to discover freedom. When people were having a hard time, he'd ask them, with a smile on his face, "Are you suffering today?" If they said no, he'd laugh and say, "Very well." When they said yes, he'd say with compassion, "Ah, you must be very attached today." It was so simple to see. If you're suffering, you're attached. And right there is the place to learn to be free.

If people were afraid, he'd direct them into their fears. If they were afraid to be in the forest alone because of ghosts or wild animals, then he would send them into the forest. His teacher told him that at night, when the mind is attacked by fear, the forest monk forces himself to do walking meditation in the open. "This becomes the battle between fear and dharma," his teacher explained. "If fear is defeated, the mind will be overwhelmed by courage and enjoy profound inner peace. If fear is the victor, it will multiply rapidly and prodigiously. The whole body will be enveloped by perspiring heat and chilling cold, by the desire to pass urine and defecate. The monk will be suffocated by fear and will look more like a dying than a living man. The threatening roar of a tiger from a nearby place or far away at the foot of the mountains only serves to increase his already desperate fear. Direction or distance mean nothing to such a monk, his only thought being that the tiger is coming right now to make a meal of him. No matter how vast the area might be, he will be hypnotized by his own fear into believing that the tiger knows of no other place to go but to the very spot where he is walking. The passages for recitation on loving-kindness to prevent fear disappear, and ironically what remains is a passage that serves only to increase it. He will recite to himself, 'The tiger is coming. The tiger is coming.'"

But simpler fears were to be overcome as well. One night Ajahn Chah had his senior-most Western monk, Ajahn Sumedho, give a dharma talk for an hour. For a new monk it was hard to give dharma talks and not be afraid of appearing foolish, boring, or insecure. So when Sumedho was finished, Ajahn Chah said, "Go on," so he talked for another forty-five minutes. Ajahn Chah said, "Go on. More." And he made him continue until he had talked for four hours. He had nothing to say, and he went on and on. It was so boring! When he'd stop, he'd hear, "More." By the end, Ajahn Sumedho learned not to care whether he was boring or foolish or not, not to be afraid of what anybody thought, but to just do it.

The first big dharma talk I ever had to give was done without preparation, in the middle of the night. On big Buddhist holidays we would sit up all night. The hall would be filled with up to a thousand villagers, and we'd alternate one hour of dharma talk and an hour of sitting. At around two in the morning Ajahn Chah said, "We will now hear a dharma talk from the Western monk." I'd never given a dharma talk before, much less in the local Lao dialect, to hundreds of people. I just got up there, and he said, "Tell them what you know of the dharma, go to it." He knew I was nervous. He said, "That's an even better reason to do it!" I talked about Westerners having material wealth—big houses, refrigerators, and cars—but not necessarily being happy. I think they were amused just to hear me try.

It is a tradition in forest monasteries to push monks into what they dislike, and over the years Ajahn Chah would find out what your weak spot was. If you were afraid to be alone, off to a remote forest with you; if you had trouble dealing with people, you might be sent to a busy city monastery. He could seem like a rascal. He'd find out just what you didn't like and make you do it. If you were bored or restless, then he'd put you in a position where you would have more boredom or restlessness to deal with, and make you feel it. He'd say, "You simply feel it until you die." That was the spirit of his practice. Whatever resists is the sense of "I," the small self, and you have to work with that until it dies. That's overcoming the difficulty.

I was extremely sleepy in my meditation practice at first. Ajahn Chah instructed me, "Sit up straight; open your eyes if you're sleepy. Walk a lot, walk backward." I'd walk backward; I'd still be sleepy. "Okay, walk backward in the forest." Then I'd really have to wake up, to avoid trees and vines. Walking backward in the forest kept me awake. But as soon as I sat down, I'd get sleepy again. Finally he said, "We have a cure for people like you. There's a well near your cottage. Go and sit right on the edge of the well." So I sat down on the edge of the well, closed my eyes, and began to meditate. I soon felt a little sleepy and started to nod. As I did, I looked down and saw fifty feet of space below me. The rush of adrenaline from the fear kept me wide awake. I learned that sleepiness was workable, like any other state.

When I got angry or restless, Ajahn Chah said, "If you want to be angry, do it right! Go back into your hot cottage, wrap yourself in your warmest robes, and spend the day being angry, and feel it, experience the body, the emotions, the stories. Just keep sitting with it." He would speak about "putting the tiger of anger in a cage of mindfulness." He said, "You don't have to take it out and butcher it. You just make mindfulness around whatever it is, and then let it exhaust itself. Let it be your teacher."

For those of us who were young monks, celibacy was especially difficult. A Westerner who had been made abbot of one of Ajahn Chah's small monasteries told him he had a lot of lust and fantasy coming up in his practice. At this particular monastery, the villagers would come every afternoon for dharma talks. So Ajahn Chah said, "Well, did you tell the villagers about yourself? Tell all the old women. Tell them." He made him get up there and admit what was in his mind. He made him look at it.

At the same time, he wouldn't push too much. He had creative ways of helping people overcome the things that they got caught in, and he did it with a lot of balance. He wouldn't allow long periods of fasting or long solitary retreats unless he thought you were ready for it. He said, "You have to know the strength of your oxcart. You can't load it up with too much or it'll break down." He made space for each person to grow at his or her appropriate pace.

The first way he taught us to work with difficulties was by being willing to face them, going directly into them, to overcome them. The second way was by letting go. This is the heart of the teachings of the Buddha.

Being around Ajahn Chah challenged any territory you were clinging to. I remember a retired wealthy man coming to the temple saying that he had made a lot of money. He was starting to give his money to charity. He said quite proudly, "I don't know whether to give it to the hospital, or to orphans, or perhaps I should give some to your monastery to provide for nuns and monks."

Ajahn Chah looked at him and said, "I know what you should do with it."

The man said, "What?"

Ajahn Chah said, "Throw it off the bridge over the river on the way to the monastery." The man's jaw dropped open. It was just the right thing for him to hear, because he was really saying, "See how great I am, how much money I have." Ajahn Chah's teaching was to look at whatever you're attached to and learn how to let go of it.

For some students, doubts would arise. Someone asked, "What can I do about my doubts? Some days I'm plagued with doubts about the practice, or my progress, or the teacher."

He answered, "Doubting is natural. Everyone starts out with doubts.

You can learn a lot from them. What's important is that you don't identify with your doubts, you don't get caught up in them. That will spin your mind in endless circles. Instead, watch the whole process of doubting, of wondering. It is only the doubting mind. Ask who it is that doubts. See how doubts come and go. Then you'll no longer be victimized by your doubts. You'll step outside of them, and your mind will become quiet. You'll see how all things come and go. Just let go of what you're attached to. Let go of your doubts. Let them be there and simply watch. This is how to put an end to the trouble of doubting." Learn to see the movements of the mind and not get caught in all of its lures, its traps, and its intricacies.

No matter where he went, Ajahn Chah taught directly about freedom. When he was in England to teach, a staid, upper-class English lady who had been part of the British Buddhist Society came to visit. She asked him a series of complicated philosophical questions about Buddhist Abhidharma psychology. Ajahn Chah asked her if she had ever done much meditation practice, and she said no, she hadn't had time, she'd been too busy studying the texts. He told her, "Madam, you are like a woman who keeps chickens in her yard and goes around picking up the chicken shit instead of the eggs."

He later explained to me that his way of teaching is very simple: "It is as though I see people walking down a road I know well. To them the way may be unclear. I look up and see someone about to fall in a ditch on the right-hand side of the road, so I call out, 'Go left, go left.' Similarly, if I see another person about to fall in a ditch on the left, I call out, 'Go right, go right!' That is the extent of my teaching. Whatever extreme you get caught in, whatever you get attached to, I say, 'Let go of that too.' Let go on the left, let go on the right. Come back here to the center, and you will arrive at the true dharma."

Ajahn Chah taught how to let go, to put down our struggle and make the heart peaceful. "Learn to let go of doubts, let go of the obsession with thinking. Let go of desires and fears," he said. "Make your mindfulness patient, like a parent with a child. Your mind is a child and mindfulness is the parent."

Maybe you have a little child who says, "Daddy, can we have an elephant?"

Rather than explaining all the reasons that would be impossible, you just say, "Yes, wouldn't that be wonderful?"

"Daddy, I want an ice-cream cone."

"Ice cream is delicious. Let's get some later."

"Daddy, can we buy a new car?"

"Yes, all right, we will get a new car in the future," you say. You attend to the child with kindness and wisdom. You don't have to directly oppose everything. Just say, "That's fine," and watch. You observe how the child of your mind can come up with a thousand desires. You see them arise, and you let them go.

The same is true for special states in meditation. Ajahn Chah used to say that one of the great difficulties in practice for people comes when they start to develop some concentration and they think, "Oh boy, I'm going to get enlightened now!" or "I must be right on the edge of one of those great experiences." When you think like that, the quiet of concentration disappears and slides away. To practice wisely, you must let go of expectations. Let things be just as they are for you. Don't try to make something happen. Simply be open to each experience as it occurs.

If judgment arises, that's fine, let judgment be there. If you have a lot of judgments, make them the subject of your meditation. There's nothing wrong with that. Being aware of the rise and fall of judgment is just like being aware of the in and out of breath. The practice of meditation is not to change anything, but to see how things arise and how they pass away, to experience things fully and yet not be caught by them. Anger, fear, doubt, sleepiness—let them come in, let them go, and rest in the pure knowing of them. Just be here and be mindful. This does not mean withdrawal, and it doesn't mean suppression. It means to rest in awareness and be open to all experience. That's how you learn to be free.

When Ajahn Chah approached the greatest forest master of his time, Ajahn Mun, it was after years of dedicated practice in mountains and caves. Ajahn Chah described his meditation experiences, looking for confirmation or guidance. The guidance was direct: "Do not focus on the many different states and experiences that arise. These are just appearances in the mind." Instead he instructed Ajahn Chah to turn directly to awareness, the essence of mind, and to make himself a witness to all that arises and passes, whether joyful or sorrowful. This Ajahn Chah called "becoming the One Who Knows," resting in the conscious awareness that knows the ever-changing conditions of life This awareness is unconditioned, the original mind. When you learn to rest in the knowing, Ajahn Chah taught, you can stop, put things down.

This radical shift, from seeking experience to being the One Who Knows, does not depend on any particular posture or form of meditation. It is the invitation to liberation wherever you are. Ajahn Chah said, "Sitting for hours on end is not necessary. Some people think that the longer you can sit, the wiser you must be. I've seen chickens sit on their nest for days on end. Wisdom comes from being mindful in all postures. Your practice should begin as you awaken in the morning, and it should continue until you fall asleep. What's important is only that you keep attentive, whether you are working or sitting or going to the bathroom. Each person has their own natural pace. Some of you will die at age fifty, some at age sixty-five, and some at age ninety—so, too, your practice will be different. Don't think or worry about this. Try to be mindful, and let things take their natural course. Then your mind will become quieter and quieter in any surroundings; it will become still like a clear forest pool. Then all kinds of wonderful and rare animals will come to drink at the pool. You'll see clearly the nature of all things in the world, see many wonderful things and strange things come and go. But you will be still. This is the happiness of the Buddha."

BALANCE

So the practices that Ajahn Chah taught were surrender and opening to experience. Then he taught how to work with difficulties by overcoming them and letting them go. This led to the fourth level of his teaching: living in balance, the simplicity of the Middle Path. Ajahn Chah rarely taught about levels of enlightenment. He didn't think the system of stages of enlightenment and levels of insight was helpful, because it took people out of the reality of the present. He said, "When you teach that, people get attached to it. They want to get there. They have a 'gaining' ideal. But freedom comes directly from letting go." He emphasized this again and again. "If you let go a little, you will have a little freedom. If you let go a lot, you will have a lot of freedom. And if you let go completely, your heart will be completely free."

I remember coming back to him after doing intensive practice in another monastery. I described a wide range of extraordinary and wonderful experiences. For him these were just something else to let go of. When I finished my account, he looked at me and said, "Do you still have any fear?"

I said, "Yes."

"Do you still have any greed and desires?"

"Yes."

"Does anger still come?"

"Yes, it comes."

He smiled. "Fine, continue." And that was it.

He wouldn't let people get stuck in practice. "Just rest here in the reality of the present, where you are," he would teach. He asked me if I had learned anything in my travels and studies with other masters. He said, "What have you learned by traveling that wasn't present at the monastery?"

I thought about it and said, "There wasn't really anything new. It was the same dharma. I could have as well stayed here."

He laughed. "I knew that before you left, but it would have done no good to tell you. You had to go on that journey to discover it. But from where I sit, no one comes and no one goes."

Learning the Middle Path, the life of balance, allows the heart's natural awareness and compassion to grow. We become free and gracious. I heard a story from the first Western monastery that Ajahn Chah set up in a forest two villages away from his main monastery. One December the Western monks there decided to have a Christmas tree. The villagers who built the monastery got upset and came to Ajahn Chah to complain. They said, "We have made a Buddhist monastery for the Western monks that we're supporting, and they're having a Christmas celebration. It doesn't seem right to us."

Ajahn Chah said, "Well, in the simple way I have been told, Christmas is a holiday that celebrates the renewal of generosity and kindness. As far as I'm concerned, that is beneficial. It is very much the spirit of the teaching of Buddhism. But since you are concerned, the monks won't celebrate Christmas anymore. Instead, we will call it ChrisBuddhamas." With that, the villagers were content and they went back home. He taught us to be kind and flexible. "The point is to learn how to let go and be free, how to be happy," he said.

Ajahn Chah encouraged us to use our dharma practice to come to what he called the natural freedom of the heart, beyond all forms and conditions. He said, "The original heart/mind shines like pure, clear water with the sweetest taste. But if the heart is pure, is our practice over? No, we must not cling even to this purity. We must go beyond all duality, all concepts, all bad, all good, all pure, all impure. We must go beyond self and nonself, beyond birth and death. When we see with the eye of wisdom, we know that the true buddha is timeless, unborn, unrelated to anybody, any history, any image. Buddha is the ground of all being, the realization of the truth of the unmoving mind."

Ajahn Chah's way of teaching combines the ultimate level of dharma with the practical level. The ultimate level invites us to rest in awareness as the One Who Knows and to see the timeless dance of existence—all arising and passing, days, experiences, aeons, and galaxies alike. The practical level teaches us to take care of the moments we are given, to live with impeccability and compassion, to sweep the paths with mindfulness, delight, and fullness, to be honest with ourselves and caring with others. He wouldn't let people get caught in either level.

To help us find freedom, Ajahn Chah taught about selflessness, the essential realization of the Buddha's liberation, in simple and remarkable ways. "If our body really belonged to us, it would obey our commands. If we say, 'Don't get old,' or 'I forbid you to get sick,' does it obey us? No, it takes no notice. We only rent this house, not own it. In reality there is no such thing as a permanent self, nothing solid or unchanging that we can hold on to. The idea of self is merely a concept. Ultimately no one exists, only elements that have combined temporarily. There is no me, there is only anatta, nonself. To understand nonself, you will have to meditate. If you only intellectualize, your head will explode. When you see beyond self, you no longer cling to happiness, and when you no longer cling to happiness, you can begin to be truly happy."

One day I had a further conversation with Ajahn Chah about this Buddhist teaching of nonself and he said, "Nonself, anatta, is not true." This was an amazing thing for a Buddhist teacher to say. "It's not correct," he said, "because self is one extreme and nonself is the other extreme. What is true is neither of those, because both are concepts. Things are as they are."

In the midst of the strict discipline and impeccable training of the monastery, Ajahn Chah had a great laugh and a playful spirit. He reminded us that the sole task of Buddhism is to help people be happy and free, develop their heart's resources, and open them to what's true. From surrender, seeing clearly, and learning how to deal with the mind in a balanced way, "you yourself can become a buddha." To know Ajahn Chah over many years brought great joy into my life. His spirit of freedom and simplicity was contagious. His maturity and delight in the dharma brought all he touched closer to liberation.

When Ram Dass, Joseph Goldstein, I, and others left Ajahn Chah in 1977, he said, "When Thai people come to me and only ask for amulets, clay buddhas, or blessing rituals, they insult themselves. Now you have come to ask me questions. You want somebody outside to teach you the dharma. You insult yourself, too, because the truths discovered by the Buddha are already in your heart. There is a One Who Knows within you who already understands and is free. If you can turn toward this ever present awareness and rest in it, then everything will become simple." He went on, "Over the years you can deepen your freedom in many ways. Use your natural awareness to see how all things come and go. Let go and live with love and wisdom. Don't be lazy. If you find yourself lazy, fearful, or timid, then work to strengthen the qualities that overcome it. With natural wisdom and compassion, the dharma will unfold by itself. If you truly dedicate yourself, you will come to the end of all doubts, you will be liberated. You will live in that place of silence, of oneness with the Buddha, with the dharma, with all things. Only you can do that."

15

The Inspiration of Dipa Ma Barua

When I was younger, my benefactor asked me a question, but I was too hot-blooded to understand it. Now I am older and I ask it of you. You must look at your life and your way, and there is no shame in dropping whatever you have undertaken, as long as it's not done out of fear or ambition. But there is one question, and one question alone, that matters. Does this path have heart?

—CARLOS CASTANEDA, *THE TEACHINGS OF DON JUAN*

IN THIS CHAPTER I'd like to share more of what I learned from my teacher Dipa Ma Barua, a woman who chose a path with heart and lived it well. Dipa Ma lived in Calcutta with her daughter and her grandson, Rishi, which is an Indian name for a sage. She lived in a simple apartment on a small, run-down street in Calcutta. She was quite poor, and her apartment was right near a metal grinding shop. She cooked like most people did in Calcutta, on a little charcoal stove on the floor in the kitchen.

She was also a teacher of many students, mostly of older women in the Calcutta Buddhist community. They would come over and bow to her and pay their respects, and then sit down and have tea and talk about who knows what in Bengali. They probably spoke about cooking and knitting and dharma practice and enlightenment—at least that was my fantasy.

I visited Dipa Ma's home in Calcutta a number of times, and once I was making a little movie about her and where she lived. At one point in the filming, I just stood on the corner of the street near her house and left the camera rolling for a while. Barefooted rickshaw pullers came by, horse carts came by (they were like stagecoaches right out of Western movies) with people leaning out of every window and piled high with various mercantile goods. People walked by carrying large washbasins on their heads, cows meandered in the traffic, and children were out bathing in the puddles in the streets, which were overflowing from broken pipes. It seemed like the whole of India was out there on her street.

I had heard about Dipa Ma from Joseph Goldstein and Sharon Salzberg, who told me that she was an extraordinary yogi and a wonderful teacher. One of the first stories I heard was from an American man who practiced in India in the late sixties and early seventies. He was an avid meditator—he shaved his head and wore white, and he spent years in temples, ashrams, and monasteries. But his parents hated his lifestyle. He was in his early thirties, and he should have been in medical school or law school or one of those places where one's parents often think we should be.

His mother in particular was very unhappy about what he was doing. To her, it was as if she had lost a son. Every time this man went to see Dipa Ma, she would ask about his mother, "How is your mother? When you do your sittings, are you doing metta for your mother? Every time you sit, you should put your mother in your heart and send her loving-kindness." Then one time when he came to see her, Dipa Ma went into her back room and got a roll of Indian bank notes from under her mattress. From this roll she pulled out the biggest Indian note there is, one hundred rupees (about twelve U.S. dollars). This was a lot of money for her. She put it in his hand and said, "Go buy a present and send it to your mother."

Her teaching was to always keep people in your heart, to give of your love to the people and the earth and the world around. She was born in British India in the early part of the century, when India, Pakistan, and Burma were all part of greater British India. She married young, probably around age fourteen. Her husband was a civil servant and they eventually had three children. After some time one of her children died, and following that, another child became ill and also died. After this, her husband got ill and also died of a heart attack. So she lost her husband and two children in a short period of time, one after another.

At age forty, she was left caring for her remaining daughter and, as one can imagine, had an enormous amount of grief and sorrow. In a way, she was facing what we all have to face as human beings, which is not just the beauty and majesty of life but also the inevitable loss and suffering of life. But she experienced this in the deepest way that a human being can: by losing the people we most love. She understood the inevitability of sorrow as a part of human life, and she wanted to find freedom. She became sick, despondent, unable to function. Then the Buddha appeared to her in a dream and she said she felt a very deep desire to practice meditation. So she went to the most famous meditation center of her day, to Mahasi Sayadaw's monastery in Rangoon, and she threw herself into practice.

Deeply motivated, she was also a natural at meditation. She had a very powerful natural samadhi, a very powerful capacity to be present and concentrated. For example, she said she was once doing a long period of walking meditation, walking very slowly, and after the third or fourth day she was walking along, just feeling the sensations of her body, which had already dissolved—there wasn't a body for her at this point after a few days of meditation. All of a sudden, she noticed that her leg was very heavy and then it became hot, and there was some painful sensation and she just couldn't walk any farther. She looked down and one of the dogs in the monastery had grabbed her leg and bitten it very hard. She wasn't aware of the actual attack, she was simply paying attention to the sensations in her body.

Ardently practicing vipassana, she experienced the deepest stages of insight and awakening, completing the most important training offered in that monastery. It took her about one week to attain this level of realization. Then she did a variety of advanced meditation exercises where you examine every aspect of body and mind as we know it, and you dissolve them to see their fundamental emptiness. She followed this by learning from one of the senior teachers all the different samadhi and jhana practices, practices of profound concentration. These states can be attained with the breath or with loving-kindness or with various objects. One can make the mind so concentrated (on the breath or on light or a visualization or a feeling) that everything disappears—all sights and sounds and sensations. The whole body and mind become filled with light, and then dissolve into a sea of peaceful, silent consciousness, infinite without any movement. Then after a time, phenomena start to arise again, all experienced with wisdom, clarity, and joy.

The teacher she was studying with, Anagarika Munindra, had several very fine students, it seems. Dipa Ma and two other women were his most accomplished yogis, so he said to them, "Since you have developed the jhana states, let's develop the psychic powers as well." Apparently these three women did so well in their training that they could disappear and appear at will. They would be sitting in the meditation hall and when it was time for an interview with their teacher, they would simply dematerialize their body, appear in his room for a little discussion about practice, and then reappear in the meditation hall. They also learned time travel. This is what Munindra told us. You can take it for whatever it's worth. Whatever you believe, Dipa Ma was an extraordinary yogi, by any standard.

She came to the United States several times to teach at our three-month retreat. One day, during a retreat at the Insight Meditation Society in Barre, Massachusetts, we took a walk together. It was one of those crystal-clear autumn days in New England when the sky is brilliant blue with puffy white clouds, and the trees are this amazing display of fall color. A group of us took a walk, and we were sitting by a lake on a rock. The lake was reflecting all these colors, and someone motioned to her and said, "This must be like one of the heaven realms." (Buddhist tradition describes many different realms of existence, including our own human realm, heaven realms, and hell realms.) Dipa Ma responded, "No, this is nothing like the heavenly realm at all. It is lovely, but it really doesn't come close."

Realms of light, the realms of infinite peace—most of us cannot imagine them. But these realms are possible, not just for her, but for all people because they are part of human consciousness, available to us when we understand how to access them. Dipa Ma became a great master of all of the possibilities and potentials for the heart and mind. She said, "I looked at the possibilities that the Buddha described in his teachings and I wanted to see if they were so; for myself I wanted to understand them. And so I did it and I discovered that they were true. I discovered that attachment, the sense of separateness of self, is false and it leads to suffering, and I discovered another way to live."

Yet to be with her, you would never know she was such a master yogi. There was no show, no pretense, nothing special. She was just a very peaceful person and she very much lived the dharma by being herself.

As I mentioned in an earlier chapter, psychologist Jack Engler studied Dipa Ma as part of his research at Harvard. He was also a meditation student of hers, and she allowed him to study her mind using a variety of Western psychological assessments, such as the Rorschach inkblot test. One of the other tests he used is called the Thematic Apperception Test (TAT), in which the subject is presented with ten picture cards that show ambiguous scenes of people doing things—men, women, and children in various situations. It's not clear whether the people in the picture are coming or leaving, had a fight or just got married, and so on. The psychologist asks you to look at the picture and tell a story about what's happening.

Jack Engler showed Dipa Ma these test cards, and for each card she told a dharma story of how these people had been entangled in some way in their lives, and how they, too, had come to freedom, understanding, and peace. In addition to that, as he presented each card to her, she wove all of the ten pictures into one long story about the path to awakening. He came back to Harvard and consulted with experts about this unusual response to the TAT. No one had heard of a subject doing this before, connecting all the images together into one long narrative with a message about awakening. (Then someone recalled a South American shaman who had been given the TAT and had done the same thing. He had told a story that knitted all ten images together to show the spiritual path, the path with heart.) Dipa Ma's response to Engler's testing demonstrates how she was constantly seeking to teach people, to help them, to show them the way to freedom.

How did she teach? It was interesting to work with her as a student and also to be teaching alongside her. First of all, she was very demanding in that role. She was a tough old grandma and she really expected you to absolutely dedicate yourself; she expected the best from people. She expected tremendous sincerity. If she developed her deep meditation in a week, the least you could do is try to do the same. Not only did she expect it, but somehow she evoked that in you. She evoked the sense that each person has a tremendous capacity to awaken, to be present, to face ourselves, to be aware, to live freely. She asked you to give your whole body, heart, spirit, and mind as fully as you could to your meditation practice, to your spiritual life as a whole, and to the way that you live. When you were around her, you started to think, What other way would one want to live? What other way is possible, other than to do it fully?

From this very sweet, mild-mannered grandmother, there was a sense of unshakable inner strength and an incredible sense of stillness and power in her being. Once, another Buddhist teacher mentioned that in some text it says a buddha must be born in a man's body. Dipa Ma sat right up and said, "Anything a man can do, I can do!" She deeply believed in the power of sitting and opening and listening, in the power of mindfulness, in our ability to discover the truth and live wisely. She would ask, "How is your sitting? How fully are you practicing and what happens? How is your mindfulness? How awake are you in your life?" Basically, the question was, are you really doing it or just kind of thinking about it?

So the first aspect of her teaching was a sense of integrity, of being very demanding, and also of evoking a sense of possibility in us. A second aspect was to get her students to see the truth of the dharma. Do you see the truth? It's right here in front of you. Wisdom is that which knows. Do you see the truth that we possess nothing? That we own nothing, that underneath all that, we are nothing, that none of it is ours? Your efforts to possess, to seek security through greed and fear, are not the way. All those things that the personality gets caught in are not the truth of our reality. We sit, walk, stand, or live with the illusion of a self, as if we were separate, solid, unchanging. Do you see the truth that you don't own this very body, these feelings, and these thoughts? Be mindful. Nothing can be possessed. It is all impermanent and selfless. With practice you can awaken. You can see what is true and be free.

A third quality of her teaching was an incredible loving-kindness. She was very grandmotherly. You would come in, especially if you came to see her in India, and she would ask, "How are you feeling, how is your health?" That was one of her first questions, and it was an important one for Westerners traveling in India. She'd ask, "Are you eating well, are you doing OK with the climate and the food?"

She worked with a lot of American students, and with whoever came to her, in whatever state they were in, whether doubting ("I can't do it, it's too hard"), or full of joy and delight; whether in fear, frustration, or even rage—it did not matter, she loved them. She would smile when people walked in the room and would offer an outpouring of welcoming loving-kindness. It didn't matter who came in or what the circumstances were or what they had to say. That level was irrelevant to her. What was important was simply that here was another person to be loved.

She had a beautiful smile. It was wonderful. My favorite scene in all the footage that I took of her is a bright morning with Dipa Ma in a white sari, hanging out her laundry. It was at our meditation center in Barre, Massachusetts, and it is like a Vermeer painting—"Saint with Laundry." I have two or three minutes of footage of Dipa Ma hanging out the laundry and smiling. She didn't use the dryer, and washed her things by hand the same way she did in India. As she hung out the laundry, she was beaming about it. Somehow, in her presence, in everything she did, was a silent integrity, a sense of completeness or rest or wholeness. She was asked whether life was boring and gray after getting rid of desire, anger, and passion. Where was the juice? Dipa ma burst out laughing. "Once greed, hatred, and delusion are gone, you can see everything fresh and new all the time. Every moment is new. Life was dull before. Now every day, every moment is full of taste and zest." Her presence was spontaneous and natural. This leads to a straightforward, joyous heart, filled with compassion. Dipa Ma lived joyfully in the reality of the present moment.

Dipa Ma was a very simple person and there wasn't any sense of pretense about her. Her wish was simply that each person be themselves—that each student, each person that she encountered or taught, be all that they could be. She wanted us to live with the deepest wisdom, to open our hearts with infinite compassion, and there wasn't any sense of how you should do that. She didn't want people to come and live in India forever or be monks or join an ashram. She said. "Live your life, do the dishes, do the laundry, take your child to kindergarten. Raise your children or your grandchildren. Take care of the community in which you live and make all of that your path. Follow your path with heart."

I remember once sitting with Dipa Ma and asking her, "What is it like in your consciousness, what's in your mind?" She smiled, as she did very often, closed her eyes for a moment, and said, "In my mind there are three things: concentration, loving-kindness, and peace." I said, "That's all?" She said, "Yes, that's all." What a wonderful sense of being she had. Let's dedicate ourselves to developing a mind like hers, a mind filled with concentration (or steadiness, presentness), loving-kindness, and peace.

16

Holding the Banner of the Dharma

Celebrating Chögyam Trungpa

THE TIBETAN LAMA and dharma teacher Chögyam Trungpa Rinpoche was a beloved friend, a benefactor, and a deeply respected person in my life. When he died in April 1987, he was the leader of one of the largest Buddhist communities in America. In July 1974, he founded Naropa University, along with many of us who taught there. He had thousands of students connected with the main meditation centers he founded in Colorado, Nova Scotia, and rural Vermont. He established centers in almost one hundred cities and small towns across North America, as well as throughout Europe. When he died at the age of forty-eight, he not only had a large following but had also brought the dharma to life in the West in a remarkable new way.

THE LIFE OF A BODHISATTVA

Chögyam Trungpa's life reminds me of one of the most creative sutras in the Mahayana teachings of Buddhism, called the Vimalakirti Nirdesa Sutra. Vimalakirti, the subject of the sutra, was a great bodhisattva and teacher who, rather than appearing as a monk or a priest, decided to incarnate as a layman and to go among the peoples of the world to teach in a way that could be understood by every person he met. In this sutra, Vimalakirti appears in different guises. At one point, he's married and has a whole flock of children. In this way he could show the merit of family life and the possibilities it offers for surrender, awakening, and practice. Later in the sutra, he works in a wine shop and teaches the dharma to those who come to buy alcohol, enlightening them in the process. In another part of the sutra, Vimalakirti makes himself sick in order to give the healers and doctors an opportunity to serve him; in this way they can learn the dharma of caring and compassion in ways that are appropriate to their situation. He goes through all of these different guises, entering into the very thick of life with a tremendous sense of joy and ease, demonstrating that each situation in life is workable as a part of one's practice.

In some ways, Chögyam Trungpa Rinpoche was closer to Vimalakirti than anyone I've ever met on my travels in the dharma. He escaped from Tibet in 1959, around the same time that the Dalai Lama and many other great teachers fled. In *Born in Tibet*, a harrowing and compelling account of his early life and departure from his homeland, Trungpa Rinpoche describes his dangerous escape over the Himalayan Mountains. He went first to India and then, in 1963, to England, where he studied at Oxford University. In 1967 he cofounded Samye Ling in Scotland, one of the first major Tibetan Buddhist centers in the West.

Chögyam Trungpa has been a tremendous supporter of the vipassana community in America. In 1974 Trungpa Rinpoche invited Joseph Goldstein, Sharon Salzberg, myself, and a number of others to join together to teach and become part of the founding faculty of the Naropa Institute (now Naropa University). After collaborating there we all began to teach vipassana in large retreats across the country.

I remember talking with Rinpoche in 1973 at a cocktail party in Cambridge, Massachusetts, when he was thinking about starting Naropa. This party was hosted by David McClelland, the chairman of the Department of Social Psychology at Harvard University, and included students, professors, and dharma practitioners. We were drinking cocktails and chatting, and he was interested in the training that I'd had as a monk and about my experiences in monasteries in Asia. Rinpoche asked a lot of questions about my training. He wanted to know what the masters and monasteries were like, how much authentic practice was still to be found in Thailand and Burma, and how I had been trained. Then he said, "I think you should join us and teach at this Buddhist university we're going to establish, Naropa Institute." I was reluctant. I had been encouraged to teach while I was in Asia, and I had begun teaching on a very small scale in graduate school. "I don't know if I'm ready to teach at that level," I told him. He was quite pleased with that, actually. He said, "Then it's clear you should come. I'll sign you up, and you'll be our teacher of Theravada Buddhism." So I went. I had met Joseph Goldstein briefly before that, but it was that first summer at Naropa that he, Sharon Salzberg, and I really struck up a deep friendship and began to teach together, and we have led our community together since then.

Besides being a supporter in those early days, over many years Chögyam Trungpa continued to value and support the community of vipassana practice. He respected all genuine teachings. When the great Burmese master Mahasi Sayadaw came to teach at our American centers in 1979, Rinpoche was in Europe, but he telephoned and tried to arrange a flight to come back just to pay his respects to Mahasi Sayadaw.

Trungpa was a follower of the path of the bodhisattva, the path of opening one's heart to all circumstances and all beings. His way combined discipline and openness in a remarkable fashion. Let me describe some of the qualities I saw and valued in him that can inform and inspire the practice of dharma for all of us.

THE QUALITY OF BRIGHTNESS

The first of the key elements in his teachings that I want to honor is the tremendous quality of brightness he had. Over many years, at Naropa and elsewhere, I must have heard a hundred dharma talks by Rinpoche. Although he might arrive late for a lecture and was sometimes in a somewhat inebriated state, there was still an amazing quality of brightness and clarity to his mind. Lama Govinda, an early Western teacher of Tibetan Buddhism, once spoke to me about Trungpa Rinpoche. While Lama Govinda was living in Almora, in the Indian Himalayas, in the 1950s and early 1960s, many people escaping from Tibet came through his household. It became a refuge, and many of the lamas would stay with him. He said that of all the young *tulkus* (reincarnated Buddhist masters) to leave Tibet, there was none so bright as Trungpa Rinpoche. He meant "bright" in the sense of the field of his being and his energy. Lama Govinda told me this at a point when he wasn't very happy with the way Trungpa Rinpoche was behaving. He said, "I still have to admit that there was no one who walked across the Himalayas and came out of Tibet who had that light more than Trungpa."

This quality of brightness in his teachings relates to what Rinpoche called "the Lion's Roar." In the Pali texts, there is a famous discourse of the Buddha, called the Lion's Roar Sutta, in which someone asks, "How do you know about all the things that you claim to know about? Have you really practiced? Have you fully experienced it yourself?" To paraphrase his reply, the Buddha responded, "If there is any ascetic practice that has ever been done on the continent of India in all of the thousands of aeons of world systems, I have tried it. I've fasted; I lay on beds of nails; I went down to eating one grain of rice, one sesame seed a day. When I put my hand on my belly, I touched my backbone." He said, "I sat up with my eyes open to the moon. I sat with my eyes open to the sun." He said, "Whatever demanding practice existed, I did. And finally, after all of those austerities and all of those practices, I discovered that self-torture wasn't the way. Liberation does not come through torturing the body, nor through indulging it. I have discovered the Middle Path, the Middle Way that brings freedom. I have seen suffering and the end of suffering. I have found the unshakable deliverance of heart, the deathless." It's a powerful proclamation of freedom.

Trungpa Rinpoche also spoke of the teachings as the Lion's Roar. He said,

> The Lion's Roar is the fearless proclamation that any state of mind, any circumstance, any part of ourselves, including the most difficult emotions, is a workable situation, a reminder in the practice of meditation. We can realize that the chaotic situations must not be rejected, nor must we regard them as regressive, as a return to our confusion. We must sit and respect whatever happens to our state of mind. Even chaos should be regarded as extremely good news . . . . We can learn to accept our states as part of the patterns of mind, without question, without reference back to the scriptures, without help from credentials, directly acknowledging that they are so, and that these things are here and are true . . . . That is the Lion's Roar, that whatever occurs in the samsaric mind [the repetitive mind] is regarded itself as the path: everything is workable.

This openness is an amazing quality to bring to one's practice. In 1977, while I was teaching at the summer session of the Naropa Institute, my first book, *Living Buddhist Masters,* was published. When I gave Trungpa Rinpoche a copy, he gave me an autographed copy of his own book, *Cutting through Spiritual Materialism.* As an inscription, he wrote, "Dear Jack, Welcome back to the West." Then the inscription continued, "Can you hold the banner of the dharma? Let us celebrate!" This inscription was written in great big letters. To me, it's been a very meaningful inscription. Can I, can all of us, hold the banner of the dharma, and can we proclaim the lion's roar?

Trungpa Rinpoche not only taught the dharma in traditional forms, he also started a secular system of presenting the practice of meditation, called Shambhala Training, which taught people meditation without the complicated Tibetan and Buddhist framework around it. When Shambhala Training is presented, the hall where people practice is hung with beautiful banners, depicting some of the symbols of what he called the state of mind of the rising sun, the Great Eastern Sun. He said that you can look at the sun and see it as either rising or setting. You see it as setting when you're depressed and feeling sad, because everything changes and it's all impermanent; there's nothing to hold on to, and it's such a shame. Or you can see everything that arises as an opportunity. The whole spirit of Shambhala is to see what arises as an opportunity in practice.

Trungpa Rinpoche had a very droll sense of humor. He could be very funny, but his jokes were usually short one-liners rather than long stories. I remember one evening when he was talking about how the practice of meditation was to not remove oneself, to not shield or armor oneself from experience, to not hide in a box or a cave or inside our fancy car or whatever. He used all kinds of metaphors for hiding from our experience, such as being inside our house and turning up the heat or the air-conditioning and closing the curtains to try to make ourselves feel safe. He said the way of the warrior, or the bodhisattva, was to have no distance between ourselves and our experience. After he finished speaking, someone raised his hand and said, "No distance? Well, what if there are circumstances where things are fearful, difficult, or dangerous?" The questioner went on for a long time. And Trungpa looked back at him and said, very simply, "No distance." Then he picked up his glass and raised it to the questioner, and he said, "Good luck, sir." And everyone laughed. That was an ending line he often used: "Good luck, madam." "Good luck, sir."

So the quality of brilliance in Rinpoche's teaching was this quality of radiating freedom like the rising sun, which illuminates a path for us. In his teachings, there was this unshakable encouragement to proceed— not out of self-confirmation, not to make ourselves into some bigger, stronger ego, but rather to be willing to stay with our experience as it presents itself, to see whatever arises as practice, and to move forward.

SHOWING THE WAY OF OPENNESS

This leads into the second quality that Chögyam Trungpa manifested in his life, which is available to all of us, as much as when he was alive. This is the quality of openness, or showing the open way, a quality of fearlessness in practice. In the 1970s, Rinpoche wrote about "dharmas without blame," *dharmas* not meaning only "the law or the teachings" but also as a term for all the elements of body and mind that make up experience. He said that all the dharmas, or the elements that arise, "are without blame because there was no manufacturer of dharmas." He continued:

Dharmas are simply what is. Blame comes from an attitude of security, identifying with certain reservations as to how things are. Having this attitude, if a spiritual teaching does not supply us with enough patches we are in trouble. The Buddhist teaching not only does not supply us with any patches, it destroys them. As ego's patches are destroyed, there comes a point where relating to the teaching means the continual death of ego. . . . Therefore the teaching of dharmas without blame should be regarded as good news. It seems that it is good news, utterly good news, because there is no choice. When you see it clearly, there is no choice whatsoever. Even praise and blame, fear and difficulty, are the conditioned experiences of a beautiful patchwork.

In the same spirit, he goes on to talk about "*buddhadharma* without credentials," which means not getting a PhD, not making oneself into a professional meditator, not turning spiritual practice into a thing that distances us from the world. His image for this is of the child:

The child's world has no beginning or end.
To him, colors are neither beautiful nor ugly.
The child's nature has no preconceived notion of birth and death.
The golden mountain is solid and unchanging.
The ruby sun is all-pervading.
The crystal moon watches over millions of stars.
The child exists without preconceptions.

Rinpoche taught this quality of openness, of finding within your own mind, within your own experience, a willingness to relate to whatever presents itself. The curriculum at Naropa included psychology and philosophy, music and art, poetry and dance. Especially in the early years, Naropa was really an expression of the breadth of his vision of dharma. It was very colorful. The banners were colorful; the way the people dressed was colorful. Gradually, they went from hippie madras and paisley to three-piece suits with a cocktail in one hand and a cigarette in the other. But there was always a real sense of theater and play with everything Rinpoche did. With anything he did, he was willing to engage in life and to play with it as a part of practice. It was anything but dull.

Out of his early talks at Naropa, Rinpoche wrote a wonderful book about the practice of Tibetan tantra called *Journey without Goal: The Tantric Wisdom of the Buddha*. Although he mentioned various tantric exercises and visualizations and so forth, the main message of his book was to encourage a willingness to touch the raw feelings of our life. The highest goal or stage of tantra is working directly with passions, fears, greed, and aggression—the emotions that fuel our action, the feelings themselves. He taught a willingness to open to all of these things. From one perspective in Buddhism, difficult emotions can be seen as hindrances and defilements, things that we get caught up in and wish to free ourselves from. However, from the point of view of the teachings of the bodhisattva, these are all qualities that have promise in them. According to how Trungpa Rinpoche taught the dharma, the way of practice wasn't to see that the things that make up our personality are a problem, but rather to see that they're part of the fabric and pattern of being, and that they become workable and in fact usable as we become wiser. Part of the playfulness of Trungpa Rinpoche was that he saw not only the difficulties but also the potential in all of the aspects of practice.

So in addition to the brightness of his teaching, there was this openness, a willingness to engage with life and play with its elements. The path of the bodhisattva in the dharma is not to withdraw from life, but to go investigate the mind and discover that which is timeless, compassionate, and free, and to bring that into manifestation in every realm of the world.

THE POWER OF DEVOTION

The next quality that Rinpoche represented was devotion. When his teachers, Dilgo Khyentse Rinpoche and the Sixteenth Gyalwa Karmapa, came to America, it was beautiful to see how respectfully and kindly he served them. In a text called *The Sadhana of Mahamudra,* which he wrote in a cave in Bhutan in the 1960s, he talks about the dark ages of the dharma and how the winds of sectarian bitterness blow between the different countries and the sects of the buddhadharma. He says that even though the dharma has been proclaimed by the Buddha and carried on by many great teachers and lamas over centuries, people get lost in the philosophy, in the psychology, in the sects, in the territoriality of it, and the true essence is often lost. Then he goes on to pray that those who receive the teachings of dharma in this age of difficulty will take them and use them to the very best of their abilities. It is a deeply devotional text that calls for wisdom in a heartfelt way. Its spirit is carried in a poem that Rinpoche and his students translated from the Tibetan, which is called, "Intensifying Devotion in One's Heart: The Supplication 'Crying to the Gurus from Afar.'" The poem says in part,

Death is certain to come, but I am unable to take this to heart.
The dharma truly benefits, but I am unable to practice it properly.
Karma and its result are certainly true, but I do not properly
   discriminate
what to accept and reject.
Mindfulness and awareness are certainly necessary, but not
   stabilizing
them, I am swept away by distractions.
Guru, think of me; look upon me quickly with compassion.

Grant your blessings so that I maintain undistracted mindfulness. . . .
Grant your blessings so that genuine devotion arises in me.
Grant your blessings so that I glimpse the natural state.
Grant your blessings so that insight is awakened in my heart.
Grant your blessings so that I uproot confusion.
Grant your blessings so that I attain buddhahood in one lifetime.

This text was originally composed by Jamgon Kongtrul Lodro Thaye, who was an earlier incarnation of Trungpa Rinpoche's root guru, or main teacher. In embodying one's practice, these kinds of supplications are recited over and over again, evoking a great sense of devotion by crying to the gurus from afar. Rinpoche talks about the quality of devotion in another way in *Shambhala: The Sacred Path of the Warrior.* He talks about devotion as the path of practice leading to the birth of a tender heart of sadness. The opening and the devotion that arise out of practice is a devotion to the dharma, to the truth, to one's teachers, to one's self, one's own being, and then through that to all the world. Rinpoche says that the practice of a warrior gives birth to a tender heart of sadness, which he likens to a reindeer who is just beginning to sprout horns. They are fuzzy and raw, and they kind of hurt. At first, the reindeer can't quite figure out what these little things on his head are for. Yet, as they grow harder and more magnificent, the reindeer discovers that he should have horns. In the same way, the warrior opens his or her heart and begins to realize that, in fact, one's heart should be able to touch all things in the world. In another place in that book, he talks about how opening the heart leaves it exposed, like a piece of raw meat. You become so sensitive that you are touched by even a mosquito landing on you. The quality of opening oneself in this way is not particularly dramatic. You're not going to weep; it's not like hearing Beethoven's Ninth Symphony. It's much more ordinary and much more human, and in that way, even more special.

Trungpa Rinpoche was a genuinely warm and charming person. He had a very big sangha, and at times it was difficult to get to see him because he was so busy. However, when one could be with him, there was a tremendous sense of warmth, caring, ease, and charm. During the first summer at Naropa, I remember going to his office to be with him. I expected to see pictures of the Karmapa and of Jamgon Kongtrul and of all the lamas of his lineage, but I didn't notice any at all. There was only one picture on the wall in his office, and it was of Shunryu Suzuki Roshi, the founder of the San Francisco Zen Center. Rinpoche met Suzuki Roshi when he first arrived in America, and they became great friends for a time, until Roshi died. I asked Trungpa Rinpoche about that picture, and he said that it was an amazing thing that he should come to America to meet his father. He said this in the most loving and respectful way. It wasn't like working something out with your father, but just that here was somebody who really loved and accepted him as he was, and saw his greatness even in the very earliest years. I was impressed by Rinpoche's devotion to Suzuki Roshi. Rinpoche had this tremendous sense of a great heart. The power of his devotion inspired other people to participate or to join in.

UNCOMPROMISING DISCIPLINE

Another quality Trungpa Rinpoche expressed was an uncompromising discipline. When he was first teaching at Tail of the Tiger (now called Karmê Chöling Meditation Center) in Vermont in 1970, he would just hang out with people. If they were taking LSD, he sometimes would take some too. If they were listening to music, or talking about transcendental consciousness, he would join in the discussion. Whatever people were doing in those early hippie days, he would get down and hang out and be willing to participate. In addition to the rural scene at Tail of the Tiger, a center grew in Boulder, Colorado. A lot of people came because they were intrigued by the stories of this open-minded Tibetan lama who would hang out with you and speak about dharma in simple, everyday language. There was very little formal practice taking place.

After a couple of years, he called his students together, especially the ones who were key in running his community, and said, "Now we will all sit two hours a day." Many of them thought he was joking. This was radically different from what they'd come to expect. In the first years, he attracted a collection of poets and artists and many other people who would never have gone to study with a regular Buddhist teacher. These were people who wouldn't be caught within miles of an official religion. Yet somehow, through his art and his calligraphy and his visionary works and his poems and his willingness to just get down and play with everybody, he attracted this remarkable group of people. There were theater people, scientists, and artists, and they were all there thinking that the dharma was some kind of groovy picnic out in the country where you talked about meditation in action, or something like that. And then Rinpoche said, "You will now sit two hours a day." They couldn't believe it. In the years that followed he strongly encouraged everyone who wished to stay in the community to do a one-week retreat two or three times a year, and he suggested that anyone who didn't have a family should do a one-month retreat every year. His students were shocked. But they did it.

When Chögyam Trungpa first came to North America, he gave instruction in mindful sitting practice. For three or four years, people were working with the breath and basic sitting practices that are very similar to vipassana practice. In 1973, the year before he founded Naropa and a year before the head of his lineage, Gyalwa Karmapa, made his first visit to America, Rinpoche accepted one hundred students for a three-month seminary in which he introduced the formal practice of tantra, or Vajrayana, for the first time in America. He always insisted that his students continue to regard sitting as the basic, fundamental practice, but he also introduced them to what the Tibetans call *ngondro,* the preliminaries of Vajrayana practice, which include one hundred thousand full prostrations (from standing to lying out on the ground and back again to standing), one hundred thousand repetitions of a purification mantra, one hundred thousand visualizations of a mandala offering, and one million seed or devotional mantras. This is the initial practice for anyone undertaking the Tibetan vajrayana path of training. At that point, he said to all his students, "You must now do your ngondro, the entire set of preliminaries," which for most people takes one to five years—sometimes longer. Amazingly, there were more than three thousand people in his community who went from talking about the dharma and having a good old time to learning meditation practice and attending and then undertaking the full training of the Tibetan path of practice. When they finished their one hundred thousand prostrations and all the other preliminaries, they went on to do the dedicated practices of various Tibetan *sadhanas.* I marvel at Rinpoche's skillful means of attracting people and then gradually seducing them, convincing them to willingly do more and more genuine practice.

He was quite uncompromising. In his foreword to my first book, *Living Buddhist Masters,* Rinpoche said that meditation begins by slowing down the speed of our culture and of neurotic mind. He spoke of meditation as an especially important discipline for the twentieth century. He wrote that "the age of technology would like also to produce a spiritual gadgetry—a new, improved spirituality guaranteed to bring quick results. Charlatans manufacture their version of the dharma, advertising miraculous, easy ways, rather than the steady and demanding personal journey which has always been essential to genuine spiritual practice." He truly knew this, and over the years he inculcated this understanding in the members of his community.

As I mentioned earlier, at one large talk in Berkeley, when many people came to listen to him, he was, as usual, very late in arriving. He told us, "If you want your money back, it's all right. Just go to the door and ask for it back. It's quite fine. In fact, if you haven't started the spiritual path, best not to begin! It's difficult and you have to face all kinds of things that you won't like. As far as the ego is concerned, it is one insult after another." And so he said, quite seriously, "If you don't start, you'll probably be better off. Best not to begin. But if you do start, best to finish!" Now that you have started, what else are you going to do? Go back and cultivate greed, hatred, and delusion? He had this great sense of humor and earthiness, with discipline about it all.

When we were in the very first summer session at Naropa, there were two big evening classes that alternated: Ram Dass taught on Mondays and Wednesdays, and Trungpa Rinpoche taught on Tuesdays and Thursdays, or something like that. Two thousand people would gather in the main hall. Ram Dass would come and teach about love and surrender, and we would sing Hindu songs and chant *kirtan* and get high on *bhakti*, opening the heart. It was great. That was Monday nights. Then Tuesday nights we'd come back. Trungpa would be a little late, and when he arrived, he would just sit there quietly for a long time. Then he would give a simple talk about how practice really meant being where you are, coming down to earth, not getting lost in all the hoopla of Eastern mysticism. He was sort of making fun of all the things that Ram Dass was doing. And then on Wednesday nights, Ram Dass would come back and talk about his guru and the yogas of the Bhagavad Gita, and we would all sing together and get high and dance with devotion and so forth. And then Thursday nights Trungpa would come back again and say, "Impermanence. The fact of death. Remember that there's also suffering in life." This went on week after week. It was driving a lot of people crazy. Finally, one night, someone raised his hand after Trungpa gave his lecture and said, "Ram Dass has been talking to us about what great power there is in the grace of the guru, and that to surrender to a guru allows you to open to the spirit of grace, the grace of God. Is there anything in Buddhism that corresponds to this sense of God's grace?" Chögyam Trungpa sat there quietly for a minute, and then he looked up and said, "Yes." This surprised everyone. Then he smiled. "Patience." That was all he said.

Trungpa was unswerving in his teaching of the dharma. He put it out directly. He taught people to practice with a great deal of discipline, year after year. He taught them to make practice a part of daily life. He taught that practice can include group and solitary retreats, long periods of meditation, short forms of practice, and studying the dharma as well. He taught that we should be willing to investigate all the possible avenues of practice and find the power and the strength of the dharma from our own practice and bring it alive in our being. I believe, as he did, that whoever undertakes a genuine practice of buddhadharma will realize the deepest truths of the Buddha's enlightenment. Whether we practice vipassana or vajrayana, we can discover the meaning of the Buddha's awakening very directly, if we're willing stay present even for one day. In sitting and walking and eating with meticulous attention, we can see that the five processes or *skandhas* (form, feeling, perception, mental formations, and consciousness) are empty of the self, that they are ungraspable, like a river. When we rest in awareness, we will see that our whole being is an ever-changing process that's ungraspable and not at all separate from what is around us. This is apparent to any person who practices deeply. All of us can touch this timeless and liberating understanding. It is our buddha nature. Trungpa Rinpoche communicated an uncompromising belief in our own awake nature, in our capacity to touch what the Buddha and every other great sage has discovered.

A MYSTERIOUS GENIUS

The final quality that I think of as expressed by Chögyam Trungpa is the quality of mystery. He was one of the most enigmatic people I have ever met. He was clearly a genius. He was a beautiful calligrapher; he wrote plays; he wrote some wonderful poetry. He was interested in photography; he was interested in science. He started a university. He started an enormous church. He wrote a brilliant best-selling book, *Cutting through Spiritual Materialism,* based on his first teachings in America. He looked around and saw that people in this country were misusing spiritual practice, which was intended to lead to freedom from self and freedom from self-involvement and self-delusion. Instead they were using spiritual practice as an imitation, to create the persona of a spiritual person, using practice as a new kind of mask or identity. He recognized this as soon as he arrived here, and he wrote a book that goes to the very heart of spiritual practice. In the first year he was here, he taught how to use practice, not to make a new improved version of our personality, but to cut through clinging and awaken to the very essence of our being.

He was also peculiar. He drank; he was a womanizer. He was very open about these things. He wasn't one of those gurus that you read about in the paper who was supposed to be celibate and then you discovered later it wasn't true. As far as I know, there was nothing hidden about him. That was part of what was so mysterious. In the later years, he also organized his community as a kind of feudal kingdom. It was as if he were the ruler of a small country. His home was transformed into a court, and there were ministers and guards and princes and princesses and things like that. I actually enjoyed visiting it. I thought it was quite terrific theater, and yet all of this was mysterious.

I feel that he gave himself as fully to the West as any Buddhist teacher that I know. And he did so in a most remarkable way. He absorbed our culture and our language and our customs. He took who we are into himself and then said, "All right, let's play. Let's take the seed of the dharma and make it sparkle and come alive in the West." He did this more than any Buddhist teacher who's come to the West so far. And he did it with his heart and his body. He gave so much that you might say it killed him. Certainly, he died at a very young age. No doubt his drinking was a big part of that as well, but he gave himself in a remarkable way. There was something completely mysterious about all that: how this person who grew up as the head of some monasteries in a remote corner of Tibet could come to America and enter into our culture so completely.

Once, a student of Rinpoche's was ill in the hospital, and the doctors thought she was dying. She later recovered, but as she felt herself fading away, she thought of the meditation practice that she had done, and she didn't know what to do at the impending moment of her death. She was thinking of Trungpa Rinpoche and wondering how one should work with *The Tibetan Book of the Dead,* or how to approach dying. As she got very close to losing consciousness—she was seriously ill—all of a sudden, the form of Trungpa Rinpoche appeared to her, seated cross-legged on her chest, and began to give her practical instructions for dying. You can take that for what it's worth, but that was her mysterious experience. I believe in this level of teaching. It has been part of my own experience, with my own teachers and even with my own students. In any case, there is a mystery around Chögyam Trungpa Rinpoche, things that I don't understand at all, many quite remarkable things. He was such a combination of qualities.

A GREAT INSPIRATION

Trungpa Rinpoche's books are like a treasure trove. Opening one of his books is like going into the basement of some wealthy museum. Every few pages there is some beautiful new explanation of some aspect of the dharma. What his books and his teaching do is invite each of us directly to become inheritors of this majestic spiritual heritage. Some of the banners he designed had a drawing on them called "the knot of eternity." It's a linking of loops that go around and around and reconnect with one another. In Tibet the knot of eternity symbolizes the eternal and timeless dharma, the undying liberation of the heart. Whatever practice you undertake, you are invited to fulfill this practice and make it your own and to carry the banner of the dharma for yourself in this world.

Trungpa Rinpoche touched a lot of hearts and a lot of people. I loved him and I miss him. I'd love to go talk to him. He's one of the few people I feel I could sit down with and say, "This is what I'm doing and teaching and the kind of community we're trying to create, and what do you think?" and he would really understand. But somehow I feel his spirit to be here, perhaps as much as anyone I've ever known who's died. Someone asked him once whether he would come back as the twelfth Trungpa Tulku in his next reincarnation. I believe his answer was that he wasn't certain whether he was going to bother to come back in that form or not, but perhaps he would come back in Japan as a businessman or a scientist or something else more interesting.

He was a wonderful person, a remarkable teacher, and a great inspiration. Rick Fields, dharma student and poet, wrote, "This man caused more trouble and did more good than anyone I ever met." I hope that what I've shared about Trungpa Rinpoche gives you a sense of the empowerment that he gave to me and to many people around him: to take the dharma and bring it into our own lives and our own hearts and our own minds and to make it true for ourselves.

PART FOUR

Practicing the Dharma in the West

17

American Buddhism

Preserving and Adapting the Dharma

WHEN I WAS ASKED to write an introduction to the book *Buddhist America*, I began with this story:

One day an old woman who lived in New York went to her travel agent and asked him to get her a ticket to Tibet.

"Tibet?!" he exclaimed. "That's a long and difficult journey. You usually go to Miami for the winter. Why not just go there?"

"I must go see the Guru," she replied.

She got a ticket, flew to India, disembarked at the airport in Delhi, and went through all the difficulties of Indian Customs. When asked where she was going, she said, "To Tibet, to see the Guru."

After this, her journey continued by train across India to Gangtok, the capital of Sikkim. Here she secured a visa and traveled by bus up to the Tibetan border, where the guards asked, and again she replied, "I must go see the Guru."

They told her, "You can only say three words to him."

She replied, "I know. I know. I must go anyway."

She then journeyed with her bags across the Tibetan plateau by bus, by jeep, by horse caravan, and finally came to a large mountain with a monastery at the top. There was a long line of pilgrims and she joined the line. After three days of waiting, it was her turn.

The guard at the door reminded her, "Only three words, now."

"I know, I know," she said.

She entered the grand chamber and there sat the Guru, a lama with a wispy beard, wearing maroon robes. She sat down opposite him and looked directly at him. After a silent period she simply said, "Sheldon, come home."

Sheldon has now been home for more than thirty years. He has been building Buddhist centers and teaching Buddhist meditation in every corner of our continent. He is engaged in the great task of North American Buddhism: bringing the heartfelt practices and awakening of the Buddha to Western soil, and teaching the dharma of liberation in skillful forms for contemporary times. In this chapter, I wish to reflect on how Buddhism is changing as it adapts to our North American culture.

First, starting in the 1850s there were traditional Buddhist temples for large communities of Japanese, Chinese, and later Thai, Cambodian, and other Buddhist people who had immigrated to this country. In the past fifty years a thousand new Buddhist centers and practice groups have sprouted up. This is a growing generation of newly inspired Buddhists for whom the dharma has already brought joy and understanding into hundreds of thousands of people's lives. Though predominantly well educated and often middle class, the new North American Buddhists are no longer a small, youthful minority. They are young and old, men, women, and children, spread across every state of the union and every province of Canada. And while it is too early to know fully what form this new North American Buddhism will take, there are many remarkable developments that have begun to give it the flavor of its new home. Let us consider these.

LAY BUDDHISM

Each time in the past that Buddhism has been integrated into new cultures, it has evolved, and new forces, flavors, and qualities have been brought to its practice. Zen Buddhism has developed along with elements of Japanese aesthetics, Shinto nature religion, and samurai culture. Vajrayana Buddhism in Tibet has been flavored by the shamanic Bon traditions and Tibet's unique blend of tantric and yogic mastery. Even with this great variety of cultures and lineages, Asian Buddhist practice has predominantly been kept alive by renunciate monks, and the most authentic Buddhist practice has been preserved in monasteries, where older monks live removed from the everyday society around them. For centuries in Asia, Buddhism has had a monastic, masculine, ascetic, and somewhat patriarchal flavor.

While many generations have benefited greatly from the excellent training received in these monasteries (and we certainly hope that a number of well-run and nonsexist monasteries for monks and nuns will grow in this country, providing opportunities for those who wish to experience the life of renunciation), it appears that monasteries with monks and nuns will not be the major focus of Buddhism in America. Instead the focus is shifting to the lay community, which is at the center of practice here. Western Buddhism is being taught, practiced, and developed by committed, nonmonastic communities.

In this predominantly lay Western Buddhism, which includes Vipassana, Vajrayana, and Zen practitioners, several new forces bringing integration and the opening of these tradition are at work. There are four key themes that I have noticed developing in the past twenty-five years.

SHARED PRACTICE

Buddhism in Asia has been divided for centuries, kept within separate traditions and lineages. American Buddhists have already begun to actively learn from one another's traditions. Many Zen masters and their students have been avidly studying the mindfulness and loving-kindness practices central to vipassana retreats. Most vipassana teachers have also practiced with Tibetan lamas and Zen masters. The American Vajrayana tradition has been profoundly influenced by teachings and practice forms from Zen and Vipassana. This is a remarkable development, one that is perhaps unparalleled since the ancient Nalanda University of early Buddhism. For the first time in thousands of years, Buddhists of each school have direct access to the practices and teachings of every other great tradition. New learnings, cross-fertilization, shared practices, and a more universal ground of Buddhist understanding have already grown. Distant strands of Buddhism are coming together in America.

With this have come unprecedented gatherings of Buddhist teachers from all traditions. In the past decades I have participated in and sponsored a series of meetings with many of the senior teachers in the West. We have met regularly in Dharamsala with the Dalai Lama, and at places like Spirit Rock Center and San Francisco Zen Center, bringing hundreds of teachers together. We have exchanged teachings and practices, considered what dharma approaches work best in the

West, confided in one another about our common problems, and gained insight in one another's company. The teachers who gather at these meetings are often struck by the remarkable similarities in their challenges and by the great help that their collective wisdom and practice experience can offer to one another.

Even the greatest remaining divide in North American Buddhism, the gap between the ethnic temples (such as the Burmese, Chinese, Thai, and Korean) and the quite separate "American" centers, is beginning to respond to this shared practice. Ethnic centers have primarily served immigrant communities with traditional Asian languages and dharma culture, most often offering devotional forms of Buddhism. But in recent years a number of ethnic temples, such as Lien Hoa Buddhist Monastery in Irving, Texas, and Wat Buddhawararam in Denver, Colorado, have begun reaching out to the broader American Buddhist community by sponsoring meditation classes and including nonethnic American teachers and programs. Some of the largest American centers have begun to reciprocate. We are learning to support one another.

DEMOCRATIZATION

Buddhism is becoming more democratic in the context of our American democracy. Traditionally, most Buddhist communities in Asia were hierarchical and authoritarian. Wisdom, knowledge, and practice were handed down from elders to juniors, and the running of monasteries and the sangha (the community of monastic practitioners) rested in the hands of the master or of a small core of senior monks. What they decided was the way things were, and there was no questioning of their authority; students just followed. In North America this has begun to change. Western Buddhists are trained to think and understand for themselves and are less suited to the hierarchical models of Asia. At present in Western Buddhist communities there are strong forces for democratization and for participation in decision making by the whole community. Rather than hierarchical structures, there are structures of mutual support and appreciation. As students and teachers have matured, our Buddhist communities are no longer totally teacher-centered. Many now are run by elected boards or use the ancient Buddhist practice of council, drawing on the collective wisdom of a group of teachers and committed students. The participation and inclusion of many dedicated voices will be a great vitalizing factor and a major force for change in Buddhism as it evolves in our country.

FEMINIZATION

A third and perhaps the most important force affecting Buddhism in America has been the force of feminization. In Asia, through the monasteries and older monks, Buddhism has been primarily a masculine and patriarchal affair: masculine by virtue of the fact that it has been mostly men who have preserved and transmitted it, and more deeply patriarchal in that its language and traditions have been predominantly in the masculine mode. Buddhism has been a practice of the mind, of Logos, of understanding, through striving and attainment, of gaining enlightenment through conquering oneself. These elements—a masculine community dominated by the mind, logic, striving, the patriarchal structures—did not allow for a full participation of women, and discounted feminine values. All of these are now being confronted by the powerful force of feminine consciousness that is growing in Western culture. This consciousness is already bringing about a softening and an opening of the Buddhist spirit and practice that allows for strength of mind and the masculine element as well as for the tenderness and earthiness of the feminine element. Not only is there a clear movement to abandon the superficial structures of sexism and patriarchy, there is also a more profound movement to develop the dharma as a practice of relationship with the body, the community, and the earth, and to stress interdependence and healing rather than conquering or abandoning. The language of the dharma is becoming more feminine and the leadership is as well. The large number of mature women who are now teaching in all American traditions is a visible reflection of this revitalizing feminization that is taking place.

INTEGRATION

The fourth major theme as Buddhism develops in the West is integration. In Asia, Buddhism was primarily characterized by ordained priests, monks, hermits, and forest dwellers who withdrew from worldly life into monasteries, ashrams, caves, and temples, where they created circumstances of simplicity and renunciation for their practice. The rest of the Buddhists, the great majority of laypeople, did not actually practice meditation but remained devoted supporters of the monks. However, here in the West, the laypeople are not content to be simply devotional supporters of other people's practice. Almost all North American students involved want to actually practice the path of liberation. The most frequently asked question in my more than four decades of teaching has been, "How can we live the practice in our American lives?" Western practice will emphasize integration, not a withdrawal from the world but a discovery of wisdom within the midst of our lives. North American Buddhists have already begun to develop the means to integrate and live the practice as householders, as family people, as people with jobs who still wish to partake of the deepest aspects of the dharma, not by moving away to caves but by applying the practice in their daily lives.

In practice, this spirit of integration has already led to new dharma forms, such as family retreats, shorter Zen *sesshin* practice periods, "sandwich retreats" (two weekends and the weekday evenings in between), urban study groups, "secularized" dharma training, such as the Shambhala centers, right livelihood groups, and much more. Integration and shared practices are being fostered by a dharma communications revolution, with popular journals such as *Tricycle, Shambhala Sun,* and *Inquiring Mind;* on the Internet by groups such as Cyber Sangha and DharmaNet; in a Vietnamese dharma ham radio network in Texas; and in Rev. Kubose's daily Dial-the-Dharma phone teachings in Chicago and a dozen popular and active Buddhist blogs.

Another powerful new stream in integrated Western dharma has been called Engaged Buddhism, encouraged by founders like Thich Nhat Hanh, Joanna Macy, Robert Aitken Roshi, and others. Engagement in compassionate action in our society as a practice has flourished. The Buddhist Peace Fellowship, which is a hub of this activity, catalogs the growing areas of direct service, from prison dharma projects and Buddhist hospices to nonviolent peace crusades, from Buddhist environmental groups to efforts to secure justice for peoples at risk throughout the world. Zen masters such as Bernie Tetsugen Glassman Roshi have created "street retreats" and projects to deal with homelessness and AIDS. American Buddhist communities are also involved in expressing their gratitude by bringing aid to Buddhist countries in trouble: to Tibet, Burma, Bangladesh, Cambodia, and Vietnam.

Buddhist trainings have made a significant entrance into mainstream American culture through teachers such as Jon Kabat-Zinn, whose work brings mindfulness training to hundreds of hospitals, and Dan Goleman, whose work with Emotional Intelligence theory has offered dharma principles for use in thousands of schools and corporations.

Along with these sweeping changes, Buddhist practitioners across America have been integrating many of the best tools of modern Western psychology into the practice. This powerful change brings a new emphasis on emotional health and wisdom into our personal lives together with the more absolute aspects of traditional dharma practice. The psychological and the spiritual, the personal and the universal, have become widely understood as complementary dimensions of the dharma liberation.

All of these themes are becoming forces in Buddhist practice as it approaches the twenty-first century in the West. This adaptation is taking place much more quickly here than it did in China and Tibet. For example, when Buddhism went from India to China, it underwent many centuries of integration with an indigenous Chinese culture steeped in Confucian and Taoist values before it became a part of the Chinese way. Here, because of the speed of communication and the rapid pace of our culture, the first developments of a unique North American Buddhism, instead of taking centuries, have become apparent in only decades.

HONEST ASSESSMENT

It is not always an easy process, and it has been a struggle for many of us—Buddhist teachers and students alike—to sort out what is valuable and ought to be preserved from Asian traditions and what is merely a "container," a structure that could be more suitably reshaped or cast off. Over the years I have struggled with this a great deal. Like a number of other dharma teachers, I had even considered quitting organized Buddhism. Here I'm not speaking of the teachings of the dharma or the discipline for renunciates; nor of the place of silence and celibacy in practice; nor of precepts, forms of bowing, or ceremonies; nor of the hardships and surrender that are, in fact, valuable parts of spiritual practice. What I have struggled with are the limitations of Buddhism as an organized religion; with the sectarianism and attachments of many of the students and teachers involved; and with the territoriality, the patriarchy, and the excessive life-denying tendencies of practice that can leave it, and some students, disconnected from their hearts.

For me, this struggle began in Asia. While traveling and practicing there, I discovered that Buddhism was a great religion just like any other—Christianity, Judaism, Hinduism, or Islam. I saw that the majority of Buddhists in Asia do not actually practice. At best, they go to temple devotionally, the way many Westerners go to church. They go once a week or once a month to hear a sermon or a few moral rules, or to leave a little money to make some merit for a better birth in the next life. In fact, even among the monasteries of such countries as Thailand, Burma, Sri Lanka, and Japan, I discovered that only a fraction of the monks and nuns actually practice—perhaps only five or ten percent. The rest are priests (some of whom are very kindly) who live simply, study and learn the scriptures (preserving the tradition, but rarely practicing it), or tend the community as monastic schoolteachers or village elders who perform ceremonies and live a renunciate existence. Other monks become part of a hierarchy of bishops, archbishops, and councils of elders, who are usually more involved in the organization of the religion than they are in the practice of liberation taught by the Buddha.

Amid this popular level of religion it was inspiring and refreshing to discover that there is also a small group of monasteries where the practices of liberation are kept alive and open to sincere followers of the Buddha's way. Meditation trainings, systematic practices of inner purification, mindful discipline, conscious development of loving-kindness and compassion, service, study, and surrender were all part of these most dedicated communities.

But even in the wisest communities it remained necessary to separate the universal teachings from the cultural container, and to overlook the problems and difficulties of certain teachers and practice temples that were "mixed bags," where good practice was mixed with power trips, blind allegiance, or other delusions. Perhaps this sorting-out process is always necessary for the maturing of spiritual students.

The struggle is always more than worth it, for the heart of the Buddha's awakening is an island of sanity in a world of delusion and suffering. What an extraordinary vision he had that night under the Bodhi tree. How unutterably marvelous that one person could sit down and see into the truth of life so deeply, with such great clarity and with such overwhelming compassion, and that this one night's vision would have the power to affect one and a half billion human beings on this earth for twenty-five hundred years. All of us involved in Buddhist practice have been touched by the depth and immediacy of this vision and inspired to continue in the face of both the external and the internal difficulties that are a part of any genuine spiritual path.

In order to have access to these teachings, there were some important lessons I had to learn. One of the first was how to "take what's good." I had teachers who were wise and impeccable, such as Ajahn Chah and Mahasi Sayadaw. And then I had other teachers who were skilled in certain yogic attainments, healing practices, or meditation techniques, but who could be unconscious or unkind, even harmful to students. When I expected them to be wise in every way, I was terribly disappointed.

Finally, it dawned on me that it wasn't necessary to expect everything to be perfect about a teacher, that I could simply take from them what was good. One was an excellent guide for certain meditations but also mean-spirited and judgmental. I learned I could take the good teachings and leave the rest for him. If a teacher had some level of realization or valuable practices, I could take advantage of it, and if his wisdom didn't encompass many other parts of his life, so be it. What a relief to learn that one can take what is skillful and leave the rest.

In the same way, it will take courage on the part of North American Buddhists to face the areas where Buddhism in its structures and practices is not working. To make a place for the dharma that is open and true, we will need to look honestly at what brings awakening and where we are asleep. We will also have to attend to such difficult issues as abuse of power and authority, alcohol, sexuality, and money; and attend to our political and social responsibilities. Already upheavals over teacher behavior and abuse have occurred at dozens of the major Buddhist centers in America. These are some of the problems that our teacher conferences had to face. Yet, if we respond with courage, these very upheavals can serve to focus our attention on those aspects of our communities that need more consciousness. They can help us build wise practice in such areas as sexuality, human relationships, and environmental responsibility, where the expression of Buddhist tradition has been weak or medieval. Similarly, we have to examine ourselves. So many of us come to practice wounded, lonely, or in fear, wanting a loving family as much as enlightenment. That is fine, for we can use the power of practice and the sangha to support, heal, and awaken. However, many people also get stuck perpetuating their neuroses in Buddhism itself, abusing practice as a means of escape, using Buddhism to hide from difficult parts of their lives, trying to create an idealistic world, or not growing and living in the world as mature individuals. The strength of our dharma will depend on the honesty with which we address these issues and on our ability to preserve what is good and leave the rest.

Those of us who helped bring Insight Meditation to America chose to simplify the practices we learned in an attempt to offer a clear, straightforward form of Buddhist practice in the West. We left much of the Eastern culture, ritual, and ceremony behind in Asia. That is not because we don't value it (I am a great lover of ritual), but we felt that for Americans it was an unnecessary barrier. It seemed to us that for our culture, the simplicity and straightforwardness of mindfulness and loving-kindness practice would speak best to the heart of those seeking practice. And, in fact, the very simplicity of Insight Meditation retreats, without foreign costumes, rituals, and bowing, or the necessity of joining an organized church, has appealed to many thousands of people over the years. Of course, there are those who prefer or benefit from practice that includes more ritual and sacred ceremony. Fortunately, the plurality of Buddhism will provide that, too. We are blessed to have so many ways made available to us.

We will need to conserve the essential texts, core practices, and rich array of trainings in each of these traditions for future generations. This will involve the dedication of a new generation of Western scholars, committed lay practitioners, and monastics. But conserving the tradition outwardly is not enough. What matters is that we also find a genuine path of practice and do it fully, that we take a practice and go to its very depths, which means going to the very depths of our own being. We must each find a practice that inspires us and follow it over and over again in whatever fashion makes it come alive in our body, in our heart, and in our mind. By doing this, we rediscover the greatness of heart, the truth, and the mystery that were discovered by the Buddha and that he declared should be openhanded and available to all who wish to practice.

Such practice, the practice of liberation, is not exclusive. There is no one tradition, one way, or one particular kind of practice that will awaken people. Although meditation practice seems especially beneficial for our times, there are many ways to realize truth. Even though D. T. Suzuki was a foremost exponent of Zen, he wrote that many more Buddhists were liberated through the practices of devotional Buddhism than through all the insight of Ch'an and Zen put together. In the traditional Pali scriptures that describe the Buddha's teaching, most people did not become awakened through the systematic process of meditation, but were opened by simply hearing the universal truths he proclaimed. When the Buddha described the truths of impermanence and emptiness and invited listeners to embrace that which is deathless, people became enlightened. As the Buddha described the happiness and freedom that comes from letting go, many beings were awakened. Yet these truths are universal and are held by other great traditions as well; enlightenment or liberation is never the possession of any one teacher or lineage.

What is unique about Buddhism is the clarity and directness of the Buddha's expression of enlightenment and the great number of skillful means that he taught to enable others to realize it. In his forty-five years of teaching and during the twenty-five hundred years of Buddhist history, a vast range of practices for liberation have been taught, encompassing many lands and many cultures. The Buddha himself taught hundreds of techniques of awareness practice, concentration meditation, discipline, and surrender. Since his time, the masters who followed have elaborated even more fully. Now that all these techniques are coming to America, how can we best receive this rich dharma feast?

First we must beware of sectarianism. The history of Buddhism unfortunately contains a great deal of sectarian pain. Zen masters put down other Zen masters. Lamas defend the turf of their own Tibetan sects, waging spiritual—if not actual—warfare with one another. The Sri Lankans or Burmese or Thais denigrate one another's practice. Buddhism has become divided into greater, lesser, and other numerous vehicles. This sectarianism has existed since the time of the Buddha himself. From the day he died, sects began springing up based on different aspects of the dharma. Out of clinging, these sects and lineages have fought with one another and continue to do so to this day. Sectarianism grows from the idea that "our way is the best," and its divisiveness is actually rooted in misunderstanding and fear. Sectarianism is never true. As the third Zen Patriarch put it, "Distinctions arise from the clinging needs of the ignorant. There is one dharma, not many." Or as contemporary Buddhist poet Tom Savage writes, "Greater vehicle, lesser vehicle, all vehicles will be towed at owner's expense."

The many practices of Buddhism are like paths up a mountain— outwardly different approaches that are appropriate for different personalities and character types. Yet, through skillful guidance and practice, these paths can lead one to awakening and freedom at the summit of the mountain.

An early story of the Buddha helps us to understand this. It takes place while the Buddha is standing in a grove at one of his monasteries. A visitor remarks on how tranquil and beautiful the scene is with so many composed monks. The Buddha points to his great disciples and the students gathered around them. He notes that there are many ways that people are practicing. Pointing to Sariputta, the wisest of his disciples, he observes, "Those who have the propensity to practice through wisdom are gathered there with my wisest disciple, Sariputta. And there is my disciple Maha-Mogallana, foremost in psychic powers. Those whose propensities draw them to use psychic powers as a part of their path to realization are gathered with Maha-Mogallana. There is my great disciple, Upali, master of the Vinaya and the discipline, and those whose tendencies would benefit by that way of practice are gathered with him. There again is another great disciple and another group of students . . . ," and so on. It is not wise to judge one practice against another; in fact, this is a detriment to practice. Our task is simply to find a practice that touches our heart and to undertake it in a committed and disciplined way.

KINDNESS OF HEART, INNER STILLNESS, AND LIBERATING WISDOM

Our understanding of different practices is also helped by understanding the structure of the Buddhist path, by seeing its essence and how it functions to bring about human happiness and freedom. The essential path taught by the Buddha has three parts to it. The first is kindness of heart, a ground of fundamental compassion expressed through virtue and generosity. The second is inner stillness or concentration. The third aspect of all Buddhist practice is the awakening of liberating wisdom.

All Buddhist traditions include ways of expressing compassion through the nonharming of other beings and a generosity of heart. All Buddhist traditions offer ways to quiet the mind, nurturing concentration, steadiness, stillness, and clarity or depth of mind. And all Buddhist paths awaken insight and the transcendent wisdom of emptiness, fostering a wise and free understanding of body and mind. The practices leading to compassion, inner stillness, and wisdom are but means to the final freedom of the heart. As the Buddha himself said, "The purpose of my teaching of the holy life of the dharma is not for merit, nor good deeds, nor rapture, nor concentration, nor insight, but the sure heart's release. This and this alone is the reason for the teaching of the dharma." The purpose of the practices of virtue, kindness, nonharming, generosity, concentration, visualization, devotion, compassion, clarity of mind, understanding, and wisdom is to bring us to freedom.

As American Buddhism becomes more mature, it will inevitably follow the historical evolution that marked the dharma's changes in Asia. The earlier forms of Buddhism expressed the path of practice in primarily a renunciatory way. They saw the body and sexuality as impure and the mind and spiritual thoughts as pure, stressing the necessity of withdrawing from the world to embrace a life of solitude as a monk or a nun, emphasizing the need to get out of the rounds of rebirth to the cessation of nirvana, and so forth. As later Buddhist schools developed over the centuries, they shifted from a dualistic approach to a nondualistic one. As the nondualistic expression of Buddhism (which was also taught by the Buddha) grew in predominance, the emphasis shifted to the interdependence of all life and the importance of discovering nirvana in the midst of samsara, or a liberation from greed, hatred, and delusion in this very life and on this very earth.

This nondualistic spirit of dharma is particularly important in our times, in a world of turmoil threatened by war and ecological disaster. The mind is able to create weapons of mass destruction and ecological disasters only when it has split off from the heart and the body. If the mind were connected with the heart and the body, with this earth, with children, with cycles of nature, it would not be possible to abstractly plan the mathematics of nuclear arms or the destruction of our environment. A nondualistic understanding, and the wisdom of interdependence, compassion, and nongreed that it teaches, are essential for the very survival of our earth. While this nondualistic flavor is spreading throughout American practice, we must honor both the old and the new perspectives, for they are part of the whole.

Lest we see one as truly separate from another, Lama Govinda gives us the image of a seed and a tree as a way of connecting the variety of Buddhist practices presented in the West. Two thousand five hundred years ago Siddhartha Gautama, through his extraordinary realization, planted a seed of timeless wisdom and compassion. Over the centuries the seed has grown and produced an enormous and wonderful tree, which has a trunk and branches, flowers, and fruit. Some people claim that the roots are the true Buddhism. Others claim it's the fruit or the flowers. They will say, "No, it's the great Bodhisattva trunk of the tree," or "the fruit of Vajrayana," or "the roots of Theravada Buddhism." In fact, all parts of the tree support one another. The leaves give nourishment back to the roots, the roots draw in moisture and minerals, bringing nourishment up the trunk to the leaves, and they in turn provide support for the flowers and the fruit. It is all part of the whole, and to understand that is to see the creative and dynamic forces that were set loose from the seed of the Buddha's awakening.

PRESERVING AND ADAPTING

Historically, all major religions, including Buddhism, have contained a basic tension—one that persists as Buddhism comes to America. This is the tension between tradition or orthodoxy and adaptation or modernization. Many people involved in Buddhism see it as their purpose and their duty to preserve and sustain the sutras, the tradition, and the practices just as they were handed down in their lineage from the original teachings and the great masters of old, from the time of the Buddha. Others have found it important to adapt Buddhist practice to new cultures, finding skillful means of allowing access to and understanding of the great wisdom of Buddhism without presenting it in old, ungainly, and inaccessible forms. This tension has been present since the time of the Buddha himself. Since the first council held after the Buddha's death, there have been those great teachers whose main purpose was to preserve, as literally as possible, the practice, style, and teaching of the Buddha without losing any aspect of the original expression of the truth. At the same time, there have been masters and teachers in many cultures who have seen the need to translate and adapt these teachings. Both of these ways, like the great tree of Lama Govinda, are parts of a whole. The ability to adapt Buddhism without losing its essence is dependent on the depth of the tradition that has been preserved. Yet, awakening new followers and gaining support for the preservation and depth of practice require that practice become truly alive in new cultures and new times. Each part depends on the other. The very diversity of views, schools, and teachings is Buddhism's health, keeping it vital and true.

In the forty years of my own study, practice, and teaching of Theravada Buddhism, I have come to recognize very clearly that our tradition contains both—masters who emphasize close adherence to the twenty-five hundred years of Buddhist tradition and masters who insist that practice must also be current, as alive today as it was at the time of the Buddha. After helping to found one center (the Insight Meditation Society in Barre, Massachusetts), which is devoted in a beautiful way to traditional retreat practice, we have founded a center with a broader purpose in Marin County, California. Spirit Rock Meditation Center offers teachings that balance the traditional and integrative aspects of practice. One the one hand, it is a center that preserves a depth of practice through intensive retreats, traditional study, a hermitage, and so forth. On the other hand, the key need to integrate practice into our times is also addressed. We have teachings on right livelihood and service, on right speech and communication, as well as training in the development and expression of compassion in all aspects of life—through Buddhist peace work, through family life, through ecology. This integrative practice has also developed in many other Buddhist centers. We are learning that our practice is not just sitting, not just study, not just belief, but that it encompasses how we actually live, how well we love, and how much we can let go of our small self and care for this earth and all beings.

As Buddhism grows in North America, a wonderful new process is happening. All of us, as laypeople, as householders, want what was mostly the special dispensation of monks in Asia: the real practice of the Buddha. American laypeople are not content to go and hear a sermon once a week or to make merit by leaving gifts at a meditation center. Zen master Suzuki Roshi observed this when he wrote in his book *Zen Mind, Beginner's Mind,*

> Here in America we cannot define Zen Buddhists the same way we do in Japan. American students are not priests and yet not completely laymen. I understand it this way: that you are not priests is an easy matter, but that you are not exactly laymen is more difficult. I think you are special people and want some special practice that is not exactly priest's practice and not exactly layman's practice. You are on your way to discovering some appropriate way of life.

As lay Buddhists, we too want to live the realizations of the Buddha and bring them into our hearts, our lives, and our times. This is why so many Americans have been drawn to the purity of intensive vipassana retreats, or to the power of Zen sesshin, or to the one hundred thousand prostrations and three-year retreats of the Vajrayana tradition. Somehow we have an intuitive sense of the potential of human freedom and the heart of basic goodness—the timeless discovery of the Buddha.

We are drawn not just to study and understand it but to practice it, realize it, and live it in our lives. Practice always involves a great deal of struggle, for it means confronting ourselves, our fears, our territoriality, and our need for security. To do this skillfully, we can use the raft of Buddhism to carry us to the shore of liberation, but we must never mistake the raft for the shore. We are called to go beyond all clinging, beyond the small sense of self to that which is selfless and timeless. When we practice with devotion and a love for truth, we can find the limitless freedom and compassion of the Buddha in our very own heart.

As the many Buddhist traditions are shared by sincere American students, a new freshness, integrity, and questioning have grown. We are open to learning from one another. In my own teaching and practice, I have benefited enormously from the privilege of studying with great masters in the Tibetan and Zen traditions. Even though my own heart has found its home in the simplicity of Theravada mindfulness practice, I now discover myself teaching what Suzuki Roshi called "Hinayana practice with a Mahayana mind." In this spirit, my teaching has shifted from an emphasis on effort and striving to one of opening and healing. So many students come to practice wounded, conditioned to closing off and hating parts of themselves. For them, striving perpetuates their problems. Instead, we now begin by awakening the heart of compassion and inspiring a courage to live the truth as a deep motivation for practice. This heart-centered motivation draws together lovingkindness, healing, courage, and clarity in an interdependent way. It brings alive the compassion of the Buddha from the very first step.

I do not want to be too idealistic. There are many problems that Buddhist communities must face—unhealthy structures, unwise practices, misguided use of power, and so forth. Still, something new is happening on this continent. Buddhism is being deeply affected by the spirit of democracy, by feminization, by shared practice, and by the integration of lay life. A North American vehicle is being created. Already this vehicle draws on the best of the roots, the trunk, the branches, the leaves, the blossoms, and the fruits—all the parts of Buddhism—and it is beginning to draw them together into a wise and supportive whole.

Some years ago we had the privilege of a visit to the Insight Meditation Society by His Holiness, the sixteenth Gyalwa Karmapa, head of the Kagyu sect of Tibetan Buddhism. His Holiness the Karmapa came during one of our three-month retreats. He sat on a gilded throne in our meditation hall, surrounded by 150 yogis and students to whom he gave a dharma talk and ceremonial blessing. Our Indian teacher Dipa Ma Barua was also visiting IMS at the time. Because she did not speak English, as the Karmapa's Tibetan was being translated into English by his translators, that English was in turn translated into Bengali by hers.

After hearing a wonderful talk by the Karmapa on the Buddhist four noble truths and on the essential teachings of compassion and emptiness, Dipa Ma turned to me, put her hand on my knee, and exclaimed with delight, "He's a Buddhist!" As an Indian Buddhist master she had been going to the Buddha's enlightenment temple in Bodh Gaya for twenty years. There she lived right across the street from a Tibetan temple, had seen tens of thousands of Tibetan pilgrims and Tibetan lamas at the Bodhi tree in India during the many years of her practice, yet she had never heard their teachings in translation and had never really understood that, like her, they too were Buddhists.

The Tibetans, the Burmese, and the Japanese had been hidden from one another for centuries by the heights of mountainous terrain and by the barriers of language and culture. Their Buddhist traditions and masters have finally met one another in the great melting pot of our

North American culture. Chögyam Trungpa Rinpoche worked with Suzuki Roshi, His Holiness the Karmapa taught Dipa Ma, Joshu Sasaki Roshi and Kalu Rinpoche joined hands . (As the story goes, they met at an airport in Arizona without their translators and could only sit there, hold hands, and smile at each other for an hour.) And now a whole new generation of North American teachers is continuing to carry the lamp of the dharma as leaders of over one thousand Buddhist centers.

In the West we are seeing the awakening of the Buddha, and the Buddha is smiling very broadly, with the wisdom of Tibet, India, Japan, Thailand, Burma, and America all joined in. We have been given the treasury of Buddhist practices, a cornucopia of compassion and wisdom to nourish and awaken us to our True Nature. It is a remarkable time in the history of Buddhism. For every practitioner it is a privilege to be part of this process. May we carry the banner of the dharma wisely and offer its blessings to all.

18

This Fantastic, Unfolding Experiment

Establishing the Insight Meditation Society and Spirit Rock

THE THERAVADA LINEAGE—"the Way of the Elders"—is the earliest form of Buddhism, still practiced and kept alive in Southeast Asia and Sri Lanka. The Theravada tradition has a rich history and tremendous diversity. Within it is a wide and often contradictory variety of teaching approaches to dharma practice and liberation. There are devotional practices, renunciation practices, community practices, visualizations and mantras, healing traditions, and hundreds of forms of meditation. The good thing is the availability of this rich and vibrant array of skillful means in the tradition. But often a problem arises because of the way many of the teachers and followers cling to their own way as the only and best one. If you go to Thailand or to Burma, often teachers will say, "We have the purest lineage, dating from the time of the Buddha. We have the original sutras and the texts." In fact, the sutras weren't really written down for five or six hundred years after the Buddha, but these teachers believe their teachings are the unchanged, pure lineage brought there from very early India. However, if you take a few steps beyond the main centers, you will notice that the countryside in Burma, Thailand, and Cambodia contains ancient Mahayana and Vajrayana temples filled with incredible iconography from the whole range of Buddhist traditions. In fact, the various traditions have been exchanging teachings for millennia. Monks in Burma believe, "In

Burma we have always been the carriers of the original true way," even though the ascendancy of Theravada Buddhism in Burma began only a few hundred years ago. So the history of Buddhism generally, and Theravada Buddhism in particular, is actually a weaving of a number of different strands.

This diversity is one of the central dilemmas in my own spiritual life and has deeply informed how I have been teaching and how the dharma at the Insight Meditation Society in Barre, Massachusetts, and Spirit Rock have unfolded. I had many teachers, but the most central were two of the wisest Theravada teachers of the past century: one in Thailand, Ajahn Chah, and one in Burma, Mahasi Sayadaw. While they were both considered deeply enlightened, these teachers did not agree at all on what enlightenment was or how you attained it. In fact, they disagreed, each believing that the other was not teaching the real way to enlightenment.

When I went to Ajahn Chah's monastery, first as a layman and then as a monk, the main form of practice was to meditate a moderate amount—two, three, four hours a day—and then to practice the dharma of letting go of suffering as you lived and worked in your dharma community. The basic instruction was to quiet your mind enough so that you could see when there was suffering and recognize the patterns of greed, hatred, and delusion in which you were entangled in the world, then let them go. Meditation was the means to support mindfulness and loving-kindness throughout the day so that you could be free in any circumstance.

When I went to a monastery under Mahasi Sayadaw, the figure and ground were reversed. There wasn't any community practice; everything focused on silent retreat. Everything you did was in the service of one thing: silent meditation. You would meditate for fifteen or eighteen hours a day (as we do on intensive retreat now) in order to have certain deep experiences in meditation that would transform greed, hatred, and delusion.

Now, there were limitations in each of these systems. The problem I found at Ajahn Chah's monastery was that while he was a fantastic dharma teacher, he was not a very precise or detailed meditation teacher. The reason was simple: he wasn't that interested in meditation experiences. If you developed samadhi or entered the jhana stages of meditative absorption, he could teach you about them because he had practiced all the jhanas. But he wasn't really interested in that. However, I was. And after I trained with him for a while, I heard, "Oh, there is deeper and more systematic meditation training at these other places. Why don't you go try that and see what happens?"

So I went to a Mahasi monastery and trained with a famous monk, Asabha Sayadaw, who was quite skillful in teaching meditation but nevertheless turned out to be a very problematic teacher. I began very ardently, the way young men do, sitting and walking twenty hours a day, with minimal sleep. I did this for nearly a year and a half. With his instruction, all kinds of cool things began to happen. My body would dissolve into light, and I had all kinds of classic insights into emptiness, just like in the old texts. My progress in insight grew, and my understanding of impermanence and emptiness deepened, and I thought, "Wow, I know this is what the Buddha meant." But then I'd looked out from the window of my cottage—he gave me a nice cottage near his because I was a Westerner—and there he would be, Asabha Sayadaw, sitting with his feet up on the table, smoking his cigar and reading the paper, belching and yelling at the gardeners because they were doing the wrong thing, flirting with the nuns and throwing rocks at the dogs to get them to stay out of his garden. He obviously had deep meditation experiences, but by temperament and character he was a very coarse and, in many ways, not a terribly kind person. So I would be getting this refined meditation instruction from this teacher who really knew how to train the mind, then I'd look at him and say to myself, "Oh my God, even though I'm grateful, I don't want to be like this person."

What I saw reflected a dilemma inherent in the models themselves. The model of intensive meditation practice is that you seek to have a certain profound experience—stream-entry, a taste of nirvana—and the idea is that it transforms you forever, and indeed there is some basis for this in the Buddhist texts. In this model (I'm not going to say whether it's true or not, I'll leave that to your own experience), people were taught that they could have a profound opening to nirvana, be assured of beautiful rebirths, and then feel like they were basically saved and would never need to do retreat practice again, or at least not very much.

U Pandita Sayadaw was an example of this belief. After very deep training, he became a skillful teacher in terms of samadhi and the higher realms of practice. When Mahasi Sayadaw died, U Pandita was the dharma successor and next abbot of Mahasi's monastery. However, there were power struggles in that monastery and U Pandita had to leave. After this loss, he went on retreat again for some deep meditation training. I'm told it was the first time he'd been on retreat in thirty-five years.

In Mahasi's model, opening to enlightenment, called "stream-entry," the first taste of nirvana comes in the form of a cessation of experience arising out of the deepest state of concentration and attention. When the body and mind are dissolved, the experience of the ordinary senses ceases, and we rest in perfect equanimity. We open into that which is unconditioned, timeless, and liberating: nirvana. Like Zen satori, this opening brings a whole new way of knowing. But there are a lot of questions around this kind of experience. Sometimes it seems to have enormously transformative effects on people. Other times people have this revelatory experience and aren't really changed by it at all. Sometimes they're not even sure what happened. Using this method of practicing, perhaps three percent of the people who went to Mahasi's monastery would have had such a stream-entry experience. If you have a thousand people practicing at a given time, that means thirty people would have stream-entry experiences and maybe another hundred would be deep in the progress of insight. A lot of people have really cool experiences, but then there are the other 870 who aren't anywhere near that level. In this system they would be told to go out and make good karma and through this, it is believed, their meditation would have better results in the next life. In fact, many of these people can just as well develop equally deep wisdom and compassion in other ways.

Even so, for most people intensive retreats are amazing. I had fantastic experiences and I learned a great deal from those intensive retreats. The insights and freedom you can touch are very beneficial. Of course when I came back to Ajahn Chah's monastery, I told him with relish about all of the experiences I had. He just looked at me and smiled and said, "Good. Something else to let go of." And that was his perspective. He appreciated the experiences, but even if they were a taste of enlightenment, they were over. He was interested in whether I could embody them moment-by-moment, here and now.

At Ajahn Chah's monastery, his language for teaching about nirvana was as the "unconditioned." He said at one point, "If you've been in this monastery for six months or a year and haven't entered the stream, if you haven't tasted the unconditioned, I don't know what you've been doing. You haven't been practicing correctly." If you followed his teachings correctly, you became mindful of the constantly changing conditions of sight, sound, taste, smell, physical perceptions, feelings, and thoughts. Through mindfulness practice you began to experience how conditioned the world is and how these conditions constantly change.

To free ourselves, we need to quiet the mind through some mindfulness in meditation. Then, instead of identifying with the changing conditions, we learn to release them and turn toward consciousness itself, to rest in the knowing. Ajahn Chah called this pure awareness, "the original mind," or resting in "the One Who Knows." Similarly, another forest master, Ajahn Jumnien talks about awareness as pure consciousness, *amattadhamma*—the deathless, the unborn. The senses and the world are always changing conditions, but that which knows is unconditioned. With practice, we discover the selflessness of experience; we shift identity. We can be in the midst of an experience, being upset or angry or caught by some problem, and then step back from it and rest in pure awareness. We let go; we release holding any thought or feeling as "I" or "mine." No problem needs to be solved. We release the whole sense of identification, and the conditioned world is just anicca (impermanent), dukkha (unsatisfactory), and anatta (empty of self)—it has nothing to do with our true nature. We learn to trust pure awareness itself. This is one of the ways Ajahn Chah taught about liberation based on the forest tradition. Awakening is always here and now. Practicing this way, your life is transformed.

Each different approach to dharma practice gives rise to teachers and students who say they have the Buddha's real true way, the very best way to practice. They let you know that others don't have the right way. You find this attitude all over the Buddhist world, and to some extent is has been imported to America. When you visit monasteries in Asia, often the teachers or their disciples will say, "Those guys in the other tradition don't know what the hell they're talking about. They won't get you to liberation." There is a kind of competition between them. But in truth, there isn't only one view or technique that brings liberation. The Buddha taught a hundred skillful means to quiet the mind and open the heart and learn to let go, and they have developed into many traditions over the millennia. Yet people often latch on to one and misunderstand the others.

The roots of this conflict can be traced to the day the Buddha died, when he said to his attendant Ananda, "When I die, you may abolish the minor rules." Alas, Ananda didn't ask which minor rules. So after the Buddha died, and they had the first Council of Elders, Ananda reported that he did not ask which rules they could abolish. Immediately, there was a fight between the disciples who wanted to adapt to the changing circumstances in India by abolishing certain rigid rules and the ones who said, "Since we don't know which rules the Buddha wanted us to abolish, let's conserve every single rule exactly as the Buddha said." From then on, it's been an ongoing dialogue. In every generation, there will be those who adapt and those whose role is to conserve. We may be those original disciples, reborn again in America, carrying on the same arguments.

You can sense the tension that comes from the clash of different models and beliefs. It happens in every religious tradition. There is the transcendent view and the immanent view. There are those who say God is best known through deep prayer, long retreat, and deep mystical experiences that transcend the mundane world. There are those who say that God is immanent, found in this very world, every day, just where we are and that everything shines with holiness all the time. Similarly, there is a tension between those who would like to adapt the teachings and those who would conserve things the way they believe they were. But meanwhile, everything is changing. When the Burmese or Thai say, "We Theravadins practice just the way it was around the time of the Buddha," they ignore the fact that Mahayana temples dot their landscapes.

When we started the Insight Meditation Society in 1975 in Barre, Massachusetts, it was primarily a Mahasi-oriented center. I brought in the flavor of Ajahn Chah as well. But because Joseph (Goldstein) and Sharon (Salzberg) had done most of their practice through the Burmese lineages of Mahasi Sayadaw and of U Ba Khin, and we shared this training, this is mainly what we taught. From the very beginning we offered the practices of both Mahasi Sayadaw and U Ba Khin, with U Ba Khin teachers Ruth Denison and John Coleman leading retreats. We also asked U Ba Khin's great disciple Goenka if he would come and teach, because Joseph, Sharon, and others were very devoted to him. He responded in a letter saying, "If you open a center and have more than one lineage there, it will be the work of Mara, and it will be the undoing of the dharma." Goenka's teacher, U Ba Khin, believed this. However, his letter came the day after we signed the mortgage—fortunately it was too late.

In fact, opening the center felt like good karma or grace, as if we were being carried by the dharma. I love the story of how we got the money for IMS. Three people who had been to India or loved the dharma each put up $15,000, which gave us enough money for the deposit on the $150,000 property. The building was almost empty and the Catholic church couldn't afford to keep paying the heating bill for this huge center with so many single rooms. So we paid only $150,000 for ninety rooms, a bowling alley, tennis courts, eighty acres of land, a huge kitchen, and all of the furnishings! When we went to the local bank, and the bank saw our name was "IMS," they thought it was the International Meditation Society, founded by Maharishi Mahesh Yogi of the Beatles fame, and they said, "Oh, sure, how much money do you want?" They lent us the money based on a complete misunderstanding!

When we started, the first principle that we got right—partly out of necessity (or out of desperation)—was that we would do collective teachings. Most often the centers that have had the most difficulty have invested all the power in just one teacher. That single teacher can get terribly isolated, and as you know, many dharma centers in the West have suffered in some fashion or another due to the misconduct of their primary teacher. When we started IMS, I was twenty-eight, Joseph was twenty-nine, and Sharon was only twenty-one. As Sharon likes to say, "It all happened without adult supervision!" In our wisdom, combined with abject terror, we said, "Let's hold hands for this one, guys." And, as a result, we created the team-teaching model that has saved us so many times. We learn from one another, support one another, keep each other straight. And students get to hear the dharma from several different perspectives. Team teaching offers a much more intelligent way of holding power, especially in a new culture here in the West.

The second principle that we got right—and I was a passionate advocate for this—was having multiple lineages. Even though there was a strong Mahasi lineage through Munindra, Mahasi Sayadaw, Dipa Ma, and Asabha Sayadaw that we shared at IMS, it was very important from the beginning that we invite other lineages and teachers. So, early on we invited Christopher Titmuss, Christina Feldman, Vimalo Kulbartz, and other Western teachers who had studied with Ajahn Buddhadasa, Ajahn Dhammadoro, Ajahn Chah, and other Theravada lineages. From my own experience, it was healthier for both students and teachers alike to have access to a wide range of dharma teachings and perspectives. It is an underlying principle at Spirit Rock Meditation Center as well.

The Buddha is described as the master of many skillful means. He taught the dharma that is gradual and sudden, practiced outwardly and inwardly, blending compassion with teachings of virtue, of generosity, of form and emptiness—all as aspects of awakening. A wise teacher, and a wise center, needs to offer a wide range of skillful practices, because people come along at different stages of inner development, with different temperaments, and with different sets of problems. If we limit ourselves to one technique, it will only serve certain people and it won't be helpful to others. Diversity of practices is an underlying vision at IMS that has also been carried through to Spirit Rock. On our retreats, though we use the basic instructions from Mahasi Sayadaw, we also draw from the teachings and perspectives of Ajahn Chah, Buddhadasa, U Ba Khin, U Tejaniya Sayadaw, and many others.

By initially adopting the intensive retreat model rather than Ajahn Chah's way of communal dharma living, we paid very little attention to the integration or the embodiment of dharma outside of retreats. In the beginning, we had no integration period at all. At the end of the first three-month silent retreat, we just said, "Three months are over; see you later." Two days later, one of our yogis was found doing walking meditation in her pajamas in the general store in Bucksport, Maine. There was no real integration and care. In fact for a number of years, James Baraz, now a teacher himself, ran a kind of halfway house in Berkeley for people coming out of the three-month retreat.

It became clear to many of us that we needed to establish a way of practice that was not just focused on retreats, because people would come back after doing a ten-day retreat or a monthlong retreat, or a three-month retreat, and say, "I'm having trouble integrating what I learned on retreat into the world out here. How do I embody this practice in my everyday life?"

After the first ten years at IMS, a group of us—James Baraz, Sylvia Boorstein, Anna Douglas, Howie Cohn, and many others—wanted to create a wider dharma stream, one that focused on both retreat experiences and on practices that would help people embody the dharma in their lives. This was the vision that drove a committed group of West Coast practitioners in the mid-eighties to look for property for a center.

We found cheap, beautiful places far out in the country, and some board members thought about buying them. But a bigger group held out for a center near the city, where silent retreats, classes, and community could grow together. Thus Spirit Rock was born. Just as at IMS, the founding of Spirit Rock involved some amazing karma. For $900,000 we bought almost a square mile of land in a gorgeous secluded valley in Marin County (some say it's a Native American sacred site), purchased from the Nature Conservancy, which in turn gave them money to save thousands of acres of rain forest in the Amazon.

Opening these beautiful centers with an array of different teachers served the students very well. But our differences in teaching styles and beliefs periodically put us in conflict with one another. At both IMS and Spirit Rock conflicts arose about the best ways to teach, because people were teaching from quite different perspectives. We started having a series of teacher meetings to try to work out our conflicts. At that time Robert Hall was our dharma psychiatrist. He would come in as a friend of the community, before he was a dharma teacher himself, sit down, listen to the arguments and problems, and help us sort them out.

One particularly instructive teacher meeting at IMS involved the center's first fifteen vipassana teachers. The dharma conflict was most strongly represented by a polarity between two teachers, one who at that time was devoted to a strict Mahasi Sayadaw style of meditation taught in a very systematic, conservative manner. The other teacher, though equally devoted to the Buddhist texts, was more formless and free, and was expressing the Krishnamurti-like questioning spirit of teachers like Ajahn Buddhadasa. He valued the radical side of the Buddha's teachings of liberation: "Throw out the bondage of tradition and live in the reality of now." The conflict between these two teachers had carried on over several years. As I look back, I now find these difficulties somewhat amusing, although it was also very painful and still can be. Nevertheless, I think conflict is part of human experience, and I'm interested in how conflict is incorporated into practice rather than avoided.

So there were conservative voices that wanted to keep things exactly the way it was done in Mahasi's retreat center in Burma, and there were voices that said, "We're in a new culture; we have to adapt and be free." We were polarized concerning how to set the wisest direction. At that point Robert Hall did a very skillful thing. He said, "I'd like to ask one of the most polarized voices to leave the room. Go out, and we will call you back later." So the most radical teacher who wanted to adapt the teachings in new ways left the room, and Robert said to the group, "Suppose this teacher was banished from the community, so that we didn't have him to bother us anymore. How would that affect you all?"

We sat in a circle and reflected on it. At first we recognized that without the conflict, our lives would be easier and more relaxed. But then something else became quite clear. If his voice wasn't here, the need for the immediate liberation that his voice proclaims would be so necessary that it would have to be supplied by the rest of us. Then Robert invited this teacher back in and sent the most conservative teacher out of the room. He asked, "Now, suppose this teacher—who at this time is the most concerned about tradition and conserving Burmese forms of practice quite strictly—was no longer part of the community. How would that affect the rest of you?"

At first we could again feel the relaxing of the tension that came from holding tightly to the conservative perspective. But then several of us said, "If this teacher were not teaching the traditional perspective that he does, we would all do more of it because it's so important that people receive this perspective. His carrying of the conservative teachings for the whole community frees us to be more creative." Robert helped everyone in the circle see that the approaches of the various teachers complement one another, that we needed each other, that we do best when we represent not one particular stream or lineage but rather a mandala or a whole, where we each have a piece to contribute.

This, then, is some of the ground on which Spirit Rock was founded. When the teachers, board, staff, and community met together in the early years to try to establish the guidelines and values a West Coast center would hold, we created a vision statement, which you can still see on our Web site. Spirit Rock is created as a mandala that includes practices in many forms, including intensive retreats, study, and the ongoing embodiment and integration of dharma in all of the dimensions of one's life. We wanted this whole range. We put the Dharma of Liberation in the center of the mandala; surrounding it are the other key elements of the mandala: retreats, with a year-round schedule; study, such as the Living Dharma retreat, Dedicated Practitioners Program, and Stephen Batchelor's study retreats; hermitage, with forest huts for very long-term practice, which will be exciting when we are able to do it; and right relationship, cultivating wise relationship with each other, with the earth, and with other beings, following all the steps of the eightfold path. This comprehensive vision provides deep training in practice. It also trains practitioners in how to integrate practice into daily life through classes and workshops that promote and support wise and compassionate action in the world.

Our mandala reflects the riches of Theravada Buddhism and of the Buddhist tradition overall. If you look at the monasteries in Thailand and Burma, retreat centers make up a tiny fraction of the Buddhist culture. Most of the Buddhist teachings in these Buddhist countries focus on generosity, on service and community, on right speech, right action, and right livelihood. The whole eightfold path is the way of practice.

There is a wonderful book about this called *Buddha in the Jungle* by Kamala Tiyavanich. From her research of Buddhism in Thailand, extending back to the earliest written records of previous centuries, you see a very wide range of meditation practices in use. You read how the forest lineages included healers, educators, schoolteachers, priests, peacemakers, and meditators; some were soothsayers and others were shamans who worked with the ghosts and spirits of the other realm. In most Theravada monasteries, along with study there were rituals and festivals and dharma arts, such as painting and music. Other monasteries trained elephants, and some held sky burials. There were monasteries on the Mekong River, where the monks used to enter into boat races with one another. There was a wide range of ways in which the Buddhist teachings were integrated into the community. The monasteries were community centers, education centers, and centers for people in every aspect and phase of their lives.

Someone might look at this and ask, "Where's the Buddhism in that?" If you simply consider the earliest Buddhist sutras, you might say, "I don't see anything about elephant training or community centers in the Buddhist texts," or "I don't see anything about Eastern and Western psychology in there; isn't the Buddha's teaching on the four noble truths enough?" And it is enough. But the four noble truths include the eightfold path, which instructs us in how to live and embody dharma in every part of life through right view, right speech, right action, right livelihood, right mindfulness, and so forth. The Buddha taught the community of followers hundreds of ways to practice based on these truths. And in thousands of years of practice these skillful means have grown. We can draw upon them all in support of awakening.

Another important principle in our community of teachers, alongside our mandala of practice, is that we have all continued to be students. Every one of us in the Teachers' Council at Spirit Rock and IMS is dedicated to continuing to practice, both within our tradition and outside of our own lineage. We have studied with many great teachers in Zen, Tibetan, Advaita, and other traditions. Our practice has taught us to value depth in the many forms, and we look for skillful means to amplify what we know in our tradition. Both at Spirit Rock and at IMS, we want to deepen our realization of liberation, our embodiment of it, and then find ways to communicate the dharma we have inherited through skillful means in this culture.

Over the decades, our way of presenting the teachings has matured. For example, in the first years we put an emphasis on great striving and effort, just as we were taught in Asia. But we learned that, in this culture, when people use great striving, they tend to judge themselves or tie themselves in knots. Feelings of unworthiness and self-criticism create huge problems, so we learned to integrate a lot of metta, or loving-kindness. Through this, people get to the same profound levels of insight but in a more integrated way.

Our range of skillful means has expanded over time. During our two-month spring retreat at Spirit Rock we use the traditional Mahasi Sayadaw form, and students go very deep, and many experience the classical inner transformative experiences of jhana and vipassana samadhi that come from long-term training. But this deepening is enhanced in other ways. By adding metta, by offering the spacious attention that comes from Ajahn Chah's nondual perspective, and by including our understanding of Western psychology, students are able to open to whatever arises. Our retreats also incorporate a sophisticated understanding of how to work with the common kinds of traumas and conflicts that come up as we open our minds and hearts. This integration serves all who come.

To preserve the strength of our tradition, the majority of Spirit Rock retreats teach vipassana as outlined in the four foundations of mindfulness. Other retreats focus on the practices of loving-kindness, compassion, sympathetic joy, and equanimity. Those are our two central streams of dharma practice. The third stream of our retreats offers an integration of mindfulness with yoga, the creative process, loving-kindness, and psychotherapy. In addition, we have hundreds of daylong practice periods, which provide teachings from our mandala of integration and how we embody all aspects of the dharma. We have a Diversity Program, which is committed to offering the dharma to as diverse a population as possible; a Program for Socially Engaged Buddhists; a Family Program for children and their parents; a Teen and Young Adult Program; a study program, and programs for yoga teachers, healers, lawyers, educators, environmentalists and artists.

To keep Spirit Rock connected to the core of our Buddhist tradition, we made a rule that when people outside our lineage come here to teach retreats, they will always be joined by one of our teachers in order to connect their teachings to our practice. In this way our core practices of generosity, virtue, mindfulness, and loving-kindness are complemented by other lineages and skillful means. This practice holds even for masters such as Tsoknyi Rinpoche. We respectfully asked him to teach at Spirit Rock because we highly value his teaching on Dzogchen. However, we explained that the way our community works is that we try to have visiting teachings relate to our own tradition, and we asked if he would be comfortable teaching with our teachers, such as Guy Armstrong or Ajahn Amaro. He said, "I love those guys. I love that monk. Sure, I will teach with them." So we have had wonderful retreats with Tsoknyi Rinpoche and both Ajahn Amaro and Guy Armstrong on different occasions.

While we are dedicated to preserving and sustaining the core teachings of our lineage, we are also willing to be innovators, as indicated by our willingness to learn from other lineages. We draw wisdom from Western psychology; we have hosted a series of international teacher meetings over the past two decades; we have honored and embraced the feminine since the early years; we have been a pioneer in our Diversity Program; and we've been innovative in our teacher training and in our Community Dharma Leader's program, a two-and-a-half-year training regimen for senior vipassana students who wish to offer classes and daylong retreats to their local sanghas. We do our best to deal with our conflicts openly, which is a lifelong process. Our teachers and staff have trained in council practices and mindful listening. In recent years many of these areas are being developed at other Buddhist centers as well. Commitment to diversity is spreading, the complementary value of Western psychology is widely being incorporated, women are becoming dharma leaders all over the West, and the major dharma traditions are learning from one another. In the 1980s, our community was one of the first in the West to create an ethics council. Our ethics statement for Western teachers and community has become a model for others.

When we established Spirit Rock, our notion was to make the governance more egalitarian than traditional dharma centers. We wanted to have a dialogue that would integrate the combined wisdom of the dedicated community, board members, and teachers to guide the center. So instead of setting up a pyramid with guiding teachers at the top who make the main decisions for the board to enact, we set up two bodies—a board of directors drawn from our own community and a teachers' council—which have now come together to jointly carry the responsibility and the vision for Spirit Rock for the century ahead. It's clear to me that we need a real coordination between teachers, community, and board members. There's a collective wisdom at the heart of Spirit Rock that we want to draw from.

The board, teachers, staff, and community members are all long-term dharma students. We have a joint responsibility to ask, "How can we bring the blessings and freedom of the buddhadharma to all who come to Spirit Rock, and how can we sustain this while working together as people who have different views? How can we make a collective of teachers and followers and practitioners who share different perspectives and yet underneath are really committed to those essential dharma principles?"

Our task is to preserve the practices of mindfulness, loving-kindness, compassion, ethics, and virtuous conduct. We want to preserve the whole eightfold path. We want to foster the deepest teachings and practices we can and bring awakening to all who practice with us. That's what will sustain a healthy center and a healthy dharma stream, and bring benefit to the world. We have embedded them in a world-renowned teacher training. We are committed to more fully supporting the hundreds of sitting groups, of *kalyanamitta* (spiritual friend) senior-student groups, and community dharma centers that are growing around the country with this same openhearted spirit. Of course, no matter what we do, we will be criticized as well as praised, so all we can do is stay true to our highest intentions.

It's a fantastic experiment that we're all engaged in, bringing the dharma to the West. We'll try our best, and if things work, wonderful, and if they seem to be unskillful, then we will stop doing them. That's what's called wisdom. No matter how it unfolds, it's been a blessing and an honor to be part of it all.

19

Sex Lives of the Gurus

The erotic instinct is something questionable, and will always be so no mat-
ter what human laws are made about it. It belongs on the one hand, to our
original animal nature, which will exist as long as we have an animal body.
On the other hand, it is connected with the highest forms of spirit. But it
blooms only when spirit and instinct are in true harmony. If one aspect is
missing then an injury occurs, there is a one sided lack of balance which
slips into the pathological. Too much of the animal disfigures the civilized
human being. Too much culture makes a sick animal.
—CARL JUNG

HOW DO SEXUALITY and spirituality fit together? They are such
powerful aspects of our lives and our culture, but we tend to separate
them. The instinctual energies of passion, of love, of desire, are often
suppressed or dealt with abstractly by those in spiritual circles. Yet we
are born out of sexual procreation. The impulse for love and connection
is so deep in us, our very life is woven together out of sexual union. Joining together sexuality, love, and consciousness is a beautiful synthesis,
and people look to Eastern spiritual teachings to help in this area. But
often they find more confusion than help. What can we learn about
sexuality by examining the major Eastern spiritual traditions and the
masters who have brought them to the West?

Few Eastern contemporary spiritual teachers offer clear guidelines
about the relationship between sexuality, love, and spiritual growth.
Nor do most American Buddhist communities address the issue openly.
This leaves most students in the dark. Unfortunately, the question of

whether one could even have a straightforward discussion of sexuality is further complicated by the disclosure, in a number of spiritual communities, of sexual misbehavior on the part of teachers that contradicts their religious vows or moral codes and traditions. These disclosures reveal many areas of confusion and concern. To understand we need to sort out the issue of celibacy versus noncelibacy and debunk the widespread spiritual myths about the dangers of sexuality. Second is a need to sort out the confusion about sexual relationship between students and teachers in the West and the expectations and/or responsibilities of each. Third, and most important, we need to find ways in which spirituality and sexuality can be consciously combined, and create of guidelines from our spiritual traditions for appropriate or skillful sexual expression. Let's attempt to clarify these issues.

To start, we might pose the question "Why do people make such a big deal about sex?" To not make a "big deal" out of sexuality is to deny the force of its presence in our lives and our culture, and to overlook its potential as a ground for suffering and confusion—or, alternatively, for wisdom and spiritual growth. It may have been easier to renounce and dismiss sexual questions in the celibate monasteries and ashrams of Asia, but as Western students and householders we cannot ignore our sexuality any more than we can ignore the issues of relationship, intimacy, and emotions in a life of conscious spiritual practice. Of course, these areas of our practice are among the most difficult. But what is the purpose of spirituality if not to deal with love and desires and freedom, with the basic energies of birth and death, body and mind? The most honest and fruitful course is to recognize the power of sexuality in our lives and to explore the beliefs we hold (true and untrue) that condition how we think and act with regard to it.

For Westerners, for whom the monastic life is an oddity rather than a common occurrence, sexual expression is considered a natural part of being an adult. Twentieth-century psychology has emphasized (perhaps overemphasized) the importance of sexual gratification, and the media often give the impression that sexual desirability and sexual success are primary goals in modern life. Returning to the United States from a visit to a more sexually modest culture like India, one is immediately struck by the powerful public displays of sexuality and seduction in our dress, our advertising, and our media.

This tendency conflicts strongly, in our society and in ourselves, with much of our Western religious heritage, in which we find strong remnants of Puritan, Catholic, and Calvinist attitudes that hold sex to be shameful, base, or sinful. Although the Western religions vary in their views on sexuality and celibacy, much of their conditioning places the pure life of the spirit high above the level of human sexuality. The body is born in sin, and Catholic clergy take celibacy as a necessary requirement of their higher spiritual vocation. Fortunately the opposite view is held by some Protestant traditions and by Judaism, where marriage and family are specifically indicated as sacred goals in life, equal in importance to the study of Torah. Nevertheless, most of our Western religious conditioning takes a negative view of sexuality, and of the body in general.

When we look, each of us can see how our own beliefs have been shaped by our religious affiliations. They have also been shaped by our peer group, our family's belief systems, cultural pressures, and even in what part of the country we were born. The sexual beliefs we grew up with may then be reinforced by our experience with Eastern spiritual practices. Since many of the Eastern traditions involve celibacy, they can reinforce the puritanical sense that "sex is not spiritual" and that, as spiritual seekers, we need to transcend or abandon our sexual impulses. We may have read that enlightened people have no sex drive and may therefore come to feel that a diminished sex drive in ourselves is a sign of increased spirituality. We may have been taught that celibacy is "higher" and healthier than noncelibacy. If, like many people, we are uneasy or fearful in relating to the powerful forces of sexuality, these teachings can provide an excuse for comfortable suppression or denial of these aspects of ourselves. Yet sooner or later they will, of course, reappear, and we may then be troubled to find that we are still motivated in large measure by desires, sexual and otherwise.

Of course we may also have been influenced by the opposite beliefs, myths fed by wild sexual tantric teachings. Or we may be confused about the teachings of surrendering fully to the teacher, or may have been told that whatever a master does is enlightened activity, always intended to teach us. It's time we examined our myths realistically and started asking questions.

Since celibacy is an important practice for Buddhist monastics, let's consider some of the reasons for this practice. Celibacy can be a liberating training undertaken by people to simplify their lives. It can help at times to step back from the involvements and power of sexual desire. Sexual relations can consume an enormous amount of our energy and attention. They also can be very complicated. For many monastics, celibacy is a relief. The discipline of sexual renunciation can support the development of inner strength and peace of mind. Beyond being a training, celibacy can also arise as the fruit of spiritual practice. In such cases, sexual renunciation is not imposed through discipline, but instead one consciously feels oneself to be already whole and content, both detached from and connected with the surrounding world. As an example, His Holiness the Sixteenth Gyalwa Karmapa, when asked about his sex life, declared himself to be a celibate monk. When asked why he had chosen celibacy, since many Tibetan lamas have wives or relationships, he explained, "I am celibate for the same reason you are not." He added that the connection and joy that people seek in sexuality was already present in his life.

Yet Buddhist teachings for lay disciples do not involve celibacy. Instead they simply instruct practitioners to be mindful, and to avoid harm through the misuse of sexuality. In this way sexuality is held to be a natural part of lay life for most Buddhists. But which way of practice is better, celibacy or mindful sex? Spiritual traditions have debated this issue for millennia and have still not arrived at a definitive conclusion. The truth is that, when consciously followed, both paths offer a powerful opportunity for spiritual growth.

Because meditation students often have doubts about the relationship between sexuality and spirituality, they look to the teachings and practices of various Eastern gurus and teachers for answers. Often their questions are motivated by their own personal confusion and the mixed messages of our culture. Sometimes they have even had sexual experiences with their teachers, or seen the inconsistencies between what a particular tradition proposes as wise or virtuous behavior and how certain teachers within that tradition do not follow these principles.

In my role as a Buddhist teacher, I have often been asked about the problems raised by sexuality between teachers and students, amplified by the many stories students have told me. How frequent are such relationships, and how harmful?

In the 1980s I collected information about this question from students and teachers (both Asian and Western) representing the major Buddhist and Eastern lineages in America. This survey attempted to answer a few simple questions: Are these teachers celibate, or are they sexually active to some degree? What are the nature and parameters of their sexual activities? And do their teachings offer any specific guidance regarding sexuality?

Of the fifty-four teachers I surveyed (six females and forty-eight males), fifteen were celibate. The other thirty-nine (including myself) engaged in sexual relationships. Significantly, thirty-four of the thirty-nine teachers who were not celibate had at least occasional sexual relationships with one or more students. Sometimes these were straightforward, honest, and open, sometimes more covert. Among the fifteen celibate teachers, some observed celibacy with delight, whereas others observed celibacy as a form of self-restraint, and a few struggled with it. Of the thirty-nine teachers who were not celibate, twenty of them had spouses and families. Of these, most lived monogamously, though seven did not. Among all thirty-nine noncelibate teachers, some were quite sexually active, others only occasionally so. Some were heterosexual, some were homosexual. Others were bisexual in preference and there were also fetishists and those interested in transgender sexuality. Yet despite all this sexual activity, few publicly taught much about sexuality.

What possible conclusions can one draw from this survey? Clearly, many accomplished meditation masters and teachers are sexually active. Indeed, as a group these teachers seem to represent the whole range of human sexuality. The birds do it, the bees do it, and many gurus do it, too. And yet when we inquire further, it turns out their Zen or mindfulness or monastic traditions offer very little specific teaching about how to work wisely with sexual relations. They are left to figure it out for themselves. Often their needs, desires, and conditioning are as unexamined as those of everyone else around them. So when we meet Tibetan lamas, Zen masters, meditation teachers, or swamis, we should not assume that they are celibate—nor, for that matter, necessarily very conscious about their sexuality. We will likely discover that a person's accomplishment as a master of meditation does not automatically ensure a similar level of sexual awareness. In fact, like the rest of us, teachers are likely to have active and complex sex lives, ones not more conscious than our own. We have to reexamine the myth that enlightenment implies celibacy, or that sexuality is somehow better and wiser for those who are spiritual teachers. I wish it were so, but it is not.

In addition, we need to acknowledge the problems involved in sexual relations between students and teachers. On occasion there can be relationships that are conscious, loving, and freely chosen. Sometimes there are more casual relationships, which while lacking in deep connection, are straightforward and harmlessly sexual. There may even be rare instances of true tantric sexuality, in which both partners are trained to use the act of sexual union as deliberate meditation practice. Nevertheless, more often teacher-student sexual relationships involve exploitation and, in a number of cases, contradict the teachings of the tradition. Such troubling relationships have happened in many communities and often they have been harmful. In part this is due to the great power imbalance. I have spoken with dozens of students who had sexual relations with their teachers. Most of them were women, and the majority report that sexual relationships with their teacher have undermined their practice, their relationship to the teachings, and their feelings of self-worth. In many cases, these relationships, by perpetuating the role of women as serving the teachers' pleasure, have caused a profound degree of pain and confusion, a betrayal that men have difficulty comprehending. These women who have undertaken spiritual practice in order to achieve true liberation have instead been met with a lack of respect and validation that has only intensified their suffering. Many have felt undermined for years.

Compounding the problem are those sexual relationships that involve secrecy or deception, for the deception has proven to be the greatest source of disappointment and pain of all in spiritual groups. The pain from covert or inappropriate sexual relations between teachers and students has happened across the traditions. Such relationships have caused major upheavals in nearly a dozen of the largest Eastern spiritual communities in America. Why? Because of ignorance, fear, and confusion. These spiritual traditions and masters have been cut off from dealing openly with sexuality for years. Their sexuality is suppressed, ignored, or feared. No amount of doing yoga or sitting on meditation cushions has touched it. The force of eros, the life force in sexuality, cannot be ignored. It has to be made a deliberate part of our practice. Otherwise we will find that unconsciousness, fragmentation, frustration, and exploitation will continue.

This means we will have to reexamine what is actually taught about sexuality and what does in fact take place between teachers and students. Ethical guidelines must be explicit. Sexuality must be openly discussed. Only then will exploitation and misuse of power be less likely to occur.

Of course, the suffering and difficulty have not been limited to students. Teacher-student sexual relations have also been a source of great suffering for many of the teachers involved as well. Sometimes the teacher's motivation for initiating such a relationship has its roots in a deliberate misuse of power, entitlement, or addiction. Other times it is a longing to step out of the isolating and lonely role of being the teacher who is not allowed to have simple human needs. Many of these teachers are isolated by their role, and almost all the people around them are to some degree their students. When such teachers do have sexual relations, students are the people who are available to them.

No doubt the seductive and rampant focus on sexuality in the West has been confusing as well, to both Asian and even American teachers. Along with this, students idealize their teachers, and it is hard for teachers not to become affected by the expectations and fantasies of their followers. As disciples project power and enlightenment onto persons in positions of authority, these projections can influence teachers as well as students. This problem of idealization and projection is familiar to practitioners of other professions, such as doctors, priests, and psychotherapists. To understand it better, one can consult the many writings in the psychological and feminist community. But Buddhism has offered little about these areas. To be honest, in most cases the Eastern traditions and teachers are silent or confused. They have not offered much help in understanding sexuality. It is up to us.

The American Buddhist community has to become clearer about our expectations of teachers and students in the area of sexuality. Teachers are responsible for openly explaining their beliefs concerning sexuality and for maintaining ethical sexual practices that are consistent with the tradition they teach. Students also have a responsibility to ask that this matter be openly addressed. In this way, we will come to understand that many teachers are still dealing with the same human energies and conflicts that we are. Fortunately in the decades since the 1980s the development of greater sexual consciousness and community ethics for teachers and students has become more widespread in the West. In the Insight Meditation community, we have had a clear ethics statement and ethics council for decades. With this greater realism there is an additional challenge. We need to let go of any falsely idealistic images or expectations. For some this may involve a sense of loss and grieving for our imagined spiritual ideals. Yet spiritual maturity and true freedom will grow as a result.

We need to accept our teachers as earthly human beings as well as bearers of wisdom and compassion. After all, who among us have not, at one time or another, made idiots of themselves with regard to sex? Our task is to discern what is true, to sort out attachment and delusion from wisdom and compassion. With an unwavering honesty, we can learn from all things. We can see our teachers with devotion and yet respect their humanness as well as our own.

WISE SEXUALITY

In spite of the problems and paucity of teachings on sexuality, Eastern spiritual traditions do offer some simple and important guidelines for skillful sexual conduct. These basic Buddhist teachings can help us understand how to relate wisely to our sexuality. Central to these are three teachings: those of precepts, those of mental states, and those of degrees of awakening.

Training precepts are instructions for nonharming, the fundamental trainings taught by the Buddha for living a life of kindness and well-being. In regard to sexuality, they direct monks and those who have chosen vows of celibacy to honor and keep their vows or else to consciously renounce them and choose the lay life. For lay people who have not undertaken celibacy, they are instructed in the householder practice of refraining from sexual misconduct. (This is one of the five traditional moral precepts taught to householders.) This precept is especially important in our sexually confusing times. It is first of all a practice of refraining from adultery, from sexual relations with those not free, and from sexual relations through coercion. Beyond this, avoiding sexual misconduct means to refrain from acting sexually in any way that brings harm to other beings. Carefully following this precept can save us from untold suffering.

The second Buddhist teaching helpful in working with sexuality is mindfulness of mental states. Any action, including sexual activity, can be associated with either skillful or unskillful mental states. We can act sexually out of greed, compulsion, aggression, or selfishness. Or we can act sexually out of love, caring, respect, and as an expression of openness and communion. It is not the sexual activity alone that is skillful or unskillful, but also the mind state that accompanies it, the intention that precedes it, the context in which it takes place, and the feelings that it brings forth. Sexual activity associated with unskillful mental states such as greed, aggression, and selfishness brings pain and bondage. Sexual activity associated with skillful mental states leads to greater harmony and freedom. With practice we can learn to release the unskillful states and follow the healthy ones.

The Buddhist teachings about stages of enlightenment can also help us understand some of the unskillful sexual behavior on the part of accomplished meditation teachers. Buddhist tradition speaks of levels of awakening, describing many degrees or steps of awakening before full enlightenment. The great Chinese master Hsu Yun taught that there are many satoris before complete enlightenment is achieved. The first tastes of enlightenment remove doubts and radically transform one's mind. But they do not eliminate all self-centered desire and aversion from the heart. It is said that these only drop away several enlightenments later. This is a critical understanding. Teachers and students as well can touch the first levels of enlightenment with profound and genuine understanding. Yet in other ways they can still be unconscious with strong needs, fears, unresolved problems, and self-centered desires. Sexual confusion may be with them and us for years, even after the first tastes of enlightenment.

Therefore, we must always use the practice of nonharming and compassionate awareness of our own mind and intentions to protect ourselves and others. When we have established a nonharming sexuality, then we can begin to develop a conscious sexuality that is loving, connecting, and potentially awakening. We can practice bringing mindfulness and caring attention to our own desires and the intimacy of sexual relation with others. Then sexuality becomes a gift. Because sexuality can bring concentration, bliss, and the natural loss of boundaries and self, we can engage in it as one of the great pleasures and mysteries of human incarnation. It can become a way to step out of our small sense of self, and experiencing oneness, freedom, and joy. The qualities of a bodhisattva can be developed through sexuality: mindfulness, kindness, generosity, virtue, truthfulness, and caring connection with all beings. We can use these Buddhist teachings to integrate sexuality into our path. In America, a new style of practice has begun to emerge. This Western style of practice is not focused on the celibate monastic forms that have been prominent for so long in the East. For most American Buddhists, the way will emphasize integrating practice into our everyday lives as householders.

Conscious sexuality requires a mindful connection to love and the body. Otherwise we will continue to divorce the mind and heart from our body. This schism is the source of confusion and suffering in our world in general. When the mind is cut off from the body's instinct and deep feeling, we treat the body as an object and we treat the physical world as less than sacred. The destruction of peoples, the environment, and the earth itself is due to this divorce. Respect for the mystery of our sexuality will have to be included in our spiritual path. Sex is not bad. It can be beautiful or terrible depending on our level of consciousness. Even the Buddha, who lived as a celibate monk, acknowledged sexuality as one of the great pleasures of lay life.

As the dharma comes to the West, we are challenged to reevaluate the myths we have held and to reawaken a spiritual vision of liberation and freedom based on dealing with all of life as sacred. As teachers and students alike, we have the opportunity to explore the mystery of sexuality in a frank and open way and thus bring it fully into our hearts and our practice. Our twenty-first-century Western, nonmonastic Buddhism must learn how to join sexuality, conscious awareness, and love, and to integrate all parts of ourselves into our spiritual life. This may prove to be one of the gifts of mindfulness for the modern world, a way of practice that honors our sexuality, our bodies, and the earth itself as the path to awakening.

20

Psychedelics, Antidepressants, and Spiritual Practice

TAKING DRUGS, for recreational purposes, for self-exploration, or to treat mood disorders, is common in our society, and this raises compelling questions for many Buddhist practitioners. How are we to regard the use of mind-altering drugs, including hallucinogens and antidepressants? Are these useful tools on the path of awakening, or do such drugs cloud the mind and hinder genuine spiritual practice?

Let's consider hallucinogens first. When I began practicing Buddhism in the 1960s, many young people were experimenting with mind-altering drugs such as LSD and psilocybin mushrooms. At that time, it was thought that altering one's awareness by taking drugs could bring about a spiritual awakening. Over the years practitioners have asked whether these substances are valued in the Buddhist tradition. It is helpful to consider these drugs in the context of the three foundations of the Buddhist path: virtue, mental training, and wisdom.

Starting from the foundation of virtue, the Buddhist precepts prohibit the misuse of intoxicants. Psychedelic drugs, though not explicitly referred to in Buddhist literature, fall into this category. This precept teaches practitioners to refrain from using intoxicants to the point of heedlessness, or loss of awareness. An alternate translation of this precept is to refrain from taking any intoxicant.

These five lay Buddhist precepts instruct us to refrain from killing, stealing, talking falsely, engaging in sexual misconduct, and misusing intoxicants. Together, these precepts instruct us to not cause harm, which is the first essential principle of all spiritual life. The tradition is telling us that we can't meditate properly after a day of lying, killing, and stealing. In order to free the heart from entanglement in greed, fear, hatred, and delusion, a nonharming relationship with the world must be developed. Only from this ground of nonharm can one properly develop meditation and wisdom.

So, living a virtuous and compassionate life is the starting point, according to Buddhist tradition. Then the second foundation of spiritual practice involves trainings to quiet the mind and open the heart. Mental training through meditation, visualizations, and yogic practices are used to "tame the wild monkey mind." These systematic practices can dissolve the fears and confusions of the mind and release our identification with a limited sense of self. Spiritual practices such as meditation unify our body, heart, and mind and open us up to vast inner realms.

By developing the foundations of nonharming and meditative training, consciousness becomes clear and open. Now the third foundation, called prajna or wisdom, can arise. With a quiet and focused mind we can see how consciousness creates the world, and thus discover freedom and compassion in the midst of it all. With these foundations as a basis for exploration, we have a capacity for deep wisdom to grow and become integrated in our life.

The use of hallucinogens in the 1960s and '70s, was essentially a reversal of the three steps in the Buddhist approach to awakening. Many people who took LSD, mushrooms, and other psychedelics, sometimes with the assistance of readings from *The Tibetan Book of the Dead* or Zen texts, had the gates of wisdom opened for them. They could see that their ordinary limited consciousness was only one plane of experience and that there were many other dimensions to discover in the mind. They opened to new realms, got profound perspectives on birth and death, and discovered the nature of mind and consciousness as a field of creation, rather than the mechanical result of having a body. They saw beyond the illusion of separation to the truth of the oneness of things.

But the transformations from these experiences tended to fade. So in order to maintain this vision, people tried to keep taking psychedelics hoping the vision would last. But it didn't. Following that, some said to themselves, "If I can't maintain the highs of consciousness by using psychedelics, let's see if there is some other way." To do this they undertook various kinds of spiritual disciplines. They did Buddhist practices, kundalini yoga, *bhastrika* breathing, raja yoga, mantra, and concentration exercises, or visualizations as a way to get back to those profound and compelling states that had come through psychedelics.

For these people, psychedelics had awakened a sense of the possibilities of opening the mind and body, and gave them a sense that they could live in a different way. Now, in order to sustain those sensitivities and visions without repeatedly taking psychedelics, they undertook some spiritual practice, such as yoga or meditation.

Soon these same people began to see that even these meditative practices could not become stable and reliable unless they found a way to bring their practice into their everyday lives. They found it was necessary to live with virtue, to make sure that their actions were nonharming and compassionate. They discovered that inner awakening must be grounded in virtuous behavior and compassion, supported by a systematic inner training, whatever the source of the initial inspiration. So those who began their spiritual journey with hallucinogens followed a reverse spiritual process that eventually led them to ground their psychedelic insights in virtue and a path of ongoing, committed spiritual practice.

However we think about them, there is no question that LSD was an important element in the importing of Eastern spiritual practices into the United States during the 1960s. Psychedelics certainly played an important part for me. I took LSD and other hallucinogens at Dartmouth at the same time I started studying Eastern religion. These interests and activities came hand-in-hand in those days. These drugs were a gateway to the inner life. In fact most Western Buddhist teachers of my generation used psychedelics at the start of their spiritual practice. Some had truly transformative experiences. Many others were inspired, and a few were damaged. It is like playing the lottery. A lot of people play, and not so many people win big, but still a potential is there for some real benefit.

When Zen master Seung Sahn came to the United States from Korea in the 1970s and began teaching Americans, he was asked about using drugs in the quest for self-knowledge. He said that there were indeed special medicines that, if taken with the proper attitude, could facilitate self-realization. "But if you have the proper attitude," he added, "you can take anything—a walk or a bath."

In the 1960s and '70s we were naive in believing that extraordinary drug experiences would bring lasting transformation. My own Buddhist training and teaching has shown me that people underestimate the depth of change that is required to transform oneself. True liberation requires a vast perspective, called by Zen "a long enduring mind." Yes, an experience of awakening can come in a moment, but living it, stabilizing it, can take months, years, lifetimes. The propensies or conditioned habits with which we live are so deeply ingrained that even enormously compelling visions do not change them very much. Therefore a complete path of liberation as taught by the Buddha, and other similar traditions, draws on many dimensions of life to support deep and lasting transformation. The possibility of human liberation is at the center of these teachings—liberation of the heart from greed, hatred, delusion, liberation from all sense of separateness and fear. This is a very compelling possibility for humans.

To come to this level of illumination, you have to face the most powerful forces in the heart and mind, those that fuel war and injustice and tribalism, that lie at the root of all human suffering. You will encounter the roots of greed, the most primal kinds of grasping; the power of hatred, finding Hitler and Attila the Hun in your own mind; and face delusion that manifests as the darkest blindness of ignorance and confusion. Deep spiritual practice—and I will include psychedelic experiences as part of that—eventually bring you to confront death. You must find ways to work with these forces and transform them in a way that leads to genuine liberation. Only if used properly will hallucinogens help with this.

A lot of people of my generation used psychedelics in casual, mindless, or misguided ways, without much understanding of these depths. The spiritual context and guidance needed to properly use these drugs was missing. If we pop a synthetic mescaline pill casually, we may have some beautiful visions, but without the two-hundred-mile prayer-filled desert walk and the months of dance and purification the Huichols used to prepare for a traditional peyote ceremony, we can't make much use of these visions. The spiritual preparations make the taking of peyote an integrated sacrament. Modern explorers of the mind such as Stanislav Grof and Ram Dass have recommended for years that psychedelics be taken in a careful and protected context. They understand the power of the forces that one may confront. Whatever our practice, we need to respect the depth of transformative experiences and make a sacred container for opening to the full range of spiritual life.

Also, even among the most conscious explorers of psychedelics, addiction and attachment can be a problem. Addiction and the unskillful actions that come from it can lead to great suffering. This is why one interpretation of the Buddhist precepts forbids intoxicants completely. But other translations of the same texts say, "Avoid using substances in any way that brings about heedlessness." If one uses any substances, whether wine, marijuana, LSD, or mushrooms, this second interpretation of the Buddhist precepts says to be very careful to not become heedless in this part of your life. Without such precepts, anyone who begins the journey will get lost or go off the track. You cannot complete the journey until you get the basics right. This is really a very simple message.

Still, many spiritual traditions in the world include the use of mind-altering substances. Whether it's the peyote used by shamans, the wine used by Sufis, or the *soma* (a visionary plant described in the Vedas) used by the Hindus, this use of drugs takes place in the context of spiritual purification. For example, the use of soma begins with the purification of one's actions, or virtue. Building on this are purifications of the body through yoga, breathwork, fasting, and other practices that prepare the body to open and touch visionary consciousness—and later to support an integration of these visions into ordinary life.

On these paths, the purifications of virtue and the body are combined with the purifications of the heart and mind. These may involve emotional transformation through the practices of extending forgiveness and opening the heart, or the release of fears, angers, and memories that have been locked within for years. Whatever the vehicle for inner transformation, the practitioner will encounter waves of desire, fear, pain, laziness, or frustration. These are the preliminary hindrances to transformation. We have to learn how to use wise attention so that we don't become caught up or lost in them. Whether mind-altering substances are used or not, there is also a need for purification of thought: confronting the nonstop inner dialogue and beginning to train a stability of mind.

All these levels of purification and stabilization grow with regular practice, using meditation, mantra, visualization, sacred movement, prayer, ritual, and other methods. As the body and mind become more open and purified, you mature in the ability to be balanced and less caught by strong emotions and thoughts, and you can use this ability to enter other domains of consciousness. With the mind stabilized you can apply the resulting clarity to discovering the laws of the mind and of consciousness itself.

Purification and the stabilization bring equanimity, the capacity to enter the domains of light and ecstasy without getting too attached. You can see it all as part of the passing show. In the same spirit, you can go through hell realms within you with the same balance. You learn how to open to all experience without grasping and attachment. In meditation you can systematically enter the vast realms of consciousness, where psychedelics may also have taken you, but now you can experience them with mindfulness and balance, and relate to them wisely. Spiritual awakening is not only about opening to the many realms of heart, mind, and body. It requires learning how to move among them wisely, compassionately, and with real freedom.

My teacher Ajahn Chah instructed us in how to work wisely with visions by saying, "Though they have come about, do not take them seriously. Do not take anything as yourself—everything is only a vision or construction of the mind, a deception that causes you to desire, grasp, or fear. When you see such constructions, do not get involved. Unusual experiences and visions are of value to the wise person but harmful to the unwise. Keep practicing until you are not stirred by them."

This understanding and the foundational trainings would be a wise approach to including psychedelics as a part of the path. First, establish virtue. Train yourself in mindfulness, equanimity, and compassion. Then create a safe and protected situation where these medicines are taken as a sacrament. Have an experienced meditator or guide with you. Know that you may open rapidly to many levels of experience. Some openings will ask for healing. You may relive past trauma, or experience the pain that is held in your body from an accident or an operation, or experience the tension from deeply stored anger or grasping as it comes into consciousness and begins to release. You will have visions; you may experience other realms and explore powerful states of consciousness, birth and death. This will call on all your meditation training in mindful presence and compassion. The healing effects of hallucinogens come through the power of bringing into consciousness that which has been below the threshold of awareness.

Sometimes with psychedelics, powerful experiences can come too quickly and you can get overwhelmed. If this happens, go back to your most grounded practice and to a place of nourishment and refuge. Take your time. Otherwise you will close down when you touch experiences that are too fearsome or too difficult. With practice you can learn to surrender and go through whatever difficulty arises, and it will release you to a larger, freer consciousness.

So, yes, LSD, mushrooms, Ecstasy, or ayahuasca can bring healing and can grant us access to visionary and mystical realms, realms of tremendous, transcendent understanding. They can bring a perception of unity, the reality of our connection with everything. Any methods that open the heart in this way and show us that we are not separate, that touch the realms of universal loving, kindness, and compassion, can be valuable. But you need to be careful. For some people, the judicious use of these substances can open the mind and reveal how consciousness creates the world, that physical reality is created out of consciousness and not the opposite. For other people these drugs are a danger, particularly if one has a history of substance abuse or a family history of drug or alcohol addiction.

Hallucinogens are powerful medicine, enormously compelling for some people as an initial opening. At later stages you may be called to use them again wisely, but always with the constraints of virtue and care. They can be easily abused if one is not careful. And remember, there are a hundred other ways to open to these realms without hallucinogens: intensive prayer, movement and breath practices, shamanic drumming, initiation rituals, ecstatic and purifying dancing, vision quests, and intensive meditation retreats. Stanislav and Christina Grof and I offer annual retreats that feature the practice of Holotropic Breathwork, a powerful breathing practice done in groups that opens the inner realms, much like psychedelics. We combine this work with Buddhist meditation. Participants interested in these forms of inner exploration seem to appreciate this combination of practices.

Sacred medicine is a part of spiritual paths on every continent. In spiritual communities, we need an honest exploration of this delicate and sometimes taboo topic. Let us approach the use of these drugs consciously. In my view, whatever leads to opening the heart and mind and letting go is beneficial.

242 PRACTICING THE DHARMA IN THE WEST

PRESCRIPTION DRUGS FOR MENTAL HEALTH

Another compelling question for dharma students in the West is whether or not to use psychoactive prescription medications such as antidepressants. In the same way that it serves us to be open-minded about hallucinogens, we need to keep an open mind about these drugs so that we can honestly inquire if they are helpful to practitioners at times, or if they undermine genuine spiritual practice.

A huge number of Americans take prescription drugs for mental support including antidepressants, antianxiety drugs, mood-regulating drugs, sleep aids, and drugs for attention deficits. In many cases these medicines bring relief and great benefit. However, because they are the least costly remedy for psychological suffering, in our dysfunctional health insurance system these medications have largely replaced psychotherapy and other forms of long-term, caring attention for grief, trauma, conflict, and difficult life situations. There are a range of drug-free interventions that can be equally effective and more supportive of patients' well being in the long run.

In addition, psychoactive medications, including stimulants to boost attention as well as antidepressants, are now prescribed to an estimated forty million children. An extensive exploration by the *Wall Street Journal* in 2011, drawing on statistics from the Centers for Disease Control and the National Institutes of Health, describes how millions of schoolchildren take prescription drugs just to get through a normal school day. Something seems very wrong with this picture, and while we know sometimes these medicines can be helpful and effective, there is also clearly a problem with overuse and misuse.

To be wise about using these medications, we need to look for the middle path. At one extreme, many people, especially children, are given powerful mood-altering medications too quickly, as an "easy" way to override the need for smaller class sizes, good therapy, critical life changes, and self-regulation skills. Instead of quickly prescribing antidepressants or antianxiety medications, psychiatrist Dan Siegel takes out his prescription pad and writes, "Forty-five minutes of strong aerobic exercise, five times a week for three months." After three months of this exercise, the depression and anxiety lifts in half of these patients, and they do not need medication.

At the other extreme are the people who never use these medications, believing that they interfere with "pure spiritual practice," even though many of these same people have no problem medicating themselves with alcohol, marijuana, or caffeine. One meditation student with epilepsy became so adamant about not using mind-altering substances that he stopped taking his antiseizure medication and had a succession of major seizures during a retreat.

Medications, like the other chemicals that make up our food and our body, can bring either benefit or harm. Yes, they can be overprescribed and used too quickly, and some psychiatric medications, in some people, can dampen access to feelings. But there are times when they can also be of enormous benefit to dharma practitioners. If our nervous system and psyche are far out of balance because of biological, genetic, or environmental causes such as trauma, sometimes we cannot simply address the problem with mindfulness and compassion training. Anyone who has meditated for a few years knows that the inner journey has many highs and lows, and that it is necessary to face and mindfully work with states such as fear, doubt, and grief. But sometimes the grief and depression are too long-lasting, the anxiety and sadness too overwhelming to work with. We are drowning, and mindfulness is not strong enough to make a difference. Then it turns out to be very helpful to use medications that help regulate our depression, anxiety, and sleep problems so that our situation becomes workable. When we feel a sense of balance and peace, we become more able to open, physically, emotionally, and spiritually. Many students and a number of dharma teachers I know have benefited from periods of using antidepressants and other such medicines because these drugs have created the stability, the ground for being able to use the tools of mindfulness and compassion training.

The Buddhist precepts speak of avoiding intoxicants that cloud the mind, but these medicines often have the opposite effect. Those who have experienced disabling or long-term depression, anxiety, or sleeplessness report that these medicines have helped them emerge from a deadly loss of vitality, a pervasive dark cloud, an ongoing sense of inner torment and of being overwhelmed.

Psychiatric researcher and longtime dharma practitioner Dr. Roger Walsh reports that preliminary studies for practitioners with significant symptoms of depression and anxiety show that prescription medications such as SSRIs can help with emotional balance and renew healthy motivation and cognitive capacities. Meditators become calmer, more attentive, and interested, and positive emotions such as joy, love, compassion, and self-esteem grow stronger. But medication is only part of the solution. In order to grow spiritually, these medicines have to be combined with regular meditation and often with psychotherapy and trauma work as well.

Like many things, prescription drugs for mental health are neither all good nor all bad. They can be used thoughtfully or misused. They should not be automatically dismissed or feared. When we are devoted to awakening, we will seek out anything that brings balance and helps us to open. And if our psyche is far out of balance, and we need medication to help serve our journey, we must respect the truth of that. We will understand that the path of inner freedom is the work of a lifetime and a return to the reality of the present with an open heart and a free mind. With wisdom we will foster that which brings awakening in ourselves and in all we touch.

21

Even the Best Meditators Have Old Wounds to Heal

TO FULLY EMBODY AWAKENING in spiritual life there is a great importance to bringing attention to our shadow side, those aspects of ourselves and our practice where we have remained unconscious. This is because the practices we undertake will often focus on specific areas of development, but may leave other dimensions untouched. For example as a teacher of Buddhist mindfulness practice for over thirty-eight years, I have seen the value of meditation. Daily meditation practice has been proven to have enormous benefits. And intensive retreats even more so. They can help us quiet the mind, dissolve our illusion of separateness, and bring about compelling insights and certain kinds of deep healing.

Yet intensive mediation practice has its limitations. In talking about these limitations, I want to speak not theoretically but directly from my own experience.

Some people have come to meditation after working with traditional psychotherapy. Although they found therapy to be of value, its limitations led them to seek a spiritual practice. This is because many forms of therapy limit themselves to insight and healing in the realm of our personal history and family. They can help us see the unhealthy patterns of our life, and release or rework them. But often these forms of therapy lack a spiritual dimension. There are neither the practices to open us beyond our ordinary sense of self nor the profound understandings and universal perspectives that connect us to the vast dimensions of wisdom, compassion, emptiness, and liberation. So even after a successful course of therapy, people can feel the limitations and turn to spiritual practice for a greater perspective.

My own course was the opposite of this. I started with meditation, and only later became interested in therapy. I benefited enormously from the training offered in the Thai and Burmese monasteries where I practiced. I learned mindfulness, compassion, virtue, and renunciation. I learned about emptiness and letting go. But then I noticed two surprising omissions. First, there were major areas of difficulty in my life, such as loneliness, intimate relationships, work, childhood wounds, and patterns of fear that even very deep meditation didn't touch. Second, among the several dozen Western monks and other Asian meditators I met during my time in Asia, with a few notable exceptions, most were not helped by meditation in a variety of important areas of their lives. Some were traumatized, neurotic, frightened, grieving, and had used spiritual practice to hide and avoid problematic parts of themselves.

When I returned to the West to study clinical psychology and began to teach meditation, I observed a similar phenomenon. Many of the dedicated students who came to our annual three-month retreats couldn't do the simple concentration and "bare attention" practices because they were holding a great deal of unresolved grief, fear, woundedness, and unfinished business from the past. I also had the opportunity to observe the most successful group of meditators—including experienced students of Zen and Tibetan Buddhism—who had developed strong samadhi and deep insight into impermanence and selflessness. But even after many intensive retreats, many of these meditators continued to experience great difficulties and significant areas of attachment and unconsciousness in their lives, including fear, difficulty with work, relationships wounds, and closed hearts. Students kept asking how to live the dharma, and kept returning to meditation retreats looking for help and healing. But sitting practice itself, with its common emphasis on concentration and detachment, often provided a spiritual bypass, a way to hide, a way to actually separate the mind from difficult areas of heart and body.

These problems exist for most meditation teachers as well. Many of us have led very unintegrated lives, and even after deep practice and initial "enlightenment experiences," our sitting practice has left major areas of our beings unconscious, fearful, or disconnected. Many American meditation teachers are now, or have recently been, in psychotherapy in order to deal with these issues.

It should also be noted that a majority of the twenty or more largest centers of Zen, Tibetan, Hindu, and vipassana practice in America have witnessed major upheavals, centering on the teachers themselves (both Asian and Western), related to issues of power, sex, honesty, and intoxication. Something is asking to be noticed here. If we want to find true liberation and compassion, what can we learn?

SOME HELPFUL CONCLUSIONS FOR OUR PRACTICE

1. For most people, meditation practice doesn't "do it all." At best, it's one important piece of a complex path of opening and awakening. I used to believe that meditation led to the higher, more universal truths, and that psychology, personality, and our own "little dramas" were a separate, lower realm. I wish it worked that way, but experience and the nondual nature of reality don't bear it out. If we are to end suffering and find freedom, we can't keep these levels of our lives separate. The personalized and the universal are two complementary dimensions of incarnation. To live a liberated life, we need to find freedom in both.

2. The various compartments of our minds and bodies are only semipermeable to awareness. Awareness of certain dimensions does not automatically carry over to the other aspect, especially when our fear and woundedness are deep. Thus we find Olympic athletes who know their bodies well but are emotional idiots, and brilliant professors with amazing minds but rudimentary, unconscious relationships with their bodies. This is true in spiritual life as well, for teachers as well as students. Thus, we frequently find meditators who are deeply aware of breath or body but are almost totally unaware of feelings, and others who understand the mind but have no wise relationship to their body.

Mindfulness works only when we are willing to direct attention to every area of our life, to our suffering and our potential. This doesn't mean getting caught in our personal histories, as many people fear, but learning how to address them so that we can actually free ourselves from the big and painful "blocks" of our past. Such healing work is often best done in a therapeutic relationship with another person.

3. Meditation and spiritual practice can easily be used to suppress and avoid feeling or to escape from difficult areas of our lives. Our sorrows are hard to touch. Many people resist the personal and psychological roots of their suffering; there is so much pain in truly

experiencing our bodies, our personal histories, our limitations. It can even be harder than facing the universal suffering that surfaces in sitting. We fear the personal and its sorrow because we have not learned how it can serve as our practice and open our hearts.

We need to look at our whole life and ask ourselves, "Where am I awake, and what am I avoiding? Do I use my practice to hide? In what areas am I conscious, and where am I fearful, caught, or unfree?"

4. There are many areas of growth (grief and other unfinished business, communication and maturing of relationships, sexuality and intimacy, career and work issues, fears and phobias, early wounds, and more) where good Western therapy is on the whole much quicker and more successful than meditation. These crucial aspects of our being can't just be written off as "personality stuff." Freud said he intended to help people to love and work. If we can't love well and give meaningful work to the earth, then what is our spiritual practice for? Meditation can help in these areas. But if, after sitting for a while, you discover that you still have personal work to do, find a good therapist or some other way to effectively address these issues.

Of course, there are many mediocre therapists and many limited kinds of therapy. Just as in meditation, you should look for the best. Beyond the traditional talking psychotherapies, many new therapies have been developed with a strong spiritual basis, such as psychosynthesis. Reichian breathwork, sand play, and a whole array of transpersonal psychologies. The best therapy, like the best meditation practice, uses awareness to heal the heart and is not concerned so much with our stories as with fear and attachment and their release, and with bringing mindfulness to areas of delusion, grasping, and unnecessary suffering. One can, at times, find the deepest realizations of selflessness and nonattachment through some of the methods of transpersonal psychology.

5. Does this mean we should trade meditation for psychotherapy? Not at all. Therapy isn't the solution either. Consciousness is! And consciousness grows in spirals. If you seek freedom, the most important thing I can tell you is that spiritual practice always develops in cycles. There are inner times when silence is necessary, followed by outer times for living and integrating the silent realizations, as well as times to get help from a deep and therapeutic relationship with another person. These are equally important phases of practice. It is not a question of first developing a self and then letting go of it. Both go on all the time.

Any period of practice may include times of samadhi and stillness, followed by opening to new levels of wounds and family history, followed by great letting go, followed by spiritual visions and then more personal problems. Working with all of these levels is our spiritual practice. What is required is the courage to face the totality of what arises. Only then can we find the deep healing we seek—for ourselves and for our planet.

In short, we have to expand our notion of practice to include all of life. Like the Zen ox-herding pictures, the spiritual journey takes us deep into the forest and leads us back to the marketplace again and again, until we are able to find compassion and the sure heart's release in every realm.

22

The Sure Heart's Release

Healing Our Personal Pain

MY TEACHER AJAHN CHAH used to say, "As the Buddha taught in the four noble truths, there is suffering, there is the cause of suffering, and there is the end of suffering. Wherever you are, is the place to realize these truths." Sometimes suffering comes through clinging to our desires, emotional pain, or certain stories. Sometimes suffering comes through not recognizing the emptiness, the evanescence of life, that nothing can be claimed as I or mine. The point of dharma practice is to pay attention wherever there is suffering, to see the clinging and identification, and to release it to find a freedom of heart.

Often traditional Buddhist texts focus on achieving perfect enlightenment and then living in an absolutely free, pure state after that. But there aren't very many beings in this era that we picture in this ideal fashion. Even great, respected, and beloved teachers like the Dalai Lama or Ven. Maha Ghosananda, the Gandhi of Cambodia, don't hold themselves in this way. These contemporary masters say, "I'm still struggling with this, or there are things that I still work on in my practice," rather than speak from the place of absolute freedom. And so in our times, even our elders and masters point to the need to live the dharma in our actual, beautiful, and difficult lives, to honor and embody it and not just focus on the ideal or absolute level.

Remember how Ajahn Chah told me, "I hope you're not afraid to suffer." And when I asked, "What do you mean, afraid to suffer?" he said, "There are two kinds of suffering: the suffering that you run away from, which follows you everywhere, and the suffering that you are willing to turn and face. There you will find the liberation that the Buddha taught for us all."

He said this with great humor. He wasn't heavy-handed. He would direct people into their difficulties without subtly increasing their unworthiness or their self-hatred. He knew how to mentor people. He would look at students and say, "I know you can do this." He would see what Thomas Merton called "their secret beauty," their buddha nature, and foster that, which is what a great teacher can do.

After tremendous benefit from my first five years in Asia I realized that I didn't want to spend my whole life as a celibate monk. Marriage, relationships, and living in the world were still important to me, and so I told my teacher that I wanted to return to the West. I felt like I had learned enough of the practices of mindfulness and compassion and now I wanted to see if I could live them in ordinary life and not only in the protected circumstances of the monastery. I had wanted to live as an expatriate in Asia for the rest of my life. I was drawn back to my own culture.

When I got back home, I found that after a time the fantastic detachment and great bliss and joy and peace that I had developed from these monastic years crumbled. I discovered to my horror that a lot of the neurotic patterns of my life were waiting back here, like old, comfortable clothes. There I was again, fighting with my girlfriend, worrying about money. So I really had to ask myself, "OK, now, how do you actually live this practice, how do you integrate it?" That became the compelling question. And what I found is that I had done a bit of a spiritual end run around a number of very painful areas of my life. All this unfinished business returned. I had spent eight or ten years in study and then dharma practice beginning in 1963 in college. I had been working primarily with my mind, through the intellect, then through monastic training in concentration and mindfulness with great ardor, but now there arose all this emotional work. I had to learn how to bring the principles of mindfulness and compassion into the pain and neurosis in my life in order to transform them in some way. I did that through meditation, using a great deal of emphasis on loving-kindness and compassion. I also did it in psychotherapy, especially body- and breath-oriented forms of psychotherapy. And I did it through gradually learning how to be more conscious in close relationships, which was a big practice for me—and not one that was focused on much in the monasteries.

What I experienced, as a practitioner and as a teacher, was a shift from a sense of struggling against the self (what in Asia was the warrior-fighting-a-battle mode of practice such as I found in the ascetic forest monastery) toward an approach that is grounded in compassion and healing. But it wasn't just my problem. In the early years of leading retreats in this country we, as teachers, encountered an astonishing amount of self-hatred and self-judgment in students. We saw that practitioners were taking the dharma language of purification—of ridding oneself of greed, hatred, and delusion—and using it to judge themselves and reinforce a deep sense of unworthiness. They were trying, in some ways, to negate who they were, which only created further suffering and tension. It became increasingly clear that the battlefield-warrior archetype did not serve those people for whom the wounds of self-hatred and self-judgment were the primary sources of suffering. To be more skillful, we shifted the forms of practice from the struggle against the self to one of radical letting go and resting in a ground of mindful loving-kindness and compassion for oneself and others.

True dharma practice is a revolutionary activity. You have to challenge the whole identity of your life. You can't do it in a comfortable way. But the strength that's asked for is not necessarily the battle to eliminate the impurities of body and mind, and fight against the coarse defilements of greed, hatred, and delusion, the inner corruptions, though this language is common in Theravada, Tibetan, and Zen Buddhism. The strength that's needed can also come from the courage of heart to remain undefended and open. This requires a willingness to face the ten thousand joys and the ten thousand sorrows of life with compassion, to open to the deepest places of our being. This is a different kind of fearlessness, one that requires as much passion and fire as any warrior path.

One of the dangers is that as the dharma becomes more mainstream in our culture, it can become too comfortable. Practitioners have become more affluent, and when you combine this with a greater emphasis on compassion and less ascetic-warrior practice, there's a danger that the true depth of commitment that's necessary for this revolutionary transformation will get lost.

The good news is that complacency is always countered by integrity, an unswerving love of the truth and a willingness to live it. If we practice with integrity, our spiritual life will deepen. If dharma teachers carry this legacy of courage from the Buddha, then they will awaken in their students the truth-loving mind. Students will recognize that liberation is their birthright and will awaken the One Who Knows, their own true nature.

It's important to see that in the West, the conditions for teacher-student relations are different than in Asia. If Western teachers treated their students in the same the harsh and punishing way that Marpa trained Milarepa, they would reinforce the American neurosis of self-hatred and judgment, and the students would either flee or file a lawsuit. In the famous story Milarepa, a Tibetan saint, had learned black magic as a youth, and to save his family's honor, had caused the death of thirty-six people. His teacher Marpa made Milarepa do years of backbreaking hard labor, and attacked him with nonstop criticism, all to redeem Milarepa from his legacy of terrible karma. This training approach is not suitable for us in the West. Yet that same radical commitment and transformation is still needed in students. Instead of creating this through a harsh and demanding teacher-student relationship, the transformative fire can be found through demanding and genuine forms of intensive practice.

The demanding nature of Zen sesshins, or of one hundred thousand Tibetan Buddhist prostrations, or of a three-month silent vipassana retreat do not require punishment and judgment, but the courage and surrender they do demand can serve to challenge and awaken practitioners very well. When students who are mature come to me during a two- or three-month retreat weeping or frightened or facing whatever demons have come for them, I let them know that inner liberation requires them to face these demons head-on. Sometimes you can feed the demons, but sometimes you simply have to experience the full force of what you have run from. I tell them that they can run away but that the demons will follow them and wait. When you are ready, you have to let yourself die. "If you die," I joke, "do you want to be cremated or buried?" Facing your demons won't actually kill you. By facing into our fears, these forms can empower us and bring genuine freedom. That is because these meditation practices are based on the truth that all our demons are empty. Seeing how our own mind creates their forms can help us let go. But it is not easy.

Sometimes our demons are addictions, or anxiety, or deep grief; sometimes they are rage or fear. Like the murders of Milarepa, Western students bring their own painful family stories and personal problems to their dharma practice. If the story is buried or half secret or confusing, it might need to be told in the presence of another person in order to accept it or let go of it. But usually a little bit of the story is enough; we don't need to go back into our whole history. Someone might say that they are suffering because of their past. But they don't have to recount their whole painful history. A few scenes will do. Then we become curious, mindful together. We might spend a little bit of time inquiring, "Where is this held in your body? What are the beliefs that you have, what are the strongest fears, memories, images that you carry?" But we're always working with an underlying awareness that asks, Does this history define you? Is this who you really are? We're not trying to solve it or go back and rework it. The true inner work is to experience the reality of contraction or fear, in the here and now, to allow it to open and release in the body and mind, and then to discover that it's not your true nature, not who you are. Knowing the story alone doesn't solve it. What brings freedom is turning to face the root of the suffering, and the identity that's constructed around it, going right into the center of it until you come to its true emptiness. Wise psychotherapy must do this in the same way that dharma practice does, because that's how liberation happens.

Let me give you an example. A woman practitioner came to me in great grief because her husband had recently left her. They had a four-year-old child, and the woman had imagined sustaining a beautiful, loving marriage, but now it was over. Her current grief was exacerbated by the fact that when she was three years old, her own father had walked out without saying a word and never returned. When he abandoned her, she had come to the conclusions, somewhere deep inside, that men were untrustworthy and that she was not lovable. So we worked first on kind attention, on holding her grief with compassion. She was not trying to get rid of anything, but to take the meditative seat and accept her situation with mindfulness and compassion. She grieved and wept and there was some necessary storytelling.

After a fair amount of inner work, it seemed time to go back to the core of this primary suffering that she carried. So I asked her to close her eyes, and through visualization meditation she went back to the worst scene, being three years old as her father left for good. She remembered herself standing at the top of the stairs, looking down, as a little girl in a blue cotton dress, while her father stood, his suitcase in his hand about to walk out the door and never see her again. Immediately, she felt grief and terror, this was a horrible scene to relive, and I had her tell me all the feelings in her three-year-old body and hold all of them with spacious attention and great compassion.

After a time I said, "See if you can shift your consciousness and enter your father's body. Tell me what it feels like." So she did. She said, "My body is rigid, I'm filled with pain and suffering and anger. But more than anything, I feel desperate." I said, "Why are you leaving?" She went on, "I'm trapped. I'm in a terrible marriage where I'm losing my life. We fight and blame and hurt each other. It feels like I'm going to die. I want to have a life and the marriage is so painful, and if I'm here another day, I'm just going to die. I have to get out of here in order to survive." She could feel the rigidity and the desperation.

I asked, "Do you know that your daughter is there at the top of the stairs, watching you?" "Yes, I do." "Well, why do you want to leave her? Why don't you say anything to her . . . ?" "Because if I look at her even for a moment—I love her so dearly—I will not be able to walk out that door. But I can't stay. I'll die. I made the wrong marriage. It's horrible. So I have to keep my eyes down, and grit my teeth, and walk out that door to survive."

This woman just sat there for a moment, stunned, and I asked her, "Now go back and be the three-year-old girl again, looking." As she saw him leave in her imagination, I asked, "What is the story that she tells herself?" She said, "'He's leaving because he doesn't love me. And because my father didn't love me, I can't be loved. There's something wrong with me.'" Then I asked her, "Who made up that story?" Somewhat astonished, she answered, "I did." "Is it true," I looked her in the eyes. After some hesitation she replied, "Well, no." "Is this really who you are?" In this moment came a whole realization of emptiness: that's not who I am.

Next I had her become her mother, filled with anger and fear, chopping carrots in the kitchen as her husband walked off. As she felt the rage that her mother carried and the anxiety that was in her mother, it made her much more sympathetic to her mother's experience. Finally, she went back to being a little girl again. And she said, "Now I can see the suffering that was there, which as a child I was asked to bear and didn't understand." I asked, "Can you see how you created a whole picture of yourself from that suffering that is not who you really are?" And from that moment, things began to change in her. She had seen her life from the wisdom Ajahn Chah called the One Who Knows. I didn't need to give her teachings about emptiness and selflessness, or have her do a special Buddhist meditation. But when the inner work is grounded in an understanding of emptiness, then we shift from the "body of fear" to inherent freedom. It's quite natural. When I'm meeting with people, the ground is emptiness. I'll say to them, "Who are you, and what is the possibility in your life of really being free?" We are working not just to change the plot of the story but to let go of all that we cling to as a false self. This isn't meditation, or therapy, it is simply the release of suffering.

But this inner work also has to be paired with outer change. To practice the dharma demands that we shift our values from an attachment to security and money and worldly success to valuing the transformation of the heart. People come into Buddhist retreat centers carrying an enormous amount of tension, worry, and stress from the complexity of living in modern consumer society, and they say, "How can dharma practice help?" They can learn mindfulness meditation to reduce their stress, and compassion practice to ease their suffering. But this is not enough. Part of the solution is that they actually have to change their lives! Dharma teaching doesn't just say only transform the vision by which you see the world, although that is one aspect of liberation. It also requires you to let go and change your behavior, change the way you live. The Buddha didn't choose to live in the midst of the marketplaces and palaces of Benares. He chose to live simply, in the forest. Yet for his lay followers who stayed in the city, the Buddha gave instruction as well. He emphasized that to free the heart, you must act ethically and generously and then create a life of balance. Ethics and generosity are the ground from which dharma practice grows. You can't meditate after a day of killing and stealing. It just doesn't work. Then on the level of balance, if you live a life that is filled with stressful complexity and are seeking peace and harmony, you may receive some benefit from changing your inner spirit but fundamentally you have to change the way you live.

Freedom is fulfilled by seeing the truth and then embodying it in every part of your life. In the 1970s I remember going to a psychology conference and giving a lecture about how I teach ethics to my clients. In traditional psychotherapy, that was a radical thing to do. Because psychotherapy was developed in response to the repressive atmosphere of Victorian culture, healing was fostered by allowing the patient's life story to be revealed with no judgment or criticism. If someone tells you that they're having a string of affairs, you're not supposed to be judgmental about it. But I said, this is ridiculous. If someone comes in and they're having one affair after another or taking money from the till, though I'll listen in a sympathetic way, and seek to help them understand the pain that is driving them, I'll also remind them there are universal laws articulated in every tradition—Buddhist, Muslim, Christian—which explain that if you steal, if you kill, or if you lie, then inevitably you will create suffering. I will not tell you what to do, but I want you to wake up to the laws of life so that you can wisely guide yourself. Some therapists were surprised, saying, "You mean you teach your clients ethics?" I said, "Of course. Aren't we supposed to be helping these people?" The boundaries between spiritual truth and conventional life are artificial. In the work that I do, what interests me most is the possibility of liberation, what is translated in one of our texts as "the sure heart's release." It's possible to be free. Freedom isn't found in transcending the world or leaving the world, but here and now, in this very moment. My own teachers demonstrated this beautifully. Even in the midst of the worst circumstances in Thailand, or Cambodia, or Burma, their hearts were free and open and their compassion seemed boundless.

To be free our dharma practice has to include attention to personal life and attention to the kind of emotional deficiencies that are common in our society. It has to bring the skillful means of awareness and compassion to our history, our relationships, our work and longings and love, to aspects of life that weren't the focus of the monasteries of Asia. In the same way, we must include in our dharma attention ecological devastation, continuing racism, and injustices perpetrated by our materialistic culture. The personal and collective problems of humanity need the medicine of the dharma more than ever at this time. The good news is that the Buddha's practices of liberation are available to use here and now.

23

Enlightenments

ON A MEDITATION RETREAT several years ago, a woman raised her hand and asked the question "Is enlightenment just a myth?" When we teachers had a meeting later that evening, we asked each other this question. We exchanged stories about the creative freedom of Ajahn Chah, the enormous field of metta around Dipa Ma, the joyous laughter of Poonja, and of our own awakenings. Of course there is enlightenment.

But the word *enlightenment* is used in different ways, and that can be confusing. Is Zen, Tibetan, Hindu, or Theravadan enlightenment the same? What is the difference between "an enlightenment experience" and full enlightenment? How do you know if someone is enlightened?

APPROACHES TO ENLIGHTENMENT

As I have explained in previous chapters, from early on in my practice in Asia, I was forced to deal with these questions quite directly. My teachers, Ajahn Chah in Thailand and Mahasi Sayadaw in Burma, were both considered among the most enlightened masters of Theravada Buddhism. While they both described the goal of practice as freedom from greed, hatred, and delusion, they didn't agree about how to attain enlightenment, nor how it is experienced.

Yet each approach was compelling. The focus of Mahasi Sayadaw was on long, silent retreats, developing a continuous depth of mindfulness until all life is experienced as instantaneous arising and passing. In this approach you pass through stages of luminosity, joy, fear, and the dissolution of all you took to be solid. The mind becomes unmoving, resting in a place of stillness and equanimity, transparent to all experience, thoughts and fears, longings and love. Out of this there comes a dropping away of identity with anything in this world, an opening to the unconditioned beyond mind and body; you enter into the stream of liberation.

Ajahn Chah's approach to enlightenment was not based on having any particular meditation experience, no matter how profound. As Ajahn Chah described them, meditative states are not important in themselves. Meditation is a way of quieting the mind so you can practice all day long wherever you are. When mindfulness is present, you can see grasping or aversion, clinging or suffering, and then let it go. What's left is enlightenment, always found here and now, a release of identification with the changing conditions of the world, a resting in awareness. This involves a simple yet profound shift of identity from the myriad, ever-changing conditioned states to the unconditioned consciousness—the awareness that knows them all. In Ajahn Chah's approach, release from entanglement in greed, hatred, and delusion does not happen through retreat, concentration, and cessation but from this profound shift in identity.

How can we understand these seemingly different views of enlightenment? The Buddhist texts contain some of the same contrasting descriptions. In many texts, nirvana is described in the language of negation, and as in the approach taught by Mahasi Sayadaw; enlightenment is presented as the end of suffering through putting out of the fires of craving, the uprooting of all forms of clinging. The elimination of suffering is practiced by purification and concentration, confronting the forces of greed and hate and overcoming them. When the Buddha was asked, "Do you teach annihilation? Is nirvana the end of the things as we know them?" he responded, "I teach only one form of annihilation: the extinction of greed, the extinction of hatred, the extinction of delusion. This I call nirvana."

There is in the texts, as well, a more positive way of understanding enlightenment. Here nirvana is described as the highest happiness; as peace, freedom, purity, stillness; and as the unconditioned, the timeless, the undying. In this understanding, as in Ajahn Chah's approach, liberation comes through a shift of identity—a release from attachment to the changing conditions of the world, a resting in consciousness itself, the deathless.

In this understanding, liberation is a shift of identity from taking anything as "self." When asked in the Sutta Nipata, "How is it that one is not to be seen by the king of death?" the Buddha responds, "For one who takes nothing whatsoever as I or me or mine, such a one is freed from the snares of the king of death." In just this way, Ajahn Chah instructed us to rest in awareness and not identify with any experience as I or mine.

I found a similar practice in Bombay with Sri Nisargadatta, a master of Advaita. His teachings about enlightenment demanded a shift from identifying with any experience to resting in consciousness wherever you are. His focus was not about annihilation of greed and hate. In fact, when asked if he ever got impatient, Nisargadatta joyfully explained, "I see, hear, and taste as you do, feel hunger and thirst; if lunch is not served on time, even impatience will arise. All this I perceive quite clearly, but somehow I am not in it. There is awareness of it all and a sense of immense distance. Impatience arises; hunger arises. Even when illness and death of this body arise, they have nothing to do with who I am." This is enlightenment as a shift in identity.

So here we have different visions of enlightenment. On the one hand, we have the liberation from greed, hatred, and delusion attained through powerful concentration and purification, emphasized by many masters from Mahasi and U Pandita Sayadaw to Ajahn Naeb and Rinzai Zen master Joshu Sasaki. On the other hand, we have the shift of identity reflected in the teachings of Ajahn Chah, U Tejaniya Sayadaw, Ajahn Buddhadasa, in Dzogchen, and Soto Zen. And there are many other approaches; U Ba Khin, Ajahn Dhammadaro, and Sunlun Sayadaw use body sensations as a path. Abhidharma teachers such as Ajahn Sujin and masters of Tibetan Gelugpa Madhyamaka and Jnana Yoga use mental deconstruction as a path. If you practice Pure Land Buddhism, which was widespread in China and Japan, the approach to enlightenment involves chanting, devotion, and surrender to "other powers," which means being carried by the Buddha's "grace."

To understand these differences, it is wisest to speak of enlightenment in the plural—as "enlightenments." It's the same way with God. There are so many forms: Jehovah, Allah, Brahma, Jesus, Kali, and so forth. As soon as followers say they know the one true God, misunderstandings and conflict arise. Similarly, if you speak of enlightenment as one thing, conflict arises and you miss the truth.

We know that the Buddha taught many different approaches to enlightenment, all as skillful means to release grasping of the limited sense of self and return to the inherent purity of consciousness. Similarly, we will discover that the teachings on enlightened consciousness include many dimensions. When you actually experience consciousness free of identification with changing conditions, liberated from greed and hate, you find it is an open field of knowing, clear, transparent, and free. Pure consciousness is multifaceted, like a mandala or a jewel, a crystal with many sides. Through one facet, the enlightened heart shines as luminous clarity; through another it shines as perfection, or as indescribable peace. It can be experienced as boundless love, vast silence, or infinite compassion. Pure consciousness is all of these qualities: integrity, joy, radiance, bliss. It is timeless, ever present, completely empty, and full of all things. Each of these qualities can fill consciousness and shine through our body, heart, and mind. This is our direct and immediate inner experience, and it happens in many ways. Do not grasp any one particular form or description. Ajahn Chah and Ajahn Jumnien would say, "Let go of striving, rest in awareness, and experience the joy of freedom here and now."

Part of the confusion about enlightenment arises when a teacher or tradition emphasizes the experience of one of these qualities over the others as if true enlightenment can be tasted in only one way. But in moments of silence, of reverence, of letting go of clinging to I, me, and mine, many of us have tasted various moments of this liberation, what Ajahn Buddhadasa calls "everyday nirvana." Sometimes it is experienced as love, sometimes as profound silence. We practice to learn to trust and stabilize this innate freedom. From the open space of awareness, the multifaceted nature of liberation becomes clear. Like the particle and wave qualities of light, enlightenment consciousness is experienced in a myriad of beautiful ways.

GATEWAYS TO ENLIGHTENMENT

So what practices lead to these enlightenments? Most centrally, Buddhism uses the liberating practices of mindfulness and loving-kindness. These are supported by the practice of virtue, which frees us from being caught in reactive energies that would cause harm to ourselves or others. Added to this are practices of composure, or concentration, where we learn to quiet the mind; and practices of wisdom, which can see clearly how all things arise and pass, how they cannot be possessed.

Through these practices come purification and healing and the arising of profound compassion. Gradually, there is a shift of identity from being the person who is caught in suffering, to the experience of liberation from it all. Releasing the sense of self and all the changing conditions of the world brings "stream-entry," the first stage of enlightenment.

The most common gates to stream-entry in the Theravada tradition are the gateway of impermanence, the gateway of suffering, and the gateway of selflessness. When we open through the gateway of impermanence, we see more and more deeply how every experience is born and dies, how every moment is new. In one monastery where I practiced, we were trained to experience how all of life is vibration. Through long hours of refined concentration, we came to sense all the sounds and sights, the breath, the procession of thoughts—everything we took to be ourselves—as a field of changing energy. Experience shimmered, dissolving moment by moment. Then we shifted our attention from the vibrations to rest in the spacious heart of awareness. I and other, inside and outside—everything dropped away and we came to know the vast stillness beyond all change. This is enlightenment through the gate of impermanence.

Sometimes we enter enlightenment through the gate of suffering. We sit in the fire of human experience, and instead of running from it, we awaken through it. In the Fire Sermon, the Buddha declares, "All is burning. The eye, the ear, the nose, the tongue, the body, the mind, the world is burning. With what is it burning? It is burning with the fires of greed, of hatred, and of delusion." Through the gate of suffering we face the fires of desire, hate, war, racism, and fear of old age, sickness, and death. We open to dissatisfaction, grief, and loss. We accept the inherent suffering in life and we are released. We discover that suffering is not "our" pain, it is "the" pain—the pain of the world. A profound dispassion arises, compassion fills the heart, and we find liberation.

My friend Salam, a Palestinian journalist and activist, passed through the gate of suffering when brutally beaten in Israeli prisons. This kind of suffering happens on every side in war. When I first met Salam in San Francisco, he was being honored for his hospice service. I asked him what brought him to this work. "One time I died," Salam told me. Kicked by a guard, he lay on the floor of the jail with blood coming out of his mouth, and his consciousness floated out of his body. Suddenly, he felt so peaceful—a kind of bliss—as he saw he wasn't that body. "I was so much more: I was the boot and the guard, the bars in the window, the goat calling outside the walls of the police station. I was all of it," Salam told me. "When I got out of jail, I couldn't take sides anymore. I married a Jewish woman and had Jewish-Palestinian children. That is my answer." Salam explains, "Now I sit with people who are dying because they are afraid and I can hold their hands and reassure them that it's perfectly safe." He awakened through the gate of suffering.

Sometimes we awaken through the gate of selflessness. The experience of selflessness can happen in the simplest of ways. In walking meditation, we notice with every step the unbidden arising of thoughts, feelings, sensations, only to observe them disappear. To whom do they belong? Where do they go? Back into the void, which is where yesterday went, as well as our childhood, Socrates, Genghis Khan, and the builders of the pyramids.

As we let go of clinging, we feel the tentative selflessness of things. Sometimes boundaries dissolve, and we can't separate ourselves from the plum tree, the birdsong, or the morning traffic. The whole sense of self becomes empty experience arising in consciousness. More and more deeply, we realize the joy of "no self, no problem." We taste enlightenment through the gate of selflessness and emptiness.

There are many other gates: the gates of compassion, of purity, of surrender, of love. There is also what is called the "gateless gate." One teacher describes it this way: "I would go for months of retreat training, and nothing spectacular would happen, no great experiences. Yet somehow everything changed. What most transformed me were the endless hours of mindfulness and compassion, giving a caring attention to what I was doing. I discovered how I automatically tighten and grasp, and with that realization I started to let go, to open to an appreciation of whatever was present. I found an ease. I gave up striving. I became less serious, less concerned with myself. My kindness deepened. I experienced a profound freedom, simply the fruit of being present over and over." This was her gateless gate.

EXPRESSIONS OF ENLIGHTENMENT

Whatever our gate to enlightenment, the first real taste, stream-entry, is followed by many more tastes as we learn to stabilize, deepen, and embody this wisdom in our own unique life. What does it look like?

The facets of enlightenment express themselves marvelously in our teachers. Each manifests enlightenment with his or her own flavors.

Dipa Ma, the wonderful grandmother in Calcutta who was one of our great masters, was a tiny person with a powerfully trained mind. Dipa Ma expressed enlightenment as love. She devotedly instructed her students in mindfulness and loving-kindness, and then she hugged them, putting her hands on their head, face, and shoulders, whispering metta phrases. They got drunk on love. Like Dipa Ma, Ammachi, a Hindu teacher from South India, manifests enlightenment as the "hugging guru." She goes into a trance, and all night long she holds people; she might take as many as two thousand people onto her lap and hug them. This is enlightenment as love.

For Zen master Suzuki Roshi, enlightenment was expressed by being just where you are. A woman told Suzuki Roshi she found it difficult to mix Zen practice with the demands of being a householder: "I feel I am trying to climb a ladder, but for every step upward I slip backward two steps." "Forget the ladder," Suzuki Roshi told her. "When you awaken, everything is right here on the ground." He explained how the desire to gain anything means you miss the reality of the present. "When you realize the truth that everything changes, and find your composure in it, there you find yourself in nirvana." Asked further about enlightenment, Suzuki Roshi said, "Strictly speaking, there are no enlightened beings; there is only enlightened activity." If you think you are enlightened, that is not it. The goal is to let go of being anyone special and meet each moment with beginner's mind.

Mahasi Sayadaw, the Burmese master, expressed enlightenment as emptiness. Watching him on his visits to America, we saw that he rarely laughed or judged. Instead, he exuded a quiet equanimity. Events and conversations would happen around him while he remained still. He was like space—transparent, nobody there. This is enlightenment as emptiness.

For Ajahn Jumnien, a Thai forest master, awakening is not only empty, it's full. His robe is covered in hundreds of sacred medallions, and he employs dozens of skillful means to teach—guided meditations, sacred chants, mantras, chakra and energy practices, forest medicines, animal stories and shamanic rituals. His dharma is all-hours, nonstop, full of life and joy. There's a sense of abundance in him, and happiness just pours out like a fountain. He expresses enlightenment as fullness.

Thich Nhat Hanh expresses enlightenment as mindfulness. When he has come to teach at Spirit Rock, two thousand people sit meditatively on the hillside and eat their apples mindfully in preparation for his arrival. A bell is rung, and he walks slowly and deliberately up the road—*so* mindfully that everyone sighs, "Ahhh." The consciousness of two thousand people is transformed just seeing this man walk, each step the whole universe. As we watch, we drop into the reality of the eternal present. This is where we awaken. Enlightenment as mindfulness.

The Dalai Lama expresses enlightenment as compassionate blessing. For instance, once at the end of his stay at a San Francisco hotel, he asked the management to bring out all the employees. This meant the people who chop vegetables in the kitchen, who clean the carpets late at night, who make the beds. The big circular driveway filled with all those who made this hotel work but who were usually unrecognized. One by one, he looked at each one with full presence, took each person's hand, and said, "Thank you," moving unhurriedly just to make sure that he connected with each one fully. The Dalai Lama personifies enlightenment as compassionate blessing.

Ajahn Chah's manifestation was the laughter of wisdom. Whether with generals or ministers, farmers or cooks, he would say, "When I see how much people are struggling, I look at them with great sympathy and ask, 'Are you suffering? Ahhh, you must be very attached. Why not let go?'" His teachings were deep and straight to the point. He'd say, "If you let go a little, you'll be a little happy. If you let go a lot, you'll be a lot happy. If you let go completely, you'll be completely happy." He saw suffering, its cause, and that freedom is possible in any moment. He expressed enlightenment as wisdom.

When people read these stories, they might ask, "How do they relate to me? I want these enlightenments. How do I get them? What should I do?" The jewel of enlightenment invites us to awaken through many skillful means. Mahasi Sayadaw would say, "To find emptiness, note every single moment until what you think to be the world dissolves, and you will come to know freedom." Ajahn Chah would say, "Just let go, and become the awareness, be the One Who Knows." Dipa Ma would say, "Love, no matter what." Thich Nhat Hanh would say,

"Rest in mindfulness, this moment, the eternal present." Ajahn Jumnien would say, "Be happy for no cause." Suzuki Roshi would say, "Just be exactly where you are. Instead of waiting for the bus, realize you are on the bus."

So, is enlightenment a myth? No. It is not far away. It is freedom here and now, to be tasted whenever you open to it. As you can see from the chapters in this book, enlightenment is available in every part of life. As a teacher, I have the privilege of seeing the blessing of enlightenments awaken in so many meditators who come to dharma practice and become transformed though its many expressions. From initial tension and struggle with life, doubt, and distress, I watch their bodies ease, their faces soften, their dharma vision open, their hearts blossom. From everyday nirvana to a deep purity of mind, they experience a taste of liberation directly.

The Buddha declares, "If it were not possible to free the heart from entanglement, I would not teach you to do so. Just because it is possible to free the heart, there arise the teachings of the dharma of liberation, offered openhandedly for the welfare of all beings."

Aim for nothing less.

PART FIVE

Practices

24

Take the One Seat

Basic Meditation Practice

BEFORE BEGINNING THIS PRACTICE, be sure to read chapter 2, "The Art of Awakening: The Way of Meditation." Once you are ready, let your body be seated comfortably in your chair or on your cushion. Take a posture that is stable, erect, and connected with the earth. Sit as the Buddha did on his night of enlightenment, with great dignity and centeredness, sensing your capacity to face anything that arises. Let your eyes close and let your attention turn to your breathing. Allow your breath to move freely through your body. Let each breath bring a calmness and an ease. As you breathe, sense your capacity to open in body, heart, and mind.

Open your senses, your feelings, your thoughts. Become aware of what feels closed in your body, closed in your heart, closed in your mind. Breathe and make space. Let the space open so that anything may arise. Let the windows of your senses open. Be aware of whatever feelings, images, sounds, and stories show themselves. Notice with interest and ease all that presents itself to you.

Continue to feel your steadiness and connectedness to the earth, as if you had taken the one seat in the center of life and opened yourself to an awareness of its dance. As you sit, reflect on the benefit of balance and peace in your life. Sense your capacity to rest unshakable as the seasons of life change. Turn your attention to the awareness itself and rest in the knowing. As the One Who Knows, relax. See with wisdom how all that arises will pass away. Reflect on how joys and sorrows, pleasant events and unpleasant events, individuals, nations, even civilizations, arise and pass away. Take the one seat of a Buddha and rest with a heart of equanimity and compassion in the center of it all.

Sit this way, dignified and present, for as long as you wish. After some time, still feeling centered and steady, open your eyes. Then let yourself stand up and take some steps, walking with the same centeredness and dignity. Practice sitting and walking in this fashion, sensing your ability to be open, alive, and present with all that arises on this earth.

25

Forgiveness Meditation

READ CHAPTER 7, "The Art of Forgiveness," before practicing forgiveness meditation. Let yourself sit comfortably; allow your eyes to close and your breath to be natural and easy. Let your body and mind relax. Breathing gently into the area of your heart, let yourself feel all the barriers you have erected and the emotions that you have carried because you have not forgiven—not forgiven yourself, not forgiven others. Let yourself feel the pain of keeping your heart closed. Then, breathing softly, begin asking and extending forgiveness, reciting the following words, letting the images and feelings that come grow deeper as you repeat them.

ASKING FORGIVENESS OF OTHERS

Recite: "There are many ways that I have hurt and harmed others. I have betrayed or abandoned them, caused them suffering, knowingly or unknowingly, out of my pain, fear, anger, and confusion." Let yourself remember and visualize the ways you have hurt others. Sense the pain you have caused out of your own fear and confusion. Feel your own sorrow and regret. Recognize that finally you can release this burden and ask for forgiveness. Picture each memory that still burdens your heart. And then to each person in your mind repeat, "I ask for your forgiveness, I ask for your forgiveness."

OFFERING FORGIVENESS TO YOURSELF

Recite, "There are many ways that I have hurt and harmed myself. I have betrayed or abandoned myself many times through thought, word, or deed, knowingly and unknowingly." Feel your own precious body and life. Let yourself see the ways you have hurt or harmed yourself. Picture them, remember them. Feel the sorrow you have carried from this and sense that you can release these burdens. Extend forgiveness for each of them, one by one. Repeat to yourself, "For the ways I have hurt myself through action or inaction, out of my fear, pain, and confusion, I now extend a full and heartfelt forgiveness. I forgive myself, I forgive myself."

OFFERING FORGIVENESS TO THOSE WHO HAVE HURT OR HARMED YOU

Recite, "There are many ways that I have been harmed by others, abused or abandoned, knowingly or unknowingly, in thought, word, or deed." Let yourself picture and remember these many ways. Feel the sorrow you have carried from this past, and sense that you can release this burden of pain by extending forgiveness whenever your heart is ready. Now say to yourself, "I now remember the many ways others have hurt or harmed me, wounded me, out of fear, pain, confusion, and anger. I have carried this pain in my heart too long. To the extent that I am ready, I offer them forgiveness. To those who have caused me harm, I offer my forgiveness, I forgive you."

Let yourself gently repeat these three directions for forgiveness until you feel a release in your heart. For some great pains you may not feel a release but only the burden and the anguish or anger you have held. Touch this softly. Be forgiving of yourself for not being ready to let go. Forgiveness cannot be forced; it cannot be artificial. Simply continue the practice and let the words and images work gradually in their own way. In time you can make the forgiveness meditation a regular part of your life, letting go of the past and opening your heart to each new moment with a wise loving-kindness.

26

Loving-kindness Meditation (Metta)

I am larger than I thought!
I did not know I held so much goodness!
—WALT WHITMAN

YOU CAN BEGIN the practice of loving-kindness by meditating for fifteen or twenty minutes in a quiet place. Sit in a comfortable fashion. Let your body rest and your heart be soft.

Begin with yourself. Breathe gently, and recite inwardly the following traditional phrases directed to your own well-being. You begin with yourself because without loving yourself it is almost impossible to love others.

> May I be filled with loving-kindness.
> May I be safe from inner and outer dangers.
> May I be well in body and mind.
> May I be at ease and happy.

As you repeat these phrases, picture yourself as you are now, and hold yourself in a heart of loving-kindness. Or perhaps you will find it easier to picture yourself as a young and beloved child. Adjust the words and images to find whatever best opens your heart of kindness. Repeat these phrases over and over again, letting the feelings permeate your body and mind.

Be aware that this meditation may at times feel mechanical or awkward. It can also bring up feelings of irritation and anger. If this happens, it is especially important to be patient and kind toward yourself, allowing whatever arises to be received in a spirit of friendliness and kind affection.

When you have established a sense of loving-kindness for yourself, you can then expand your meditation to include others. Choose a benefactor, someone in your life who has loved or truly cared for you. Picture this person and carefully recite the same phrases:

May you be filled with loving-kindness.
May you be safe from inner and outer dangers.
May you be well in body and mind.
May you be at ease and happy.

Whether the image or feelings are clear or not does not matter. Simply continue to plant the seeds of loving wishes, repeating the phrases gently no matter what arises. Some people find loving-kindness for themselves so difficult that they choose to begin their practice with a benefactor or someone they find easier to love. This too is fine. The rule in loving-kindness practice is to follow the way that most easily opens your heart.

When loving-kindness for your benefactor has developed, you can gradually begin to include other people you care about in your meditation. Picturing each beloved person, recite the same phrases, evoking a sense of loving-kindness for each person in turn. After this you can include a wider circle of friends. Then gradually extend your meditation step-by-step to picture and include community members, neighbors, people everywhere, animals, all beings, the whole earth.

Finally, include the difficult people in your life, even your enemies, wishing that they too may be filled with loving-kindness and peace. This will take practice. But as your heart opens, first to loved ones and friends, you will find that in the end you won't want to close it to anyone.

Loving-kindness can be practiced anywhere. You can use this meditation in traffic jams, in buses, and on airplanes. As you silently practice this meditation among people, you will immediately feel a wonderful connection with them—the power of loving-kindness. It will calm your mind, open your heart, and keep you connected to all beings.

May the blessings of these practices awaken your own inner wisdom and inspire your compassion. And through the blessing of your heart may the world find peace.

Credits

PART ONE: BECOMING WHO WE ARE

"The Liberating Practice of Mindfulness" originally appeared in the *Shambhala Sun*, July 2007, under the title "Doing the Buddha's Practice."

"The Art of Awakening" is from *Breath Sweeps Mind*, edited by Jean Smith. Every effort was made to contact the rights holder of this material, however these efforts were unsuccessful.

"A Mind Like Sky" originally appeared in the *Shambhala Sun*, May 2003.

"Realizing Our Full Potential" is from *The Wise Heart: A Guide to the Universal Teachings of Buddhist Psychology* by Jack Kornfield, copyright © 2008 by Jack Kornfield. Used by permission of Bantam Books, a division of Random House, Inc.

"Our Children Will Learn What They Live" reprinted by permission from *Inquiring Mind*, Vol. 8, No. 2 (Spring 1992). www.inquiringmind.com

The poem "Children Will Learn What They Live" is excerpted from the book *Children Learn What They Live*, copyright ©1998 by Dorothy Law Nolte and Rachel Harris; poem "Children Learn What They Live" copyright ©1972 by Dorothy Law Nolte. Used by permission of Workman Publishing Co., Inc., New York. All rights reserved.

"The Art of Forgiveness," is from *The Art of Forgiveness, Lovingkindness, and Peace* by Jack Kornfield, copyright © 2002 by Jack Kornfield. Used by permission of Bantam Books, a division of Random House, Inc.

PART TWO: TAKING UP THE SPIRITUAL PATH

"Spiritual Initiation" is reprinted by permission of Open Court Publishing Company, a division of Carus Publishing Company, Chicago, IL, from *Crossroads: The Quest for Contemporary Rites of Passage* by Louise Madhi, Nancy Geyer Christopher, and Michael Meade, copyright © 1996.

"Perils, Promise, and Spiritual Emergency" is adapted from "Obstacles and Vicissitudes in Spiritual Practice" by Jack Kornfield, copyright ©1989 by Jack Kornfield, from *Spiritual Emergency* by Stanislav Grof and Christina Grof. Used by permission of Jeremy P. Tarcher, an imprint of Penguin Group (USA) Inc.

"The Near Enemies of Awakening" originally appeared in *ReVision*, Fall 1993.

"The Bodhisattva Way" is from *The Wise Heart: A Guide to the Universal Teachings of Buddhist Psychology* by Jack Kornfield, copyright © 2008 by Jack Kornfield. Used by permission of Bantam Books, a division of Random House, Inc.

"Samadhi" is excerpted from *The Experience of Samadhi* by Richard Shankman, copyright © 2008 by Richard Shankman. Reprinted by arrangement with Shambhala Publications, Inc., Boston, www.shambhala.com.

"Spiritual Maturity" is from *A Path with Heart* by Jack Kornfield, copyright ©1993 by Jack Kornfield. Used by permission of Bantam Books, a division of Random House, Inc.

PART THREE: LESSONS FROM MODERN MASTERS

"Natural Freedom of the Heart" is from *Voices of Insight* edited by Sharon Salzberg, copyright © 1999 by the Dharma Foundation. Reprinted by arrangement with Shambhala Publications, Inc., Boston, www .shambhala.com.

"Holding the Banner of Dharma" is excerpted from *Recalling Chögyam Trungpa*, edited by Fabrice Midal, copyright © 2005 by Fabrice Midal. Reprinted by arrangement with Shambhala Publications, Inc., Boston, www.shambhala.com.

The untitled poem that appears in "Spiritual Maturity" is from *The Tassajara Recipe Book*, by Edward Espe Brown ©1985 by the Chief Priest, Zen Center, San Francisco. Reprinted by arrangement with Shambhala Publications, Inc., Boston, www.shambhala.com.

PART FOUR: PRACTICING THE DHARMA IN THE WEST

"American Buddhism" is from *The Complete Guide to Buddhist America* by Don Morreale, copyright © 1998 by Don Morreale. Reprinted by arrangement with Shambhala Publications, Inc., Boston, www.shambhala.com.

"This Fantastic, Unfolding Experiment" originally appeared in *Buddhadharma: The Practitioners Quarterly*, June 2007.

"Sex Lives of the Gurus" originally appeared in *Yoga Journal*, July/ August 1985.

"Psychedelics, Antidepressants, and Spiritual Practice" has been revised and adapted from an essay by Jack Kornfield that originally appeared in the book *Zig Zag Zen*, copyright © 2002 by Alan Hunt Bediner. Permission granted by Lowenstein Associates, Inc.

"The Sure Heart's Release" is adapted from an interview with Jack Kornfield © 2000 *Tricycle: The Buddhist Review*.

"Enlightenments" originally appeared in *Inquiring Mind*, Fall 2010.

About the Author

Jack Kornfield trained as a Buddhist monk in the monasteries of Thailand, India, and Burma. He has taught meditation internationally since 1974 and is one of the key teachers to introduce Buddhist mindfulness practice to the West. He graduated from Dartmouth College with a degree in Asian Studies and then joined the Peace Corps in northeast Thailand, home to several of the world's oldest Buddhist forest monasteries. He studied under the Buddhist master Ven. Ajahn Chah, as well as Ven. Mahasi Sayadaw of Burma.

After returning to the United States, Jack cofounded the Insight Meditation Society (www.dharma.org) in Barre, Massachusetts, with fellow meditation teachers Sharon Salzberg and Joseph Goldstein. He is also a founding teacher of the Spirit Rock Center (www.spiritrock.org) in Woodacre, California, where he currently lives and teaches. Over the years, Jack has taught in centers and universities worldwide, led International Buddhist Teacher meetings with the Dalai Lama and worked with many of the great teachers of our time. He holds a PhD in clinical psychology and is a husband, father, and activist. His books, including *A Path with Heart* and *After the Ecstasy, the Laundry,* have been translated into twenty languages and sold more than a million copies. For more information, visit www.jackkornfield.org.